The
Flower Farmer

GARDENER'S SUPPLY BOOKS

Eliot Coleman, *The New Organic Grower: A Master's Manual
of Tools and Techniques for the Home and Market Gardener*

Leandre Poisson and Gretchen Vogel Poisson, *Solar Gardening: Growing Vegetables
Year-Round the American Intensive Way*

Lynn Byczynski, *The Flower Farmer: An Organic Grower's Guide
to Raising and Selling Cut Flowers*

GARDENER'S SUPPLY COMPANY was founded in 1983 in Burlington, Vermont, to make available innovative tools and equipment that would bring the joys and rewards of gardening to as many people as possible. Gardener's Supply serves gardeners of all interests and abilities with seasonal catalogs that offer earth-friendly methods for growing plants in all climate zones and seasons. Four seasonal and specialty catalogs; a retail store and the renowned community and demonstration gardens in Burlington's "Intervale"; and a complete line of high-performance home greenhouses combine to make Gardener's Supply "America's Gardening Resource."

To further its mission as the leading source of new ideas and information for gardeners, Gardener's Supply has joined Chelsea Green Publishing Company to co-create and co-publish a series of gardening books. The books in this series are written by pioneering individuals who have firsthand experience in using innovative, ecological techniques to grow healthy food and flowers that enhance our lives—and the well-being of Earth.

Ian Baldwin, Jr.
President, Chelsea Green

Will Raap
President, Gardener's Supply

The *Flower Farmer*

An Organic Grower's Guide to Raising and Selling Cut Flowers

Lynn Byczynski

Illustrations by Robin Wimbiscus

CHELSEA GREEN PUBLISHING COMPANY

WHITE RIVER JUNCTION, VERMONT

Printed in the United States of America

First printing, March 1997

00 99 98 97   1 2 3 4 5

Library of Congress Cataloging-in-Publication Data

Byczynski, Lynn, 1954–
        The flower farmer : an organic grower's guide to raising
    and selling cut flowers / Lynn Byczynski.
                            p.   cm.
        Includes index.
        ISBN 0–930031–94–6
        1. Floriculture. 2. Organic farming. 3. Cut flower industry.
    I. Title.
    SB406.53.B93   1997
    635.9'6684—dc21   97–3553
                                                            CIP

CHELSEA GREEN PUBLISHING COMPANY
P.O. Box 428
White River Junction, Vermont 05001

For Dan,
who always encourages me
to plant more.

Echinacea,
Coneflower

Syringa,
Lilac

Acknowledgments

THIS BOOK WAS MADE POSSIBLE BY MANY PEOPLE WHO HAVE SUPPORTED AND inspired me as I've made my way—first, growing flowers, and later, writing about them. I have visited and interviewed countless people who generously shared their ideas and knowledge. To name them all would be impossible, but I hope that those who have answered my questions and opened their gardens to me will recognize themselves and accept my thanks.

I owe much to David Porterfield, the owner of Porterfield's Flowers in Topeka, Kansas. His willingness to buy my flowers has contributed to my family's determination to remain in farming. And I believe that his contributions to this book will help other small farmers establish relationships with florists.

I also am indebted to Pamela and Frank Arnosky of Texas Specialty Cut Flowers in Blanco, Texas. Pam and Frank have written the monthly flower column for *Growing for Market* for the past two years, freeing me up to spend more time farming. They are extremely knowledgeable about flower production, and they generously share their information with *Growing for Market* readers every month. Besides that, they're good writers and funny, too.

I'm grateful to Ben Watson, my editor, for his steady guidance and botanical expertise, and to Jozie Schimke, who helped compile the flower list in appendix 1.

To paraphrase Thomas Alva Edison, success is 1 percent inspiration and 99 percent perspiration. It is my hope that aspiring flower growers who read this "how-to" book will find their inspiration in the profiles of successful farmers. The people who agreed to be featured in this book are true philanthropists. None of them stands to benefit directly from participating in this project, but all have been generous with their time and knowledge. They welcomed me warmly to their farms and held back nothing when I asked questions. Their openness reflects a genuine commitment to the ideal of small-scale farming. My thanks go to Linda Arietta, Pam and Frank Arnosky, Chris Banthien, Eric and Katie Coburn, Will Fulton, Tom Gumbart, John Hurd, the Jackson and Harimon families, Howie Myers, Billene and Richard Nemec, Karen and John Pendleton, Paul Sansone and Susan Vosburg, and John Zehrer.

Similarly, several growers contributed their Top Ten lists so that others in their regions could be successful with their first flower gardens. Thanks to

MaryLee Johnson, Cass Peterson, Betsy Hitt, Lorraine Billeaud, Faye Jones, and Beth Benjamin.

Finally, I want to recognize the contributions of my children, Will and Laurel. They have been involved in the flower business since they were babies, playing in the garden and accompanying me on deliveries. They have cheerfully gone along on many trips to other farms to gather information for this book. Having them always nearby has made farming and writing worth all the hard work.

Introduction

WHEN I FIRST STARTED THINKING ABOUT QUITTING MY CITY JOB FOR LIFE ON a small farm, I didn't plan to become a flower farmer. I thought I wanted to be an herb grower. For a time, after my husband and I started farming, I did grow herbs for upscale restaurants. But then I put in a few rows of zinnias to sell at a farmers' market, and was surprised at how well they sold. The next year, I grew a dozen varieties of flowers to make into mixed bouquets and was again impressed with the demand. I discovered that, acre for acre, flowers were more profitable than produce. We still grow vegetables, but flowers have become an important part of our market garden.

As my business relationship with flowers has expanded, so has my affection for them. I find myself unendingly intrigued by the colors, fragrances, forms, and movement of flowers. I take pleasure in almost every aspect of growing flowers, from winter's work of studying catalogs and planning new varieties to summer's work of harvesting, bouquet-making, and delivering. Even after a decade of growing flowers, I still am mesmerized by the sight of my own fields, and still feel a thrill when my customers exclaim over the beauty of my flowers.

I also feel a deep regard for flowers because I have seen the important role they can play in the survival of the small farm. This country needs family farmers—for their work ethic, their independence, their understanding of nature, their neighborliness, their rootedness. Yet all the demographic indicators point to the demise of the small farm, and our leaders in government and education haven't done much to prevent that from happening. Fortunately, through ingenuity and hard work, many idealistic people are making small farms viable again. The model that is meeting with the greatest success is the organic market garden, where a wide array of crops is grown and marketed locally. Since 1992, I have been writing about organic market gardening in my monthly newsletter, *Growing for Market*, and I have visited and interviewed hundreds of successful small farmers who grow flowers as all or part of their income. You will meet some of these growers in profiles throughout this book, and through them, you will get a sense of the many directions a flower business can take and the ambitions it can fulfill.

Whatever the reason that you picked up this book, I hope you will find the key to your own dreams here. Perhaps you're interested in growing flowers for a living, or at least for additional income. Or perhaps you're a serious gardener who wants to know the secrets of professional flower growers so that you can duplicate their exuberant bouquets. Whatever your level of interest in flowers, this book holds something for you. It is intended to be a thorough introduction to both the production and marketing of cut flowers. It starts with the very basics of selecting what varieties to grow and where to dig your first flower beds, and takes you through the specifics of where to sell your flowers. Everything I have written in this book has come from my own experience and the experiences of others that have been explored in the pages of *Growing for Market*.

WHY ORGANIC FLOWERS?

Many people who understand the importance of growing food organically have asked me why I use organic practices for flowers. After all, you don't usually put flowers in your mouth, so what difference does it make if they have been sprayed with chemicals?

First, agricultural chemicals not only endanger the people who eat food sprayed with them, but can directly harm the workers who handle them. Agricultural chemicals can disperse in the air, drifting onto your neighbors, their pets, and their gardens. Methyl bromide, a fumigant widely used by fruit and vegetable farmers, contributes to the depletion of the stratospheric ozone layer, which protects life on Earth from ultraviolet radiation. Chemicals can also contaminate your water supply. For example, the herbicide atrazine, which is a known carcinogen, has been found in drinking water in many communities throughout the Midwest.

Organic farming practices, in contrast, protect the health of both people and the environment. Organic growers view crop protection in a holistic way; they are as concerned about prevention as about cure. First and foremost, organic practices focus on building soil fertility and growing healthy crops that are better able to withstand pests. Cover crops, composting, appropriate fertilization, skillful timing of planting, and proper irrigation are all essential to the organic grower because it is these practices that make plants thrive. When a problem does arise, the organic grower seeks the method of control that is most closely targeted to the problem. The organic grower doesn't turn to a broad-spectrum insecticide—one that kills everything—at the first sign of an insect attack. Instead, the organic grower identifies the pest, assesses the damage, and seeks a solution that will affect only that pest and not the beneficial insects that coexist in the garden. In certain rare circumstances, the organic grower may use a botanical pesticide as a last resort when threatened with the loss of a crop. However, the only pesticides acceptable for organic use are those that are derived from natural sources and that remain active for only a short time.

Organic flower growing, then, is important because farming practices can affect the environment. But there are a few other good reasons to grow flowers organically.

First, many of the flowers sold by florists and supermarket floral departments have been imported from countries where the pesticide regulations may not be as stringent as they are in the United States and Canada. As a result, many imported cut flowers have been sprayed with toxic chemicals to keep them cosmetically perfect—and those chemical residues are still on the flowers when they reach this country. (Florists, in particular, regularly have their hands immersed in a chemical soup of water, floral preservatives, and pesticide residues. Some florists develop dermatitis on their hands and worry about what other effects their exposure to chemicals is having on their health.)

Second, although most organic flower growers admit that there is, at present, no premium price for organic flowers, they also agree that the organic label can hold added attraction for new customers. After all, who wouldn't want to buy flowers that were grown without toxic chemicals—and still were beautiful, fresh, and long-lasting?

Finally, one more reason to grow flowers organically: You're growing them at your home, in the place where your children play, where you entertain friends, where you yourself come for solace and respite. A flower garden should be a place that nourishes your soul, not a place where you have to feel cautious and tense. In the organic flower garden, you will be free to enjoy your flowers with all your senses, and to experience the true joy of gardening that comes from working as a partner with nature.

WHAT DO YOU NEED TO GET STARTED?

Flowers have the same requirements as vegetables. They need fertile, well-drained soil, adequate water, sunshine, and protection from weeds and pests. Variety selection, timing, and post-harvest handling are equally important for success with cut flowers.

But above all, I believe, the most important qualification for success is a genuine love of flowers. Not long ago, I was at a flower growers' conference, in a workshop about some business aspect of flower farming, and the speaker said, "Flowers—everybody thinks they're so romantic, but when you're a commercial flower grower, they're just another widget, right?" I froze in my seat, dismayed by the notion that flowers could be considered just another commodity to produce and sell, like bathtub faucets or tape dispensers.

In fact, I don't believe you can grow flowers successfully if you think of them only as a commodity. I am convinced that you must love flowers in order to grow them well. You must have empathy for them and you must be as attentive as a parent.

This is not to say that you have to have a natural talent for flowers, like playing music by ear. The "green thumb" isn't born—he or she is bred by constant exposure and patient observation. With flowers, familiarity is sure to lead to love. And with the right heart, anyone can grow beautiful flowers.

CHAPTER 1

Choosing Varieties

$\mathcal{A}$S YOU BEGIN YOUR JOURNEY INTO SERIOUS FLOWER GROWING, THE first thing you should determine is where you hope to go. Do you want to grow enough flowers to keep your house full of bouquets all summer long? Do you want to raise flowers for dried arrangements to sell at craft fairs? Do you want to quit your present job and become a full-time flower farmer?

All of these options are possible with flowers. It helps to have clarified your goals before you start digging beds and ordering seeds, because hundreds of flowers are available to you. But since you can't grow them all (not all at once, anyway), you should narrow your selection to those that best meet your needs.

I recommend that you request catalogs from several of the seed companies listed for this chapter, in appendix 2, "Sources and Resources." Many of them have excellent color photos that will serve as a guide while you're becoming acquainted with flowers. Of course, all blooms look great in the catalogs, which is why this book gives you the names of the easiest, most reliable varieties to get you started as a cut-flower grower.

In this chapter, you will find recommendations of foolproof flowers for the novice grower. If you've never grown flowers before, these suggestions will help you get some experience before you make the leap into a full-fledged commercial venture. In subsequent years, you can expand your plantings to include the many other varieties recommended throughout the rest of this book. In the alphabetical list of recommended cut flowers in appendix 1, you'll find specific information about the uses, desirability, cultivation, and handling of more than one hundred kinds of specialty cut flowers. They are considered "specialty cut flowers" because they transcend the standard floral fare of roses, carnations, and chrysanthemums. They are considered good cut flowers because they have long stems and a vase life of at least five days. These recommended varieties are, in short, reliable in both the home and the marketplace.

However, many hundreds of other plants can be grown as cut flowers—for yourself or for sale—even though they don't meet the stem-length and vase-life standards of those most commonly grown. For example, lilies of the valley are in some demand for weddings, despite their short stems. Some floral designers will use just about anything from the garden, including petunias, geraniums, and the grasses you may think of as weeds. Many British and old American books on flower arranging give no thought to vase life—if a bloom lasts two or three days inside, it's worthy of cutting.

This book, then, is just an introduction to the topic of cut flowers. The flowers you will find here are reliable and will serve you well as you get started in flower farming. But don't let them limit your creativity. Sometime down the road, you will want to try new cultivated varieties or explore antique flowers. You might want to experiment with post-harvest handling to find a way to get better vase life out of a short-lived flower. You might want to branch out into greens or unusual flowering branches. Once your flower skills are firmly rooted, you'll want to stretch.

PLANT NAMES

Before we can talk about which flowers to plant, we need to consider the matter of how plants are named. You've no doubt heard that a rose is a rose is a rose; however, that's not exactly true. There are *Rosa rugosa, Rosa multiflora, Rosa damascena, Rosa eglanteria, Rosa gallica, Rosa moschata, Rosa chinensis,* about one hundred other *Rosa* species, and literally thousands of cultivars (named cultivated varieties). If you hope to grow the same rose your grandmother grew, or plant the same type that does so well in your city parks, then you must learn the precise name of the rose involved.

The fact is that common names, however picturesque, just aren't very useful to a serious gardener. Common names differ widely across the country. What's called "kiss-me-over-the-garden-gate" in Georgia is something quite different from the plant that goes by that name in California. Common names also convey no information about refinements that make a plant worth planting. "Yarrow" might refer to any one of several species of flowers, from a small white wildflower to the stately gold flower grown for drying. Similarly, "coneflower" might be the native species, with its drooping purple petals—or it could be the new, improved 'Magnus' cultivar, with deep pink petals that face outward, making a superb cut flower.

To be absolutely clear about plants, you must use their scientific or Latin names. Many people get nervous when they see Latin names because they think they can't pronounce them. Don't worry about it. Most people mispronounce Latin names, and you won't be criticized if you say them wrong. The important thing is to understand what the parts of the scientific name mean, and to be able to recognize them in plant catalogs and gardening books.

The Latin name can consist of two, three, or four parts: the genus, species, and, in some cases, variety or cultivar name, in that order. Thus, in the name *Echinacea purpurea* 'Magnus', the genus is *Echinacea,* the species is *purpurea,* and the cultivar is 'Magnus'. Here's an explanation of each part of the name:

- The *genus* is the broadest category in the Latin name, and refers to a closely related and definable group of plants. Similarity of flowers or fruits is the usual characteristic that defines a genus, although some plants are grouped into the same genus based on similarity of roots, stems, buds, or leaves.

  The plural of the word "genus" is "genera."

- The *species* is a subcategory, a more narrowly defined identity for the plant. A species is a group of plants sharing essential features that are different from those of other types of plants within the genus, and that are passed down from one generation to the next. This is a vague definition, but necessarily so, because nature doesn't adhere to human definitions and you will find variations within a species.

  The abbreviation for one "species" is "sp."; the plural is abbreviated "spp." Accordingly, "*Echinacea* spp." referes to the group of species within the genus *Echinacea.*

  When you see a genus and species name separated by an "×," you're looking at the name for a hybrid. For example, one of the most commonly grown cut-flower delphiniums is *Delphinium × belladonna.* A hybrid is simply the offspring of two different species.

- A *variety* is yet a narrower category, in which plants exhibit one or more common characteristics that differ from other plants in the same species. A cultivar is a term for a "cultivated variety" that was produced in cultivation rather than in the wild. The words "variety" and "cultivar" are often used interchangeably. However, sometimes you will see both variety and cultivar names after the genus and species. *Celosia argentea,* for example, is usually followed by variety and cultivar (*Celosia argentea var. cristata* 'Chief').

  The cultivar name always is written within single quotation marks (for example, *Zinnia elegans* 'Blue Point') and is probably the most important bit of information for your purposes. Cultivars are improvements over the wild or species form of the plant; they have been selected for bigger flowers, clearer colors, stronger stems, and other useful features. So when you have a recommendation for a certain cultivar, don't buy a plant unless you see that cultivar name on it. With commonly grown flowers, nurseries often list plants by their genus name followed by the cultivar name, making identification easier for you. If you're looking for rare plants, however, you will need to use the species and possibly the variety names as well as the genus and cultivar names.

Of course, new cultivars of cut flowers are introduced every year, so it pays to read the descriptions when you see a new cultivar. You may be the first in your area to discover a great new cut flower.

A GARDEN OF ANNUALS

Many of the best flowers for cutting are annuals, which live only one season and therefore can devote all their energy to blossoming. Perennials, in contrast, have to spend much of their energy developing roots and foliage to sustain them year after year. That's not to say they aren't good cut flowers; some perennials are, and we'll get to them later. But it will be the annuals that at first form the foundation of your cut-flower garden and provide the greatest number of stems for your bouquets.

Many of the best annuals can be direct-seeded into the garden. Others that need to be started in a greenhouse are readily available at garden centers because they're also good bedding plants. However, you need to be careful when purchasing from a garden center. Many of the flowers that I recommend for cutting are also available as dwarf cultivars, so always check the tag to make sure that the cultivar you're buying will be tall enough for cutting. For example, one of the nicest blue flowers for cutting is a tall ageratum called 'Blue Horizon'. Most of the ageratums you'll find in garden centers, though, are the small creeping types used in the front of landscape beds.

For the garden of annuals, I recommend that you set aside a special area: in the vegetable garden, along a fence, or beside the garage. Although annuals are beautiful to behold individually, they won't look great from a distance. You'll be cutting them constantly, and they'll never display the intense spread of color you might want in a landscape. Also, you'll probably want to grow a wide range of colors, and you may get some clashing combinations in the garden. So give annuals their own spot where you won't be reluctant to cut them for indoor use, or to deadhead fading blossoms to encourage new blooms.

In the accompanying beginner's garden plan (see pages 6–7), you'll find a list of the most basic, reliable, cheerful annuals that you can grow for a long season of cut flowers. This represents just a tiny portion of the annuals that look great in bouquets. Depending on your expertise, you may also want to grow more difficult annuals such as sweet peas, lavatera, and lisianthus. But even with the very basic flowers listed in this sample garden, you'll be able to make colorful informal bouquets or select color themes for more formal arrangements. The varieties have been carefully chosen to provide a wide range of colors and shapes over a long season. In fact, the annuals in this plan can supply all the cut flowers you need. However, it never hurts to vary the menu in your arrangements, which is why you might want to plan for cut flowers in the other parts of your garden. You can always prune a few branches from your shrubs, steal a couple of rosebuds, and snip flowering herbs from the vegetable garden.

PERENNIAL BEDS

If you're a serious gardener, you probably have given considerable thought to the plantings around your house. If you have a perennial bed, you may have planned the selection and placement of the flowers to combine colors, season of bloom, height, and texture into an eye-pleasing whole. And the idea of going in there and snipping flowers for a bouquet may seem nothing short of sacrilegious. If that's your reaction, then you've just found an excuse to plant new perennial beds.

Many perennials make beautiful cut flowers that last a long time in the vase. They tend to have a more delicate, ethereal quality than the robust annuals listed in the sample garden. A few delphiniums or campanulas, for example, can turn a country bouquet into a work of art. Peonies will provide a romantic feel and sweet fragrance. Phlox will add brilliant colors unlike any annual flower.

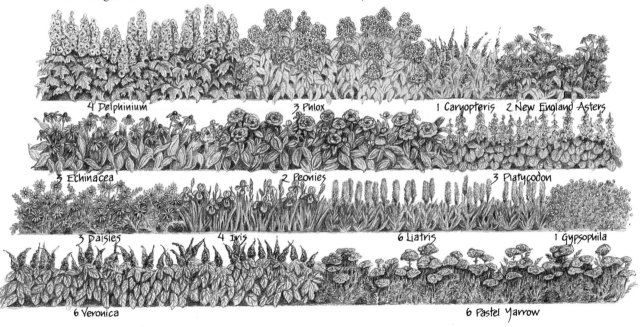

4 Delphinium   3 Phlox   1 Caryopteris   2 New England Asters

3 Echinacea   2 Peonies   3 Platycodon

3 Daisies   4 Iris   6 Liatris   1 Gypsophila

6 Veronica   6 Pastel Yarrow

5 x 12 Perennials

Even a small perennial border can provide cutting material all season long. In this sample garden, the iris, daisies, peonies, gypsophila, and veronica bloom in late spring. In early to mid-summer come the delphinium, yarrow, balloon-flower, and liatris. By August and into September, full production can be expected from the purple coneflowers, Phlox paniculata, *caryopteris, and New England aster.*

A BEGINNER'S ANNUAL GARDEN

This sample garden is designed for a new flower grower who wants to gain experience with growing and harvesting flowers without being overwhelmed by the diversity and size of a commercial garden. About 60 square feet of annuals—a bed 5 feet by 12 feet—will provide enough stems to fill your house with bouquets throughout the summer and give you a feel for the work.

The flowers in this plan are basic, but they all have many qualities to recommend them. All of them bloom prolifically, most of them providing multiple stems for cutting each week. They also bloom for a long time, although you may find some of them dying out if your summer gets too hot. This selection of flowers also provides a wide assortment of colors and shapes, and many varieties can be used as cut or dried flowers. Finally, this plan uses plants in quantities of six, because most garden centers sell six-packs. If you have to buy more flowers, you can always expand the garden by a foot or so and squeeze them all in. Here's what you'll need for a 5- by 12-foot bed:

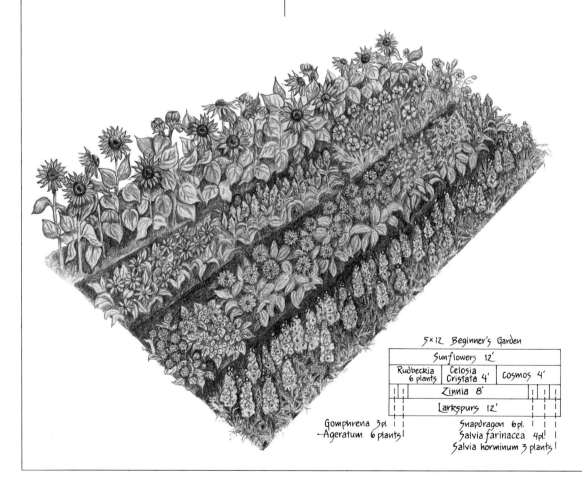

5 × 12 Beginner's Garden

Sunflowers 12'		
Rudbeckia 6 plants	Celosia Cristata 4'	Cosmos 4'
Zinnia 8'		
Larkspurs 12'		

Gomphrena 3 pl.
—Ageratum 6 plants

Snapdragon 6 pl.
Salvia farinacea 4 pl.
Salvia horminum 3 plants

- *Consolida ambigua* (larkspur). In many areas, larkspur should be direct-seeded in fall. You also can freeze the seed for two weeks and direct-seed in spring. You'll need enough seeds for a 12-foot row, or buy eighteen plants. Larkspur can be used fresh or dried.
- *Salvia horminum* (tri-color sage). This heavily branching plant sends up spikes of what look like pink or blue leaves; they're actually bracts around the inconspicuous white flowers. They can be used fresh or dried. Because they branch so profusely, you'll need only three plants.
- *Antirrhinum* (snapdragon). Be sure to get a tall cultivar, such as 'Rocket' or 'Liberty'. You'll need six plants.
- *Ageratum* 'Blue Horizon'. Don't mistake low-growing varieties for this tall cultivar. Buy six plants.
- *Rudbeckia* 'Indian Summer'. The blooms on this huge-flowered black-eyed Susan actually look better a few days after they've been in the vase. Get six plants.
- *Zinnia*. Grow 'State Fair', 'California Giant', or some other cultivar that's 30 inches tall. Direct-seed an 8-foot row or buy twelve plants.

- *Gomphrena* spp. (globe-amaranth). 'Bicolor Rose' is a great soft pink-and-white color, or you can buy the clear pink, dark rose, or red varieties. (I don't recommend the pure white.) These branching plants produce an astonishing number of flowers, and since you'll use them only as fillers in bouquets, buy just three plants. They can be used fresh or dried.
- *Cosmos* 'Versailles' or 'Seashells'. These can be direct-seeded. Grow a 4-foot row or buy six plants.
- *Celosia cristata* (cockscomb). 'Chief' is a good variety for its long stems, and can be used fresh or dried. Direct-seed a 4-foot row or buy six plants.
- *Salvia farinacea* 'Victoria' or 'Blue Bedder'. This lovely blue spike can be used fresh or dried. Buy four plants and cut them hard to encourage branching.
- *Helianthus annuus* (sunflower). Buy seed for a 12-foot row. Grow one of the branching, multicolored varieties, such as 'Autumn Beauty', to get the most versatility. Or go for one of the exotic dark-red sunflowers, such as 'Velvet Queen' or 'Prado Red'. ❧

This sample garden of annuals is filled with easy, prolific flowers that will provide cutting material from late spring until frost. Early in the season, larkspur, snapdragons, and Salvia horminum *will bloom for a month until the weather turns hot. By then, the zinnia, ageratum, rudbeckia, and sunflowers will begin producing. They will bloom until late summer, and will be joined during that time by cosmos, gomphrena,* Celosia cristata, *and* Salvia farinacea.

There are scores of perennials that make good cut flowers. Many may surprise you, because you don't normally think of them as cut flowers, such as the blossoms of the shade garden: Hostas are lovely both for their foliage and their blooms; the tiny flowers of coral bells *(Heuchera sanguinea)* make a wonderful addition to a country bouquet; and arching sprays of old-fashioned bleeding-heart *(Dicentra spectabilis)* look exquisite in an arrangement. The extensive list in appendix 1 will give you a complete picture of recommended flowers you can choose from when planning a perennial cutting bed. The sample garden illustrated on page 5 will give you a specific plan for a small perennial cutting garden that you can double or triple in size if you wish.

THE BEST CUTTING FLOWERS FOR YOUR REGION

To guide those of you who are beginners, I asked some experienced growers to name their Top Ten varieties, that is, those that are easiest, most reliable, and most productive. I called one expert from each region of the country and asked which flowers he or she considered foolproof. Several flowers were Top Ten choices in every region. Zinnias and larkspur, for example, were listed by growers from the cool coast of Maine to the hot heart of Texas. That says something about how tough they are. In the lists that follow, each variety is listed by Latin name first so that you can easily find it in appendix 1.

Northeast

MaryLee Johnson manages the flower trials for Johnny's Selected Seeds in Albion, Maine. She has traveled the world looking for new flowers for the Johnny's catalog and says the most popular looks that will be coming our way soon include green-and-white bouquets and colorful amaranths and other grains. MaryLee also has worked as a florist, and likes to incorporate many kinds of materials into her designs. Her Top Ten cutting flowers are:

> *Achillea millefolium* 'Cerise Queen' and 'Colorado Mix'
> *Consolida ambigua* (larkspur) 'Giant Imperial', 'Snow Cloud', and 'Blue Cloud'
> *Cosmos bipinnatus* 'Sensation' and 'Versailles'
> *Dianthus barbatus* (sweet William) 'Hollandia' mix and 'Messenger'
> *Gomphrena* spp. (globe-amaranth)
> *Helianthus annuus* (sunflowers)
> *Limonium sinuatum* (statice) 'Pacific Strain' series
> Ornamental grasses, including *Setaria* spp. (foxtail millet); *Briza maxima* (large quaking grass); and *Pennisetum* spp.
> *Veronica longifolia* 'Sightseeing' mix
> *Zinnia elegans* 'Blue Point' and 'Sunbow'

Mid-Atlantic

Cass Peterson of Flickerville Mountain Farm in Dott, Pennsylvania, makes bouquets to complement her vegetable sales at farmers' markets in the Washington, D.C., area. For farmers' market sales, bright flowers pull in more customers than pastels. Cass says, "Our farm stand is known for its rather loud and funky flower bunches. The general rule is lots of purple, red, and orange; a little bright yellow; few pastels; and absolutely no white. Not much filler, either, except for purple statice." Here are her favorites:

Buddleia davidii (butterfly bush)
Celosia cristata 'Fire Chief' and 'Persimmon'
Centaurea macrocephala (golden basket flower)
Delphinium 'Standup'
Echinops ritro (globe thistle)
Eustoma grandiflorum (lisianthus) 'Echo' mix
Helianthus annuus (sunflower) 'Giant Sungold' and 'Velvet Queen'
Helichrysum (strawflower) 'Frosted Sulfur' and peach/apricot shades
Liatris spicata (gayfeather) 'Floristan Violet'
Lilium (lily), Asiatic varieties 'Enchantment' and 'Red Knight'
Zinnia elegans 'California Giant'

Southeast

Betsy Hitt grows two acres of cut flowers near Chapel Hill, North Carolina. She and her husband, Alex, have been growing vegetables and flowers for market since 1981. At farmers' markets, Betsy sells flowers as "grower's bunches," that is, one type of flower in bunches that vary in size. She also sells about three hundred mixed bouquets each week to natural foods supermarkets. Here are her best performers:

Agastache barberi 'Tutti-frutti'
Ageratum houstonianum 'Blue Horizon'
Agrostemma githago (corn cockle)
Consolida ambigua (larkspur)
Dianthus barbatus (sweet William) 'Messenger' and 'Electron'
Digitalis (foxglove)
Eustoma grandiflorum (lisianthus)
Helianthus annuus (sunflower)
Nigella damascena (love-in-a-mist)
Zinnia elegans 'Burpee Giant'

South

Lorraine Billeaud grows flowers in Lafayette, Louisiana, as a complement to her landscaping business. She sells mixed bouquets to a produce stand and a meat market, and also sells to retail florists and a wholesaler. Lorraine says her bouquets are big—the plastic sleeves measure 24 inches across the top and 7 inches across the bottom. Here are her most reliable flowers:

Buddleia spp. (butterfly bush)
Celosia plumosa and *cristata*
Consolida ambigua (larkspur)
Coreopsis tinctoria (calliopsis)
Delphinium
Dianthus barbatus (sweet William) 'Hollandia'
Salvia 'Indigo Spires'
Salvia leucantha (Mexican bush sage)
Tagetes (marigold) 'Gold Coin'
Zinnia elegans

Midwest

I pulled together a Top Ten list of the flowers that I consider absolutely foolproof at my farm in Lawrence, Kansas. I sell primarily to florists, so I'm looking for flowers with stiff stems that can be poked into floral foam. But I also sell mixed bunches to customers in our vegetable subscription program, so I also like to grow some thin-stemmed but voluminous plants, such as *Salvia horminum*. These varieties have done well for me, even during the summer when I blatantly neglected them to get this book written. Here are my champions:

Achillea millefolium 'Cerise Queen'
Ageratum houstonianum 'Blue Horizon'
Antirrhinum (snapdragon) 'Rocket' mix
Celosia cristata 'Chief'
Consolida ambigua (larkspur) 'Giant Imperial' and 'Early Bird'
Cosmos bipinnatus 'Seashells' and 'Versailles'
Salvia farinacea 'Blue Bedder'
Salvia horminum (tri-color sage)
Veronica longifolia 'Sightseeing'
Zinnia elegans 'Blue Point' and 'Oklahoma'

Upper Midwest

Faye Jones of Morning Glory Farm in Spring Valley, Wisconsin, grows flowers for a bouquet business. She sells to a bouquet maker who supplies supermarkets in the Minneapolis–St. Paul area. Here are her most useful flowers:

Ageratum houstonianum 'Blue Horizon'
Antirrhinum (snapdragon) 'Red Stone,' 'Bronze', and 'Rocket' mix
Celosia cristata 'Chief' and *C. spicata* 'Flamingo Feather'

Consolida ambigua (larkspur) 'Giant Imperial'
Dianthus barbatus (sweet William)
Digitalis (foxglove) 'Foxy'
Liatris spicata (gayfeather)
Limonium sinutatum (statice) 'Excellent'
Salvia farinacea 'Blue Bedder'
Zinnia elegans 'State Fair'

Southwest

Pamela and Frank Arnosky of Texas Specialty Cut Flowers in Blanco, Texas, make bouquets for an upscale supermarket in Austin and for florists. They have five acres in field-grown cut flowers and four greenhouses where they grow flowers in winter. Their bouquet style is big and bold, and these are their Top Ten picks for reliability and ease of culture:

Celosia cristata 'Chief'
Consolida ambigua (larkspur)
Coreopsis tinctoria (calliopsis)
Echinacea (coneflower) 'Bravado'
Gomphrena globosa (globe-amaranth) 'Bicolor Rose'
Helianthus annuus (sunflower) 'Superior Gold'
Polianthes tuberosa (tuberose), Mexican single
Rudbeckia 'Indian Summer' and 'Gloriosa Double'
Tagetes (marigold) 'Gold Coin'
Zinnia elegans 'Blue Point'

Coastal California and Pacific Northwest

Beth Benjamin was for many years the flower expert at Shepherd's Garden Seeds in Felton, California. As part of her job, she sought out new flowers to add to the catalog and grew them in the company's trial gardens. She has recently left Shepherd's to devote more time to her gardens and other interests. Although almost everything grows well in her temperate coastal climate, she was able to name her Top Ten:

Consolida ambigua (larkspur)
Coreopsis tinctoria (calliopsis)
Dianthus barbatus (sweet William)
Helianthus annuus (sunflower)
Nigella damascena (love-in-a-mist)
Lavatera trimestris
Phlox drummondi 'Grandiflora'
Salvia coccinea 'Coral Nymph'
Zinnia elegans 'Blue Point'

Sunflowers

Choosing Varieties

During the early 1990s, sunflowers achieved fad status. Their cheery yellow faces could be found on everything from hats to welcome mats, and their popularity in the garden kept pace.

Although sunflowers are departing as a decorating motif (replaced by pansies), they're still holding strong as a cut flower. That's because the seed companies did some truly remarkable work in developing cultivars of this American native flower. The results are so beautiful that sunflowers have become a standard in floral design.

When research on breeding work started, the biggest problem with sunflowers as cut flowers was that they produced abundant amounts of pollen. Although the yellow powder is beautiful as it develops on the dark disc, pollen sheds on everything, from the grower's T-shirt to the flower buyer's tablecloth. (In the garden, the bumblebees that arrive after the dew dries normally sweep up the pollen as soon as it develops; that's why you don't really notice the pollen until you bring the flowers indoors.)

Several pollenless varieties have addressed that problem. 'Sunbright' is a single-stemmed variety with a dark center and bright gold petals. When given plenty of space, fertility, and water, it can produce flowers 8 inches across. Grown more closely, the flowers measure 4 to 6 inches in diameter. Other early pollenless cultivars include the single-stemmed 'Sunrich Lemon' and 'Sunrich Orange', and the wine-red branching 'Chianti'.

Pollenless sunflowers are F_1 hybrids, meaning that two different parents are used to produce every seed crop of the pollenless generation. Pollenless flowers will not develop seeds if pollination is prevented by covering the flowers with netting. However, in the field, insects move pollen around indiscriminately, not caring that they're mixing up the genetic material. Those pollenless sunflowers, once pollinated by some other type, will produce seeds. If you plant those seeds the next year, you'll get some interesting combinations of cultivars. My favorite accidental sunflower was a big 'Sunbright' type with the red and gold petals of 'Autumn Beauty'.

Other breeding work has focused on colors. Cultivars are now available in every shade of yellow, gold, bronze, red, maroon, and brown, plus many bicolors. At this writing, there are at least three dozen cultivars on the market.

Sunflowers are easy to grow. In most places, you can just push the seeds into the ground, water them, and expect to see blooms in just two months. If grasshoppers or other insects endanger your seedlings, you may want to start the sunflower seeds indoors and transplant out when they have a few sets of leaves. They can be planted oudoors every two weeks until midsummer (about two months before you normally get a frost) for a long season of flowers.

Sunflowers are big plants, and require quite a bit of fertility. Enrich the bed with compost before you begin, and scratch in a bit of bloodmeal if your soil tends to be deficient in nitrogen. Side-dress the plants with compost, or water them with manure tea just before they bloom, to keep them productive.

Sunflowers can be cut as soon as the petals (the ray flowers) start to unfurl. If cucumber beetles are present in your garden, you can try to cut blossoms even sooner to prevent those insects from nibbling on the petals. Sunflowers will do fine if you put them in plain water—research shows that only a few cultivars do better in floral preservative than in tap water. Vase life can range from five days for some cultivars to thirteen days for others. For commercial growers, here are some cultivars that will last more than ten days in the vase: 'Sunbright', 'Sunrich Lemon', 'Sunrich Orange', 'Happy Faces', 'Taiyo', 'Golden Pheasant', 'Sunbeam', 'Giant Sungold', and 'Teddy Bear'. ∽

The most popular sunflowers grown commercially are the non-branching, pollenless varieties such as 'Sunbright' (below). This variety will produce flowers up to 8 inches across if given 12 inches of space between plants; planting closer will produce smaller flowers. Commercial growers harvest the entire 5-foot stem and make bunches of five. 'Sunbright' is also a good choice for drying.

FLOWERS FOR DRYING

Nearly any flower can be preserved by one method or another, and you will learn later in this book how to preserve those special flowers that make your arrangements extraordinary. But you still need large quantities of easily dried flowers for the filler or base of your designs. When I made wreaths for farmers' market sales, I would bring a brown grocery sack full of dried flowers from the barn every time I sat down to make an 18-inch wreath. Here are my choices for the best flowers to grow for drying; complete instructions for growing and drying them appear in the alphabetical list of recommended cut flowers in appendix 1:

Celosia cristata (cockscomb)
Consolida spp. (larkspur)
Gomphrena spp. (globe-amaranth)
Gypsophila paniculata (baby's breath)
Helichrysum bracteatum (strawflower)
Limonium sinuatum (statice)
Limonium suworowii (pink pokers)
Limonium tataricum (German statice)
Nigella damascena (love-in-a-mist)
Salvia farinacea 'Victoria'

HERB BOUQUETS

Many of the plants that we think of as herbs and edible flowers can be used in bouquets. An herb-and-flower arrangement will be a fragrant and utilitarian addition to your kitchen counter. You can pluck leaves from the plants for cooking or garnishing plates while enjoying their fragrance and subtle beauty as you work. More elaborate arrangements of herbs are popular for luncheon centerpieces. And market growers may find the herbal bouquet to be a good choice for selling to cafés and gourmet food shops.

Of course, you have to be careful when selecting plants for your edible bouquets. Because so many plants—even those closely related to edible ones—are actually quite poisonous, you should use only those listed below, which are known to be safe and are widely used as food ingredients. Never mix in unknown flowers with an herb bouquet, because it would be too easy to mistakenly use the ones that aren't safe to eat.

Here are a dozen edible herbs and flowers that hold up well in the vase and should, in combination, provide you with bounteous herbal bouquets over a long season:

14

- Anise hyssop *(Agastache foeniculum)* is a member of the mint family and is a tender perennial that self-seeds. Both the foliage and the flowers have an anise scent. The foliage is a bit coarse, but the lavender flowers are quite nice in mixed bouquets.
- Basil *(Ocimum basilicum)* varies in its ability to be used as a cut flower. The large-leaved green varieties often wilt quickly, but some of the smaller-leaved varieties will hold up for days. The dark opal basil, with its purple-and-green–streaked foliage, is a good choice. So is cinnamon basil, which has glossy green leaves, purple stems, and pink flowers. Thai basil is shorter, but has interesting flat clusters of maroon flowers held above the green leaves.
- Calendula *(Calendula officinalis)* has yellow or orange flowers, and the petals are often sprinkled on food. Grow one of the tall cultivars such as 'Prince' or 'Kablouna'.

Herb bouquets, with their fragrance and subtle colors, are popular for casual decorating. Dress them up with a raffia bow.

- Chives *(Allium schoenoprasum)* produce lovely purple or pink flowers that bloom in early spring. Garlic chives *(Allium tuberosum)* have starry white flowers in midsummer. The blooms of either type can be pulled apart and the individual florets sprinkled on salads or soups for a chive or garlic flavor. Kept in the vase, these flowers emit only the faintest garlicky smell.
- Dill *(Anethum graveolens)* produces a broad umbel of tiny yellow flowers. A variety of the common "dill weed" used for pickling is sold as a cut-flower filler. So it's a natural for your herb bouquets.
- Fennel *(Foeniculum vulgare)* is an anise-scented herb that resembles dill and can be used as an airy filler for bouquets.
- Lavender *(Lavandula* spp.) is traditionally used in perfumes and soaps or, dried, as a sachet for perfuming clothes and table linens. But it also has a place in the kitchen and can be used sparingly in baked goods, sauces, and condiments. 'Lavender Lady' blooms the first year from seed, but its dwarf stature makes it useful only in small bouquets. English lavender *(L. angustifolia)* is taller and is considered the best kind for eating, but the other lavenders can also be used.
- Bee balm or bergamot *(Monarda didyma)* belongs to the mint family, with bright, shaggy flowers that grow in whorls around the stem. The foliage has a minty, citrusy flavor.
- Nasturtium *(Tropaeolum majus)* is widely used as an edible flower, and its peppery round leaves are often added to salad mixes. In the vase, the flowers will last only two or three days, but the attractive foliage will last for up to two weeks. Be sure to grow a tall variety, such as 'Jewel'.
- Oregano *(Origanum* spp.) is a terribly misunderstood genus. Several species and many varieties go by the common name "oregano," but their appearances and flavors vary widely. The best one to grow for bouquets is *Origanum vulgare,* known as wild oregano or marjoram. It doesn't have much flavor, but it produces attractive clusters of pink flowers that can be dried.
- Sage *(Salvia* spp.) in its several forms, is an important ingredient in herb bouquets. The common garden sage *(Salvia officinalis)* has pebbly, silver-green leaves that look wonderful in bouquets anytime, and its purple flowers in early spring are particularly attractive as cut flowers. In addition, several cultivars of *S. officinalis* are highly ornamental. 'Aurea' has leaves of green and gold, and 'Tricolor' has leaves of cream, purple, and green. *Salvia elegans* is pineapple sage, which bears bright red flowers.

Whether you plant herbs, perennials, annuals, or a combination, the success of your flowers will depend on the proper location and preparation of the beds—the topic of the next chapter.

Dos Osos Multifloro ⮘ Watsonville, California

WHEN WILL FULTON STARTED HIS OWN FLOWER SHIPPING BUSINESS IN 1989, he defied the experts who said he needed to sell the three most common cut flowers—roses, carnations, and chrysanthemums—to survive in the floral industry. His company, Dos Osos Multifloro, sells only the unusual.

Touring his cooler in Watsonville, California, is like taking an introductory course in specialty cut flowers. Just about every type of plant that can be used as a cut flower—*except* roses, carnations, and chrysanthemums—goes through his doors. Sweet pea, tweedia, allium, sunflower, godetia, dill, artichoke, hydrangea, bachelor's button, horsetail—from the delicate to the robust, the common to the exotic, flowers and greens of every description are available to fulfill the creative whims of floral designers.

Shipping a wide selection of specialty flowers is a formula that has worked well for Dos Osos Multifloro. Will now buys from several hundred California flower growers, and ships to floral wholesalers and retail florists throughout the United States year-round. He faxes price lists every night and has his own page on the World Wide Web. He's experimenting with putting a camera in his cooler and showing the photos on his Web page, so customers can see the actual flowers that are available before they order them.

Recently, Will took another road less traveled in the cut-flower industry. He switched to organic production on his twenty-one-acre flower farm, even though he had to buy out a partner who was reticent about making the transition. This time, though, the market wasn't driving his strategy.

"I don't see any demand for organically grown cut flowers," he says. "The only time I've ever been asked whether my flowers were organic was when they were going to be eaten. There really is no marketing justification for switching to organic. I'd like to say there was, because maybe more people would start growing organically, but it's not true."

So why then *did* he switch to organic production?

"I wanted to sleep at night," Will says. "The notion that we rent our land from our descendants is one that resonates for me. I want to try to make the land I farm into better farmland than it is now, for the sake of future generations. I want to learn to grow healthy soil. I want the plot to which I'm assigned in this lifetime to live on after me, nurtured rather than depleted."

Will's farmland is surrounded by hills, but the cries of sea birds overhead and the smell of salt air reveal that the Pacific Ocean is just beyond view. His land is near one of the last remaining estuaries, or coastal wetlands, in California. Conventional chemical farming on such a piece of land, he says, could damage the fragile wetlands that provide habitat for birds and other wildlife. "There used to be so much wetland in California that the skies were frequently darkened by flocks of birds," Will says. "There are still birds in California, but not so many. I recently visited Albania, a country climatologically and geographically similar to California, but one with virtually no birds. I don't want to be a party to a similar catastrophe in California."

His fields don't get nipped by frost until January, so Will focuses on growing flowers for fall, when supplies elsewhere are diminishing. In summer, he says, it's cheaper to buy flowers than to grow them himself. Although most of the flowers he buys from other U.S. growers are not raised organically, he says they are still safer than flowers grown in many other countries.

"We have the strictest environmental regulations in the hemisphere here in California," he says. "If the consumers were going to vote with their dollars the same way they do at the polls, we would have a larger share of the market. But they don't know where flowers come from—they have no way of knowing."

Will supports the idea of a labeling law for cut flowers. A sticker that reveals the country of origin would help sell domestic flowers, if it were coupled with an educational campaign to tell consumers that U.S. pesticide regulations are much more stringent than those in South America and many other flower-growing regions.

Although the domestic flower market isn't clamoring for organically grown flowers, Will says he's confident that he's doing the smart thing.

"As a marketer of cut flowers for eighteen years, I have learned that if I try my best to provide a quality product for my customers, then a profit will be forthcoming. It just proceeds. I may not get rich, but I'll earn a living. Similarly, I have to believe that if I attend to the health of my soil, I'll enjoy good crops. Maybe they won't be bumper crops, but they'll be okay. I guess what I really believe is that if I do the right thing, I'll get what I need." ∾

CHAPTER 2

Site and Soil

*I*F YOU'RE A CITY OR SUBURBAN GARDENER, CHANCES ARE YOU DON'T HAVE much choice about where you will plant your flowers. You probably have just one site that's eligible for a garden. And that's fine: You will just have to focus all your energy on making that particular site as hospitable as possible for flowers.

For those of you who do have some options about where to place your garden, consider them carefully, because your choice of location may make the difference between success and failure. When my husband and I started market gardening, we originally planned to plow the meadow north of our house because it was the biggest stretch of open land on our farm. Later, we decided to plow instead an area in front of the barn because it was closer to water. After we hacked through the head-high weeds, we realized we had stumbled on a gold mine. The area was an old corral, and the soil there was much better than any other field on our farm. I shudder to think how difficult flower growing would have been on that windblown meadow; I probably wouldn't be speaking now as the voice of experience.

The following factors are the main ones that you should consider before determining where to put your flower gardens.

Soil

Where is the soil most fertile and friable—that is, crumbly and even-textured? If your property is extensive, get a soil map from the local Soil Conservation Service office. If you're dealing with just a few acres, take your shovel out and dig holes in many places to get a sense of the soil patterns, which can vary significantly over a small area. On our hillside farm, for example, there's a layer of sandstone close to the surface on the hilltop, but the topsoil is deep and rich just a few hundred feet away. Areas of your property that have been excavated in the past for septic systems and water lines may be heavy with clay. Likewise, if you live in an area of new houses, you may find that the developer stripped the topsoil before beginning construction, leaving you with lifeless clay for a garden. In either case, you're going to have to have new topsoil trucked in before you can start.

The ideal soil for growing flowers is a well-drained sandy loam with a neutral pH, adequate fertility, and abundant organic matter. Most people aren't blessed with this perfect soil, but they can improve what they have and make it productive with cover crops, compost, and organic soil amendments.

Water

Where is water most accessible? Flowers need water, so consider irrigation in your site selection. Are you on a well, or on a municipal or rural water line? Do you have access to a spring, stream, or pond, and, if so, is the water clean or will it require extensive filtration? Is there electricity for pumping, or can the water be siphoned or gravity-fed? Before you determine your garden site, figure out how you can get the water to your garden, either by laying a pipe below the frost line and installing a new faucet by the garden, or by physically hauling the hose. Hauling hoses is hard work, and you don't want to have to pull them any farther than necessary.

Wind

Where is the ground most protected from wind? Flowers can handle a surprising amount of adverse weather, but they do not like to be battered by wind. Research has shown that winds of just 7 miles per hour can damage plants. Seedlings can be sheared off at ground level by wind-whipped soil particles, and wind can tear blossoms, blow over plants, or sear their tender growing points. Flowers are susceptible to even short periods of windy weather because they exhibit growth responses known as tropisms: Some plants turn away from gravity (negative geotropism), and others will quickly will grow toward light (phototropism). When they are pushed by wind off-vertical, their tips will turn upward, creating a nasty bend in their stems. So try to pick a site that has trees, shrubs, or buildings to shield your flowers from the prevailing summer wind.

If you don't have a naturally protected area for your flower garden, plant one. Select shrubs or trees with flowering branches or interesting foliage that you can use for your bouquets. And while you're waiting for them to grow tall, plant a barrier of wheat or rye, which can be used fresh or dried in your arrangements. (To find out the best planting date for your area, call your regional Cooperative Extension office.)

How many windbreaks do you need for your field? The rule of thumb is that the area of calm behind the windbreak extends for a distance six to eight times the height of the windbreak. Thus, a strip of rye 4 feet high would provide good protection in the 24 to 32 feet behind the windbreak. Some level of protection extends for a distance of twelve to fifteen times the height of the windbreak, so in the case of the 4-foot grain, there would be a lesser degree of protection for about an additional 20 feet. Your best strategy, therefore, would be to plant a strip of wheat or rye, leave 30 to 50 feet open for flowers, and plant another strip of grain. Make your strips 5 to 10 feet wide to provide enough density to really slow the wind.

If wind is a problem only in spring, you can harvest the windbreak crop for drying. Wheat, rye, and triticale are all popular ornamental crops.

Your long-term goal might be to plant a row of 10-foot-tall flowering shrubs every 100 feet in your flower garden. When fully grown, the shrubs would provide a good level of wind protection for your young plants.

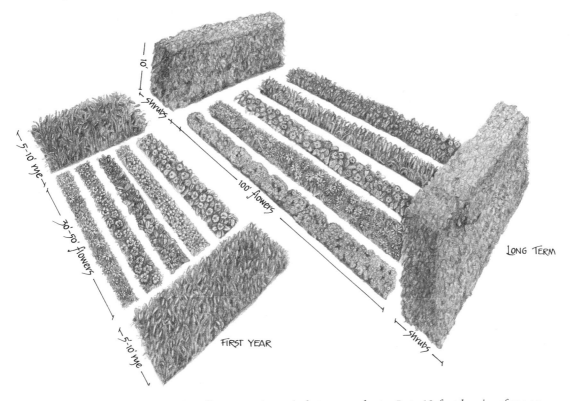

As a temporary measure to protect flowers against wind, you can plant a 5- to 10-foot barrier of rye or wheat every 30 to 50 feet. For a long-term solution, plant a line of tall shrubs about every 100 feet. Choose varieties with foliage or flowers that are good for cutting (see chapter 6).

SOIL PREPARATION

One of the most commonly heard myths about flowers is that they do not need good soil, that too much fertility will lead to lush foliage and no flowers. In truth, the needs of flowers are no different from the needs of vegetables. Some flowers need abundant nitrogen and others need less, but all will benefit from a fertile soil with good tilth, or texture, and high organic matter. If you doubt this fact, transplant some daisies or coneflowers from a meadow or roadside into a well-prepared garden. They will grow far bigger and prove more robust.

Soil preparation is the most important job you will do in the flower garden. I can't emphasize this enough. If I could, I would take you on a tour of my flower gardens to show you what a difference proper soil preparation can make. In one bed located over the septic field (a bad place to plant anything), delphiniums struggled mightily, but just barely survived in the hard, pale clay soil. Fifty feet away from the septic field, I double-dug a new bed and filled it with compost and topsoil, then transplanted some of those delphiniums. Within sixty days, those same sorry plants were covered with tall, stately blooms. And that was not an isolated case. Over and over again, I have seen the power of good soil preparation. You can't expect flowers to thrive in poor soil, so take the time to create good soil.

Your best tools for soil improvement are cover crops and compost. Let's look at how each one might fit into your gardening schedule.

Cover Crops

Cover crops, also referred to as green manures, can increase your soil fertility while creating a mellow, crumbly texture that your plants will love. Some cover crops are legumes that fix nitrogen while they're growing, helping supply the nutrients your flowers will need and providing organic matter when they're plowed down. Cover crops that are not legumes will not add significant amounts of nitrogen to the soil, but they will improve the soil tilth, prevent erosion, and smother weeds.

Cover crops can be either annual or perennial plants. In general, perennials are used in areas that won't be disturbed every year, such as orchards, berry patches, and paths between raised beds. Annuals are usually sown right in the area where you want to grow flowers in subsequent years. This discussion will focus on the annual cover crops, which will do their job in one season and then be plowed down.

If you are planning to start your flower-growing career in the fall, plow or dig your garden area, then seed it with an overwintering cover crop. The list on the next page includes the best cover crops for each season, but there are regional differences based on winter temperatures. To find the best choices for your area, ask your Cooperative Extension agent, fellow farmers in local organic groups, or regional seed suppliers. With overwintering cover crops, the seeds will germinate and plants will begin to grow in fall, then go dormant when the weather turns cold. They'll resume growth again in spring. You should plow them down or turn them under with a shovel or tiller about two to four weeks before you intend to start planting flowers. If they are beginning to flower before that time, mow them to prevent them from going to seed; otherwise, they may reseed themselves all over your garden.

If you are starting your garden in spring or summer, you will benefit from putting in a cover crop during the growing season. You don't have to plant the entire garden with a cover crop. In fact, farmers do their planting in rotations: One year, they put one field in a cash crop and the next field in a cover crop; the following year, they plant the cash crop where the cover crop had been, and vice versa. You can do small rotations in your garden by seeding just one or two strips in a cover crop this year, while growing flowers in the rest of the garden, then switching next year. Plant these warm-season annuals after your last frost and nurture them along just like any other crop, but be sure to mow them before they flower to prevent them from spreading their seeds. You can grow the same annuals again in the same place, or you can turn them under and start a different cover crop there. The point is to get as much organic material decomposing in your soil as you can.

For the home gardener, most cover crops can be planted by broadcasting the seed, then raking it in, and turning on the sprinkler. On a com-

Cover Crops for the Home and Market Garden

Many of the cover crops listed below are used by farmers for rotations or as cash crops, so you may find the seed at your local farmers' co-op. You also can purchase cover-crop seed by mail from many of the seed companies and suppliers listed in the notes for this chapter in appendix 2, "Sources and Resources." If the name of the cover crop is followed by (L), that means the plant is a legume, which adds nitrogen to the soil. You should also purchase the proper bacterial inoculant to treat the seeds of legumes before planting; this helps to increase the amount of nitrogen the plant can produce in the soil.

Spring-seeded:
Black-eyed peas (L)
Buckwheat
Cowpeas (L)
Crotalaria juncea (L)
Lablab (L)
Pinto beans (L)
Soybeans (L)
Sudan grass

Fall-seeded:
Annual ryegrass
Austrian winter peas (L)
Barrel medic (L)
Bell beans (L)
Berseem clover (L)
Common vetch (L)
Crimson clover (L)
Fava beans (L)
Garbanzo beans (L)
Hairy vetch (L)
Kenland red clover (L)
Lana Woolly-pod vetch (L)
Miranda peas (L)
Mustard
Oats
Purple vetch (L)
Rape
Rose clover (L)
Rye
Subterranean clovers (L)
Sweet clover (L)
Wheat

mercial scale, some crops may require a seed drill for planting, but most seed can be broadcast and then "disced in," incorporated with a disc pulled by a tractor. Ask the seed supplier how to plant each type you buy.

Compost

Gardeners often refer to compost as "black gold," and with good reason. A well-made compost will do more for your soil and your plants than you would ever expect. It doesn't seem pos-

sible that just an inch or two of deep brown organic matter worked into the soil should be so beneficial, but it is. Dull, lifeless soil seems more alive; clay turns mellow; plants grow robustly.

Composting is basically an accelerated version of nature's recycling system, which, with the help of microorganisms, decomposes complex organic materials into humus, macronutrients, trace elements, enzymes, and other substances used in plant growth. Although composting will eventually occur on its own, it takes some human effort to do the job quickly and in such a way that the maximum amount of nutrients are retained.

To make high-quality compost, your raw materials need a carbon-to-nitrogen (C:N) ratio of about 25 to 1. (The chart at right gives you an idea of the C:N ratio of commonly used materials.) Materials that are high in carbon include straw, hay, and grass clippings. Kitchen scraps and vegetable wastes are high in nitrogen. You also need to water the compost pile to make it hospitable to the bacteria that will do the work of decomposition. And you need a way to turn the pile, in order to ensure that decomposition occurs evenly throughout it.

If you're a backyard gardener, you can make your own compost using an inexpensive and easy-to-maintain bin. There are countless variations available commercially that will take your yard waste and kitchen scraps, and convert them into soil-building organic matter; you'll find advertisements for these in gardening magazines. Or you can build your own com-

---

COMMERCIAL COMPOST

Here is a basic formula that will help you know, without weighing your pile, how much compost you can make from the raw materials you have accumulated and pushed into a windrow.

1. Multiply the height of the windrow of raw material by the width at its base. Then multiply that by ⅔ to figure the square footage of the windrow. Let's say you have a rounded windrow, 8 feet tall by 14 feet wide at the base: $8 \times 14 \times \frac{2}{3} = 74$ square feet

2. Next, multiply the square footage by the length of the windrow to get the total cubic feet of raw material. Let's say the windrow runs 50 feet long: $74 \times 50 = 3,700$ cubic feet

3. Divide the total cubic feet by 27 to get the total cubic yards: $3,700 \div 27 = 137$ cubic yards

4. Divide the total cubic yards by 2, because volume will shrink by as much as 50 percent as the raw materials decompose: $137 \div 2 = 68$ cubic yards of finished compost

5. A ton of compost is equal to 1.5 to 2 cubic yards, so your 8- by 14- by 50-foot pile will make about 34 to 45 tons of finished compost. ∾

C:N Ratios of Compost Ingredients

Many factors influence the C:N ratios of various compost ingredients; the C:N ratios listed below are only general guidelines. Backyard composters can usually achieve the desirable C:N ratio of 25:1 or 30:1 by simply alternating layers of high-nitrogen materials such as kitchen scraps with layers of high-carbon materials such as straw or leaves. Commercial growers who want to make compost on a large scale should consult one of the references listed in appendix 2 for more precise instructions on blending materials.

Sawdust–400:1
Rice hulls–120:1
Pine needles–100:1
Straw–80:1
Leaves–80:1
Wheat straw–78:1

Weeds–30:1
Mature grass clippings–29:1
Rotted manure–20:1
Young grass clippings–12:1
Kitchen scraps–15:1

post pile with a small investment of time and effort. See the notes for this chapter, in appendix 2, "Sources and Resources" for books that provide more details about composting.

Another option for backyard gardeners is to buy bagged compost at your local garden center. I was skeptical about the quality of this material, because there's so little information on the label. But I used bagged compost and bagged topsoil from a discount store one year, in a garden that was built in midsummer after our usual supply of compost was exhausted. I was pleased with the results: The tilth of the soil in the bed was good and the flowers did well there.

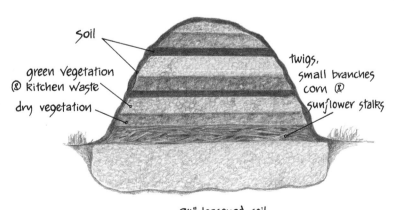

soil

green vegetation & kitchen waste

dry vegetation

twigs, small branches corn & sunflower stalks

24" loosened soil

Compost can be made in a variety of containers, or it can be piled up in a windrow, as shown here. The proportions of materials in the compost pile are approximate and can be varied.

If you're growing flowers on a commercial scale, you will need to either make or buy large amounts of compost every year. Some growers apply 5 tons of compost per acre between crops, although you can safely add up to 50 tons per acre if your soil is depleted. To get a sense of how to make that much compost, see the box (on page 24) for the formula for predicting your yield from raw material.

We make a small amount of compost every year using leftover vegetables, plant debris, greenhouse potting mix, and our kitchen scraps. But it's a pretty haphazard affair—we just pile it up behind the greenhouse and let it rot for a year. To be sure our soil is getting a high-quality annual boost, we buy compost from a certified organic compost-maker who delivers it, 4 tons at a time, in a dump truck. We found our supplier through our organic certification agency, which is a good place for you to look, too, if you would like to purchase compost. Most composters will either be certified themselves or will be known to the people at the organic agency. If you don't know the organic agency nearest you, contact your state department of agriculture's marketing division or your Cooperative Extension agent for a referral.

A GARDEN IN YOUR LAWN

You've chosen a site, made or purchased compost, and are ready to get your hands in the soil. Now it's time to build the garden where your plants will grow. Your mantra, as you head outdoors, should be "double-dig." Repeat that rhythmic phrase as you pick up the shovel, and keep saying it when your shoulders start to ache—it is the key to your success as a flower gardener.

Double-digging is a pretty simple concept: First you dig, then you dig again. Your goal is to loosen the soil to a depth of 18 to 24 inches. You must remove the soil down to a depth of one shovelful; next, use a spading fork to loosen and aerate the soil below that. Then you replace the top layer of soil, mixing in compost with it at the same time.

Here are step-by-step instructions for double-digging. Each numbered step refers to the same numbered panel in the illustration on the next page.

1. First, spread an inch or so of compost over the entire garden surface. Working in a line the length of your garden, remove the top layer of soil and compost, creating a trench the depth of your spade. Put the soil in a wheelbarrow or on a tarp nearby.
2. Standing in the trench you have just dug, plunge a spading fork into the lower level of soil. Wiggle and rock the fork to loosen the soil.
3. Start the next trench behind the first. This time, when you remove the top layer of soil, drop it into the first trench you created, breaking up the clods as much as possible. Again, use the spading fork to loosen the lower soil. When you have reached the end of your garden, and loosened the lower layer of soil with the spading fork, fill in the trench with the soil you reserved in the wheelbarrow or tarp.

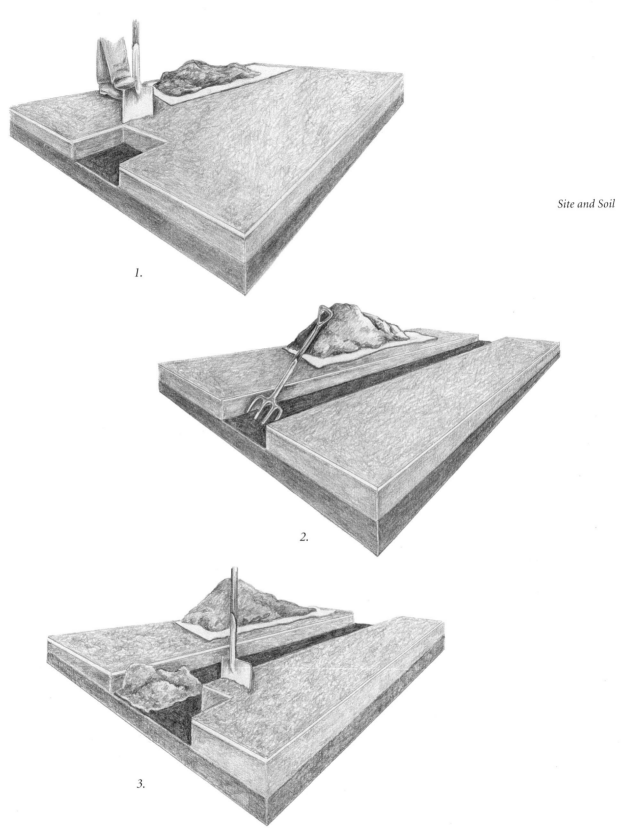

1.

2.

3.

An economical and attractive way to keep grass from encroaching on flower beds is to edge the bed with flat rocks dug down into the soil so that the top of the rock is just slightly higher than the surrounding lawn.

Double-digging and adding compost will raise the height of your soil. If you're preparing a bed or border in the lawn, you can install some type of edging to keep the grass from encroaching on your garden. My favorite technique is to use a layer of flat rocks or bricks set slightly above ground level, which allows you to roll the wheels of your lawnmower right over the edging. This type of mowing strip is attractive and takes less work than an upright plastic edging, which will require you to trim the grass along the garden's edge.

MAKING RAISED BEDS

If you are putting your flowers into an existing garden plot, or perhaps plowing a whole new field for flowers, you will want to make raised beds. The advantages of raised beds are many: They allow the soil to drain better; they allow for more intensive planting, and therefore more square-foot efficiency; they allow you to target fertilizer and compost to the soil where your plants will grow. During many rainy springs, the soil in our raised beds dries out quickly enough to let us plant, even while the soil in the paths is still gummy.

If you're building a small garden—say, anything under 1,000 square feet—you can create raised beds with a spade and your own muscle power. After you have double-dug your garden, make one or more 4-foot-wide raised beds by shoveling the soil from the path onto the adjoining bed. By shoveling 6 inches of soil from the path and throwing it up onto the bed, you create a raised bed 8 or 9 inches high.

If you have a rototiller with a hilling attachment, the job is much easier. After you have tilled the garden to a depth of about 4 to 5 inches, put on the hilling attachment and push the tiller where you want the paths to go. The wings of the hilling attachment will push the soil up off the path and onto the adjacent beds.

Some people go to the trouble of enclosing their raised beds with boards or cement blocks or some other structure. Frankly, I don't think it's worth the effort, unless you're doing it for the landscaping effect. The uncontained raised beds *will* break down over the course of the season, but that is not a bad thing. By the time the heat of summer arrives, you will be less likely to need the raised bed to provide drainage, and having a lower mound of soil means your soil won't dry out as quickly. In annual gardens particularly, it's much easier to make new beds every year than to build and tend permanent ones.

Raised Beds on a Commercial Scale

If you're growing a half-acre or more, you might want to invest in mechanized equipment for preparing your fields, or at least in hiring out the work to a neighbor with a tractor.

First, you should plow the ground to a depth of about 6 inches, using a moldboard plow. If time allows, let the plowed ground sit for a few weeks to allow the vegetation to begin to decompose. Then go over the field with a disc, which breaks up the clods of soil and smooths the surface. To make the raised beds, you can purchase a specialized piece of equipment called a bed shaper, which pulls the soil up into a mound and flattens the top. Some bed shapers can be adjusted to varying bed widths and heights. They also can be combined with tools to lay plastic mulch and drip irrigation tape simultaneously. Farmers who use plastic mulch say that mechanical mulch layers are essential on a large scale, because it's nearly impossible to get hand-laid plastic mulch taut enough to resist wind.

You also can make raised beds using just your plow. We have been doing it this way for many years and we find it to be slightly more time-consuming, but far less expensive, than purchasing a bed shaper. Here's what we do: Using a two-bottom plow, we plow the length of the field in one direction, which creates a furrow while mounding the soil on the right. Then we turn the tractor and plow in the opposite direction, about 6 feet away from the first furrow. The plow pushes the soil to the right again, toward the mound that was made by the first pass. By the end of this second pass, the first raised bed will be formed. Then we reverse directions again, with the left tractor tire on the bed we just made, and the plow slightly widening the furrow and throwing soil to the right onto the next bed. And so on. You have to be a pretty skilled tractor operator to keep your furrows straight and to space the furrows evenly every 6 feet, but precision comes with experience.

These mounds will be rough and not flat on top. To achieve smoother texture and a flat planting surface, you can either disc the field lightly or rototill the beds. If you use a small walk-behind tiller, you should hold it on top of the bed while you walk alongside in the furrow. With a large tiller, you're going to have to walk on top of the bed to maintain control of the tiller. Your beds will be about 4 feet wide on top—just the right size for rolls of paper or plastic mulch and support netting.

*Making
raised beds
with a plow.*

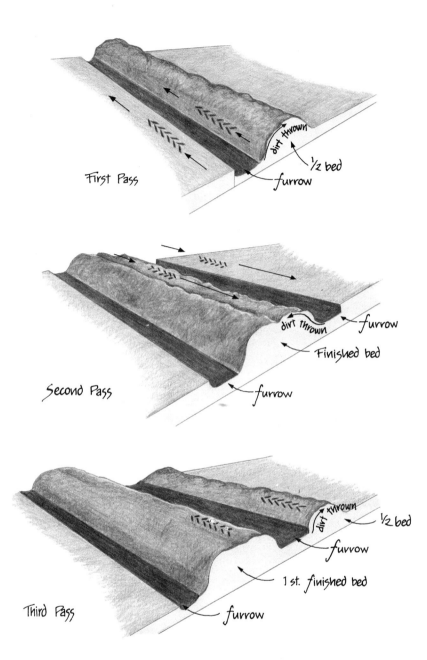

First Pass

dirt thrown
½ bed
furrow

Second Pass

dirt thrown
furrow
Finished bed
furrow

Third Pass

dirt thrown
½ bed
furrow
1 st. finished bed
furrow

Here & Now Garden ⤚ Gales Creek, Oregon

*A*T HERE & NOW GARDEN IN GALES CREEK, OREGON, PAUL SANSONE AND SUSAN Vosburg have found a way to blend idealism with business, small scale with big revenue, and high touch with high tech.

Paul and Susan grow cut flowers for the wholesale market, propagate new cut-flower varieties for a Dutch breeder, and sell plant material to other cut-flower growers. They do it organically, according to a system known as biodynamics that was pioneered by the German philosopher Rudolph Steiner in the 1920s. But they have adapted Steiner's practices to fit the needs of a 21st-century farm. Their equipment is sophisticated, their marketing intense.

"Steiner used the tools that were available in the twenties," Paul says. "We follow his principles, but we use the tools that are available to us today."

This successful business was created by serendipity rather than by a business plan. Paul and Susan, both now in their forties, met at the University of California at Santa Cruz, where they studied under Alan Chadwick, who introduced the French intensive method of horticulture to the United States. Paul helped design a solar heating system for the university's greenhouses, which launched him on a career in renewable energy. For ten years, he ran a company that built renewable-energy plants. By 1988, though, he was ready to abandon his city job for full-time work on the farm he and Susan had already occupied for twelve years. During that time, their two

31

children, Anthony and Sophia, were born.

Paul and Susan got their start selling at Portland farmers' markets. Competition was tough, especially in flowers. One market day, as Paul was left with several hundred bunches of unsold flowers, he was approached by an older man who brought along shipping boxes and started packing Paul's flowers in them. The man asked Paul what he planned to do with the flowers. Paul looked at him, dumbfounded, as the older man gave him the number of a wholesaler in Minneapolis who would buy them. The wholesale flower business was on its way.

In the years since, Paul and Susan have become well known for their skill as flower farmers. Their farm is meticulously neat, their equipment and techniques cutting-edge. Paul is a frequent speaker at conferences, and not at all shy about promoting his organic system, even to a roomful of conventional farmers. He lectures about the importance of soil fertility and advocates compost to anyone who asks him how he grows such great flowers. He pioneered the use of heavy polypropylene landscape fabric as an organic weed control, a system that has been widely adopted across the country.

So it was no surprise that Here & Now should be selected by the famous Dutch breeder Bartels Stek to propagate and market plant material. The Dutch company ships "mother plants" of its cut-flower varieties to Paul and Susan, who take cuttings to send to a greenhouse that specializes in rooting cuttings. The rooted plants are then returned to Here & Now Garden, where they are either sold in the tray or planted out in the field to grow for six to eight months. Small-scale commercial growers generally order the plants in lots of twenty-five.

Paul says that selling plants has become 50 percent of the business in just three years.

It's a perfect complement to the wholesale business, because he can sell the flowers of the plants he is propagating.

The work is year-round at Here & Now Garden, in part because Paul believes that winter work will alleviate summer's problems. He has all systems ready to go as soon as the weather moderates in March. The black polypropylene fabric, which allows water and air to penetrate but keeps out the light that would germinate weed seeds, is removed from some beds, and early perennials such as solidaster, phlox, and delphinium are planted. Some perennials, such as gentian and scabiosa, which can't be divided in fall, are dug and moved to other beds.

In May, the flower harvest begins with single peonies, polygonum, campanula, heuchera, delphinium, and Siberian iris. It continues through October, with late-blooming gentian, 'Monte Casino' asters, and the last of the pods such as montbretia (*Crocosmia*), turtlehead (*Chelone*), and obedient plant (*Physostegia*). In all, Here & Now Garden produces more than one hundred cultivars of specialty cut flowers on thirty acres. All are sold on the wholesale market. Some flowers yield as much as $20,000 in revenue per four-tenths of an acre.

However, Paul doesn't sing the praises of any flower too highly. The market is too volatile, too easily glutted by growers following a fad. He prefers to grow a diversity of unusual flowers and find his own markets for them.

The buyers "won't give you a dime extra" for growing organically, Paul says. But Paul and Susan remain true to their organic roots, because they believe that the quality of their flowers and the long-term success of their farm depend on their good stewardship of the land. ❧

CHAPTER 3

Buying and Starting Plants

*T*HE COMPLETE FLOWER GARDEN WILL HAVE A MIXTURE OF ANNUALS, perennials, and bulbs; plants that are seeded directly into the garden and those that must be started in a greenhouse; and plants that are purchased from suppliers. There's a broad spectrum of work that can be done in flower gardening. If you're a fanatical gardener or a full-time professional grower, you can be planting something practically every week of the year from January through October (and longer using greenhouse production). At the other end of the spectrum, you can spend a week or two in spring doing all your planting and still have a pretty good garden. Whatever your inclination, this chapter will tell you everything you need to get that garden started.

BUYING PLANTS

The easiest way to start your garden is to buy plants, both annuals and perennials, from a reputable grower. Unfortunately, few of the plants you will find on the market have been cultivated under strict organic standards: Nearly all have been grown in a potting mix that contains synthetic wetting agents; most have been grown with synthetic fertilizers; some have been sprayed with pesticides. To be an absolute organic purist, you are pretty much consigned to growing your own transplants. However, there really are no "organic" standards for flowers; the federal law pertaining to organics applies only to food and fiber crops. Many flower growers are content to start the organic process in the field, and not worry about the few weeks when the plant may have been exposed to nonorganic materials. Others don't want to support businesses that use or manufacture pesticides. It's a judgement call, and only you can decide where you want to draw the line.

If you're a small grower, you'll be buying retail either from your local garden center or from a mail-order nursery, and you'll find that prices are about the same wherever you go. Here are some of the pros and cons of various types of suppliers:

Local greenhouses and nurseries. I think it's important to support locally owned businesses, so I would recommend that you shop around in your community for the plants you want. Many greenhouses grow their own plants from seeds or plugs, giving you the benefit of getting plants that have never been stressed. However, many others just buy the plants, particularly perennials, from distant suppliers, so there's no particular advantage to those plants. Also, their selection may be limited because most garden centers are geared toward bedding plants rather than flowers for cutting. It never hurts to check, though.

Local farmers. You'll find many small farmers who sell plants in spring at the local farmers' market or their own farm stands; that's the time of year when farmers really need cash to get the rest of their production going, so you'll be helping local agriculture twice over by buying plants from them. If you don't see what you want, make suggestions. Some small farmers will grow to order for you next year, or at least experiment with the plants you're seeking.

Mass merchandisers. Chains of discount stores, hardware stores, home centers, and supermarkets have all gotten into the business of selling plants in spring. I would caution you strongly to inspect these plants closely before buying them. Generally speaking, they're fine when they first come off the truck, but they can quickly deteriorate after sitting out on a sidewalk or parking lot. In addition, there is a belief in the greenhouse industry that consumers will buy plants only if they can see them in bloom, so many mass-market growers use growth-regulating hormones and synthetic fertilizers to force those tiny plants to flower. Common sense will tell you that a plant that's supposed to grow to 2 feet should not be flowering when it's 6 inches tall, with a tiny cube of soil for its roots.

Mail-order suppliers. If you don't find what you want locally, there are thousands of mail-order nurseries to provide your plants. You will find a list of dependable suppliers in appendix 2, "Sources and Resources," and nearly all the gardening magazines run buyers' guides in late winter, in which you will find even more names and addresses. Most nurseries specialize in perennials, but some seed companies now offer small annual plants. Try to find a nursery in your region, if not your state, to cut down on shipping time and costs. Be careful of the huge, mass-mailing operations; their plants tend to be pretty generic and sometimes of poor quality. Instead, look for companies that put out a good catalog (not necessarily filled with glossy, full-color photos) with thorough descriptions of the plants, along with their Latin names. Read what suppliers have to say about how their plants are packed and shipped, too; experienced nurseries have shipping down to a science. I buy perennials from a nursery that sends them in pots inside plastic flats, with mounds of moist, shredded newspaper separating the pots from one another and cushioning their tops. Then the flats are separated by pieces of strong corrugated cardboard and packed in big, heavy boxes with the top clearly marked. Because I buy from a nursery just one state away, the plants arrive two days after they've been shipped, and they're always in great shape when I clear away the packing material.

For the Commercial Grower

Most commercial-scale farmers buy in sufficient quantities to qualify for a wholesale price. The required minimum purchase varies, but most suppliers ask for an order of at least $100 (and require you to show them a sales tax number or other proof that you're in business). Don't be put off by that kind of minimum; if you find a supplier with a good selection, you can surely order that much and get three or four times the number of plants you would get for the same amount from a retail supplier. For example, my perennial supplier—who also supplies most of the nurseries and garden centers in my area—sells a flat of thirty-two plants for $22 and a flat of seventy-two plants for $25. (Shipping adds a few dollars more per flat.) For the same $25, I could buy only a dozen perennials at a retail price.

Most commercial growers will buy a flat each of the perennial plants they want to grow, then propagate them to increase their supply. That's much less expensive than buying a few hundred plants of each type, and you can produce the quantities you need within two or three years.

The "Sources and Resources" appendix contains the names and addresses of a number of reputable wholesale plant suppliers. In most areas, you can also find a wholesale nursery that supplies the small garden centers in your region. To find those growers, ask the people who buy the plants—the employees working at your local greenhouse or other garden-center store. If you make it clear that you are a commercial cut-flower grower trying to find a new supplier, they will realize that you're not in competition with them, and they should be willing to share the names of their suppliers. Using these resources, it should be easy for you to find a good supplier of perennials and bulbs.

Annuals can be a bit more difficult to locate. Nevertheless, there are many good commercial suppliers of annual flower plugs, and you can contact them directly using the annotated list in appendix 2; or you can order through one of the commercial seed companies also listed there. Most of these companies grow to order, so you'll have to place your order late in the preceding fall or very early in the year that you need them. Some flowers, such as lisianthus, are quite slow-growing, so you'll need to place your order a full three months or more before you want to have plants shipped to you.

GROWING UNDER LIGHTS

In an ideal world, every avid gardener would have a little greenhouse to putter about in. You may be lucky enough to have a greenhouse or sunspace where you can let sunlight grow your transplants. But if not, you can still grow good transplants with the help of artificial lights. Before we got a greenhouse, we grew thousands of transplants every year in a space no bigger than a refrigerator. Our setup required only shop lights, boards and concrete blocks. Here's how to do it:

1. Buy a few shop lights, the 4-foot-long kind with fluorescent tubes. You can buy special "grow lights," or you can use one warm light and one cool light to provide nearly a full spectrum of light for your plants. Then buy an equal number of 4-foot-long 1 x 12 boards. Attach the shop lights to the boards with the chains provided, leaving about 6 inches between the board and light.
2. Place a couple of concrete blocks 4 feet apart on the floor. Balance the board and attached shop light across the blocks. Adjust the chains on the shop light so that the tubes are about 5 inches above the floor.

Board-and-block shelves can be outfitted with shop lights for an inexpensive, effective seed-starting system.

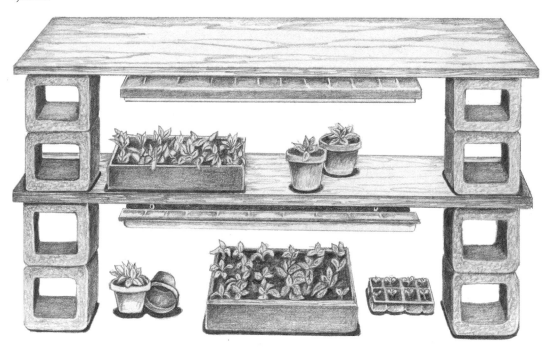

3. You now have a miniature greenhouse on your floor. You can slide two flats of plants under the lights. As the plants grow, you can raise the light by its chains so that it always remains about 2 inches above the top of your plants.

4. To increase the number of plants you can grow, just stack up more blocks, boards, and shop lights. (The setup will eventually look like the bookshelves you may have had in college.) In a space 4 feet wide, 1 foot deep, and about 5 feet tall, you can grow 576 transplants: Use four layers of lights, with two flats under each light, and seventy-two plants in each flat.

You can germinate seeds in the dark, or on a warm windowsill, but you need to get them under those lights just the minute you see the leaf emerging from the seed. Then keep the lights on, sixteen hours a day.

STARTING TRANSPLANTS

Once you have your lights set up, it's time to plant. You can buy complete seed-starting systems, including flats, inserts, plastic covers, heat mats, and potting mix. If thrift is more your style, you can make do with many materials that are probably already around your house, such as paper cups, plastic wrap, and pie tins. We've always taken a middle-of-the-road approach, assembling the components ourselves from garden centers, and we've produced beautiful plants. Here are the basic components of a seed-starting system:

1. **An organic growing mix.** This may be the most difficult ingredient to find, because most of the ready-mix stuff available at garden centers and discount stores has fertilizer added to it. As an organic gardener, you don't want to start with synthetic fertilizers. If you're just growing a few flats, I recommend that you buy an organic potting mix from one of the suppliers listed in appendix 2. If you plan to grow a large number of seedlings, it will pay to mix your own growing medium. Using a 1-gallon bucket or other container, mix:

   • 2 parts sifted compost
   • 2 parts sphagnum peat moss
   • 1 part perlite
   • 1 part coarse river sand

   Use this mix to germinate your seeds. When the seedlings have two sets of true leaves, mix up another 6 gallons of the recipe above and add:

   • ¼ cup blood meal
   • 1 cup bone meal

2. **A tray to hold your seedlings.** You can make a wooden one (the standard size is 3 inches deep by 11 inches wide by 22 inches long). Or buy plastic ones; get the kind without holes so you can bottom-water your plants.

3. **Small boxes or cups for germinating seeds.** You can use paper cups with small holes punched in the bottom for drainage if you're only doing a dozen or so seeds. Or you can buy plastic boxes that fit into the plastic seed flats. You need a large enough surface to spread the seeds so that they don't touch. If you give the seeds some space, they will be easier to transplant and you'll reduce the risk of the fungus disease known as damping-off.

4. **A clear plastic cover to keep humidity high while germinating the seeds.** You can use plastic wrap or buy plastic domes that fit tightly on the plastic flats. Remove the plastic cover as soon as the seeds germinate, however. You don't want water condensing on the plastic and dripping down onto the leaves, because plants that are constantly wet will be susceptible to disease. And even clear plastic will reduce the amount of light that reaches the seedlings.

5. **An electric heating pad or heat cable to provide bottom heat.** For most seeds, soil temperature should be 75 degrees Fahrenheit (29 degrees Celsius) to ensure optimum germination. This is important. If you don't have a temperature setting on your heat source, buy a $15 soil thermometer to make sure your soil is as warm as it needs to be. Damping-off, which can shrivel your tiny plants overnight, is more likely to occur in cool soil.

   If you're starting more than one tray of seeds, you can stack them on top of the heating pad. Put the summer-loving seeds, such as globe-amaranth and strawflower, on the bottom, and the spring seeds, such as bachelor's button and nigella, on top. Once you've transplanted the seedlings into

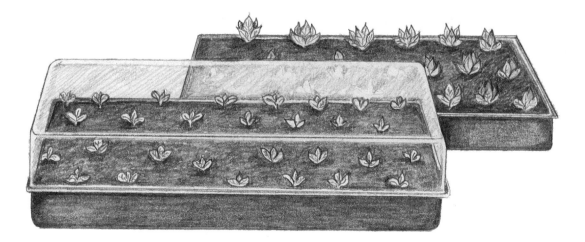

Any type of container can be used to start seeds, but the most most efficient system uses purchased plastic flats covered by clear plastic domes.

individual pots, you can leave the hot-season plants on the heating pad and keep the temperature at about 70 degrees Fahrenheit (21 degrees Celsius).

6. **Larger cell packs or peat pots to grow on the seedlings.** We buy plastic cell packs, which can be reused for many years if handled carefully. You may even have some of these left over from plants purchased last spring; just clean the cells well before using. The trays come with various sizes of cells, but a good size is seventy-two cells to a tray. If you go much smaller, the little plants might not withstand spring winds and rains. If you have enough space, though, go for bigger plants—fifty to a tray, or even 4-inch pots.

7. **Fertilizer.** As the plants grow, they'll need more nutrients than those provided by your mix. Most organic growers use a combination of fish and seaweed emulsion to water their plants every few days. Check your plants often, because they are living in a tiny amount of soil that can dehydrate quickly in the dry air of a house.

8. **Nurturing.** These baby plants like to be fussed over. Honestly. When you visit them, you bring them carbon dioxide, which is necessary for plant growth. It's also been shown that brushing the tops of your plants for a few minutes every day (gently, when they're dry, with an empty paper-towel roll or similar wand) will make your plants stockier and hardier.

Don't start your plants too early, because they're likely to get rootbound and suffer nutrient deficiencies. And some plants, once set back, will never produce to their full potential. Six weeks before they can be planted out is, in general, about all the time plants need to grow indoors.

If you've never started seeds before, just play around with these instructions on a few varieties of flowers. If, on the other hand, you're ready to go all out, you will no doubt be spending quite a bit of money on seeds, so it will be worth your while to consult a few books and magazines for more details. See "Sources and Resources" (appendix 2) for recommended titles and plant suppliers.

Commercial-scale transplants

At some point in the growth of your business, you may think you need a greenhouse for starting your own transplants. From a strictly business perspective, you should think long and hard about buying a greenhouse. Try to pin down the costs of operating it—you may find it's cheaper to buy plants, even if you're purchasing many thousands every year.

Consider the following questions to help you decide whether it's smart to take the plunge into greenhouse ownership:

- How much space do you need? In all but the gentlest climates, growers prefer to go to the field with transplants grown ninety-eight to the flat or even fewer. Smaller plants just may not survive spring winds, rains, cutworms, cold snaps, and all the other hazards awaiting them. With that in mind, calculate how many flats you'll need for the number of plants you want to grow. A standard-size flat measures 11 by 22 inches, so figure out how many linear feet of unobstructed light you'll need to accommodate the required number of flats.

- Which greenhouse design(s) would fit the greatest number of flats into the smallest amount of space? You don't want to heat more greenhouse than you really need, so look at various designs.

- Can you get a real, permanent greenhouse from a commercial supplier? It's worth it. We've made the mistake of buying a small hobby greenhouse from a garden center, only to learn later that we could have gotten twice the space for the same amount of money from a commercial greenhouse company. We've also made the mistake of trying to grow transplants in a hoophouse that was basically intended as a cold frame for overwintering or hardening off plants. It's worked fine most years, but we've lost plants when the weather turned bitterly cold.

  You may find that some greenhouse companies don't exactly bend over backwards to help a small grower who only wants a 24- by 48-foot house; after all, many of them sell greenhouses by the acre. But you also may find some smart sales reps who will recognize that you might be buying more in the future, and they will welcome your business. To find the names of greenhouse companies, consult the greenhouse-industry publications listed in appendix 2.

- What would it cost you to heat the greenhouse? Before you commit to purchasing one, ask the sales rep to help you calculate heating costs. He or she should be able to do this, having had experience with other growers in your particular climate. The answer you get may well be the determining factor in your decision, so check the details for as many variables as you can, too. We know growers whose heating bills quadrupled from one winter to the next simply because of increased cloud cover.

- Finally, do you really want to work in the winter? One of the most common complaints I hear from small-scale farmers is that they've been *too* successful at extending their season; now they don't have the rest time they really need in order to renew their energy and enthusiasm for the hectic growing season.

*Greenhouses are available in a bewildering range of styles and prices. The most
expensive are the permanent houses with concrete footings and rigid plastic or glass
glazing, like the one pictured here. For a commercial grower, such expense is usually
justified only if the greenhouse will be used year-round or if it needs to be an attractive
retail space. Also, local building codes may dictate more solid construction for retail
greenhouses.*

*For growers who need a greenhouse only to produce their own transplants, a less
expensive alternative is a hoop or quonset-style frame covered with a double layer of
poly. Although they cost less and are easier to erect, double-poly greenhouses can be
outfitted with the same kinds of equipment used in a permanent structure, such as
ventilation, heating, supplemental lighting, and much more. A good book that
explains the many variations in greenhouse structures and equipment is* Greenhouse
Engineering *from the Northeast Regional Agricultural Engineering Service, 152 Riley-
Robb Hall, Cooperative Extension, Ithaca, NY 14853-5701.*

*In milder climates, many commercial growers start their transplants in unheated
cold frames. These can be hoophouses with a single layer of poly, or in-ground boxes
covered with glass or taut plastic. Once freezes are no longer a threat, a heating cable
or heat mat is all that is needed to germinate seeds.*

Coburn's Flower Farm ❧ Carmel Valley, California

Coburn's Flower Farm in Carmel Valley, California, is a small flower business, surrounded by some of the biggest flower farms in the country. Yet, for twenty-two years, this small-scale operation has been providing a livelihood for Eric Coburn.

Eric, now in his forties, got started with about 600 square feet of flowers. "When I was twenty-one, I had the blindness of youth," he says. "As I've gotten older, I've managed to move along with this thing."

The keys to his success, he says, have been to diversify into a large number of markets and to grow flowers that no one else is growing on a large scale.

Eric and his wife, Katie, grow six acres of flowers today. They sell to florists and wholesalers and do their own design work for weddings, parties, corporations, hotels, restaurants, bed and breakfasts, and doctors' offices. They do some retail sales, but by appointment only, as they don't want to keep shop hours. Eric and Katie sell rootstock to nurseries and other growers. Recently, Eric also has been doing a fair amount of garden consulting.

The Coburns' production focuses on flowers not normally found in the trade, particularly perennials. They'll grow a new flower for several years, then start to sell the rootstock, and eventually move out of growing it as it becomes more available in the California markets. For example, the Coburns

say, a decade ago they were one of the first commercial growers to produce spuria iris, which is a hybrid of three iris species. The flowers of spuria iris look like Dutch iris, but the plant is much taller—ranging in their fields from the 3-foot cultivar 'Protege' to the 10-foot 'Angel Wings'. Spuria iris also have four to thirteen flowers per stem, compared to the one or two flowers on a Dutch iris.

In recent years, spuria iris have become more widely available to commercial growers. Although they aren't yet a staple in the floral trade, Eric has decided to stop growing so many and, instead, to increase production of Pacific Coast hybrid iris. These relatively new iris are hybridized mostly from *I. douglasiana*, which grows wild on the West Coast. Although the stems are much shorter than spuria iris, the flowers are similar in form and in numbers. The Pacific coast hybrids, though, are available in an unusual range of colors, including lavender, magenta, yellow, blue, rose, purple, and shades of white with intricate markings.

Many of the Coburns' favorite varieties are flowers that are usually considered too short for the floral trade.

"The flower industry is dominated by males who want to see big flowers with long, straight stems," Eric says. "They're all sent in 44-inch boxes, and then the florist chops them down and you wind up with a 12-inch bud vase. Many of the flowers I grow are short little things."

Some examples: *Arum italicum*, which has white-veined, arrow-shaped leaves 15 inches tall, with orange and green seedpods in the fall; *Campanula medium* (Canterbury-bells), which can be from 15 to 30 inches tall; *Geum*, which grows to 24 inches; and *Heuchera sanguinea* (coral-bells), which are 18 to 24 inches tall.

Since the beginning, Eric has made novelties his specialty. "Back in the seventies, the flowers that were grown were roses, chrysanthemums, and carnations," he says. "A novelty cut flower back then was statice." So Eric started growing statice, along with many other garden annuals such as salpiglossis, schizanthus, nemesia, calendula, centaurea, and zinnia. "Growing novelties was good and bad," he recalls. "The bad part was that nobody knew what they were. A lot of it was trial and error, finding different things that would grow and sell." Needless to say, he has left behind the statice and other common annuals of his early years.

He has modified his farming practices over the years, too, to get away from using pesticides.

"One of the keys to farming without pesticides is cleanliness. If you keep a clean farm, you reduce a lot of problems," he says. "We try to keep things weed-free and to remove spent foliage. We also grow beneath a pine hedge, which attracts birds, and they really help keep down our insect levels."

Over the years, the Coburns have worked hard to stay a step ahead of the crowd. "I'm a small operation, but extremely diversified," Eric says. "I have to compete against these huge operations. I do it by growing flowers other people don't have and carving a niche out of the market for myself. There are many parts of the country where you could be doing this exact same thing." ❧

CHAPTER 4

Growing in the Field

ONCE YOUR PLANTS HAVE ESTABLISHED A GOOD ROOT BALL, IT'S TIME TO start hardening them off. Withhold fertilizer, cut back on watering, and move them outside for longer periods of time each day to help them adjust to field conditions. You must bring the plants back inside to protect them from storms or late frosts, and you need to water them enough to keep them from wilting. But try to toughen them up as much as possible. One week to two weeks of this treatment should make your plants ready for the field.

Some plants can withstand and even enjoy temperatures near freezing, but most flowers should not be planted out until your frost-free date has passed and the soil has warmed to about 70 degrees Fahrenheit (21 degrees Celsius). When in doubt, wait.

Finally, the day arrives when the soil is tilled, the raised beds are made, the weather is settled, the plants are hardened off, the seeds are all purchased, and you're ready to start farming.

TRANSPLANTING

If you are starting with transplants, take a ruler to the field. Measure and mark your spacing along several feet of the bed until you recognize how far apart to plant. You can use a trowel to dig holes, or just your hand if your soil is freshly tilled. Holding the plant stem gently in one hand, squeeze the plastic cell with your other hand to loosen the root ball, and tip or gently pull the plant out of the cell. Place the plant in the hole and pull the soil around the root ball, covering it completely to prevent the roots from drying out. It's important to then press the soil around the plant to eliminate pockets of air that can rob the roots of moisture.

Work your way down the row, and when all your transplants are in the ground, water them in with a rose sprinkler on a long wand that allows you to deliver a gentle stream right to the area around the plant's stem. Water gently so that you don't dislodge the plant, but thoroughly so that soil washes up against all the roots. Don't water from the top of the plants on this first watering.

Mechanical Transplanting

Commercial growers with more than a few acres in production usually end up buying a tractor-pulled transplanter. They come in various configurations, but basically are tools that have a space for holding flats of plants, a pair of seats for workers, a dibble that makes holes into which the workers drop the plants, and a tank and hose for watering the plants.

MULCHING

To prevent weeds from crowding out new plants, many growers use some kind of mulch around their plants. In some cases, the mulch is laid before the transplants are set into the ground; in other cases, mulch is applied after

Newly-planted seedlings need to be watered carefully so that soil washes up against the root ball. Use a wand and a nozzle with a soft spray, and deliver the water in a circle right around the base of the transplant.

LANDSCAPE FABRIC

Landscapers have long used heavy black woven polypropylene fabric to keep weeds out of their plantings. Now, organic cut-flower growers are turning to this fabric as a solution to their weed problems, particularly with perennials.

Unlike plastic mulch, the black landscape fabric lasts many years and allows water and nutrients to percolate through to the plants. It also heats the soil in spring, which is a benefit in cool climates. However, landscape fabric is not the answer to everyone's weed problems. First, it's expensive, and although it will pay for itself over many years of use, it does require up-front capital. Second, it may heat the soil too much in hot climates, stunting the growth of some plants. Growers who are interested in using the fabric should experiment on a small space before investing in large amounts.

The landscape fabric is available in several thicknesses and widths. Many growers use one thickness on their beds and a heavier type in the paths. Planting holes can be cut in the fabric easily with a pair of scissors, but, for precision placement, commercial growers use a plywood template with approximately 6-inch squares cut through it in the desired spacing. The template is laid over several thicknesses of the landscape fabric, and a square branding iron is used to burn holes through the plastic fabric.

The fabric is then laid over raised beds and anchored with metal "staples," either purchased from the landscape supplier or made by bending pieces of wire. Irrigation tape can be laid either under or over the fabric, and compost can be applied right on top of the material. Plants are then planted into the holes. The bare soil around them is either left open or covered with wood chips or other mulch to prevent weeds from germinating.

The landscape fabric can be removed from the bed in winter after the plants have spread enough to outcompete the weeds. If handled gently, the fabric can be reused on new beds for a decade or more. ❧

planting. Following are some advantages and disadvantages of various kinds of mulches:

Black plastic. Many commercial growers use black plastic mulch, and lay it with a special implement pulled by a tractor. These mechanical mulch-layers do a great job of unrolling the plastic flat, pulling it taut across the soil, and anchoring the sides.

For the smaller grower, you can lay plastic mulch by hand, but it's a lot more difficult. You'll need two to three people: one to walk ahead, unrolling the plastic, and one or two to follow behind, shoveling soil onto the edges to hold the mulch in place. Later, you'll want to walk down the row, doing a more thorough job of covering the edges, because any loose piece of plastic is likely to catch the wind.

The real trouble with plastic is that it is not biodegradable, so you have an awful mess to pull up at the end of the season. Also, there's no way to recycle it because it's covered with soil, and most recycling companies won't take dirty plastic. If you're going to be a certified organic grower, be aware that the proposed federal organic laws will require growers to pull up plastic mulch at the end of the season.

Black paper. A fairly recent innovation, black paper mulch does everything that the black plastic does, but it biodegrades over the season; by fall, you'll never know it was there. Because the paper can tear, it's a little more difficult to apply with a mechanical mulch-layer, but I find it easier to lay by hand than the plastic. Use the same technique of one person unrolling the paper while the other comes behind and throws shovelfuls of soil along the edges.

Whether using black plastic or paper, you should be sure the soil is thoroughly moist before you cover it. Once the mulch is in place, cut holes in the desired spacing and plant your seedlings through the holes.

Straw, hay, and grass clippings. These natural materials have the added benefit of decomposing during the season and adding organic matter to the soil. We have found that alfalfa hay adds a lot of nitrogen to the soil as it decomposes; beds that were mulched the previous season with alfalfa hay are much more fertile the following year. However, straw and hay often contain weed seeds that may germinate in your beds and cause problems in the future.

Grass clippings, if they're still green when you apply them, can deplete nitrogen from the soil to aid in their own decomposition. So let your natural materials dry out or, better still, compost them before using as mulch. Be sure to apply a thick enough layer to prevent light from reaching the soil and any weed seeds in it. Plant your seedlings first, then pile the mulch around them.

Wood chips, cocoa shells, etc. These are excellent mulches for the ornamental beds in your yard, because they look and smell good while keeping down weeds.

FLOWERS YOU CAN DIRECT-SEED

Most flower seeds are started in a greenhouse, because soil temperatures outside are too low in spring to ensure germination or because the new seedlings are tiny and frail. Some species, though, germinate best in cool temperatures, which makes them good candidates for direct-seeding. Other seeds are just so quick to germinate and send up such big seedlings that they, too, can be seeded right into the field.

There's more to consider in direct-seeding than soil temperature and days to germination: You need to be able to supply moisture to the seeds before and after germination; the soil in the seedbed must have a fine enough texture that tiny seedlings can push their way through; and you must protect the emerging seedlings from chewing insects, if those are a problem in your garden, with floating row covers (see page 49). If you can provide these precautions for your plants, here are some of the cut-flower varieties that are often direct-seeded:

Agrostemma githago (corn cockle)
Amaranthus (Joseph's-coat, love-lies-bleeding)
Ammi majus (bishop's weed)
Carthamus spp. (safflower)
Caryopteris incana (blue spirea)
Celosia spp. (crested, wheat, plumed)
Centaurea cyanus (bachelor's button)
Consolida spp. (larkspur)
Cosmos spp. (cosmos)

Emilia javanica (tasselflower)
Helianthus spp. (sunflower)
Helichrysum spp. (strawflower)
Lunaria annua (honesty)
Moluccella (bells-of-Ireland)
Nigella spp. (love-in-a-mist)
Scabiosa spp. (pincushion flower)
Tagetes spp. (marigold)
Zinnia spp. (zinnia)

The more finely shredded the mulch, the more quickly it will decompose. Shredded hardwood, such as oak, isn't as pretty as some wood chips, but it lasts longer and is a good choice for mulching paths between perennials. Because wood chips will use soil nitrogen while decomposing, use a little extra compost on beds that will have wood mulch, and be sure to pile on the mulch thickly.

DIRECT-SEEDING

For small patches of direct-seeded flowers, you can just make a small furrow in the soil with an edge of a hoe. Drop the seed in the furrow, according to the spacing directions on the package. Then run your hand along the furrow, using your thumb and forefinger to gently push a small amount of soil from the piled-up sides onto the seeds. Firm the soil over the furrow to ensure that the seeds will be in contact with soil.

For larger gardens and commercial gardens, it is imperative that you direct-seed in straight lines. Otherwise, weeding later will be a nightmare. You can create straight furrows by running a string between two stakes at either end of the bed. Once your plants are up, you'll be able to run down between those straight rows with a hoe in half the time it would take you to hand-weed a wobbly line or a broadcast planting of seeds.

Larger seeds can generally be planted with a push seeder. I plant larkspur and zinnias with an Earthway seeder. For larger commercial growers, there are tractor-pulled seeders that make short work of direct-seeding.

Seeds, however they are planted, should be watered in gently immediately afterward to bring moist soil in contact with the seeds to help them germinate.

PLANTING UNDER TUNNELS

Flower gardeners can take a lesson from vegetable growers and get a head start on the season with the use of plastic-covered tunnels, which warm the soil and protect young plants from late frosts. With protection, some flowers can be blooming a month earlier than they would be if planted after the frost-free date.

It is important to use the tunnel system only for plants that are cold-tolerant, and even then, you're taking a calculated risk. A tunnel can protect flowers down to about 28 degrees Fahrenheit (−2 degrees Celsius), but if you get a freeze harder than that, you may lose your plants. So don't invest a huge amount of money in the system. If you're a commercial grower, you may do little more than break even—but you'll start your season earlier, which can be a marketing advantage when early customers continue to buy from you all season long. Tunnels also may give you the mass of flowers you need, when added to spring bulbs and perennials, to start selling bouquets earlier.

Good choices for planting under tunnels include statice (*Limonium sinuatum*), pink pokers (*Limonium suworowii*), snapdragons (*Antirrhinum*), acroclinium (*Helipterum* spp.), bishop's weed (*Ammi majus*), and *Salvia horminum* (*S. viridis*). The transplants can be quite small—about two hundred plugs to a tray—but they need a good root system, and must be hardened off before transplanting.

The tunnel system requires four components: an irrigation hose, a mulch for the soil, a row cover, and hoops to hold the row cover above the seedlings. Here's how to construct these little greenhouses for early flowers:

1. After you've prepared the soil and raked it smooth, lay down a soaker hose or drip tape to water the plants.
2. Next, lay down mulch. Mulches are essential because the warm, protected environment under a tunnel is as hospitable to weeds as it is to seedlings. If you don't mulch, you'll have a bumper crop of weeds crowding out your new plants within a week. Black plastic, black paper, or organic mulches such as hay or grass clippings can be used.

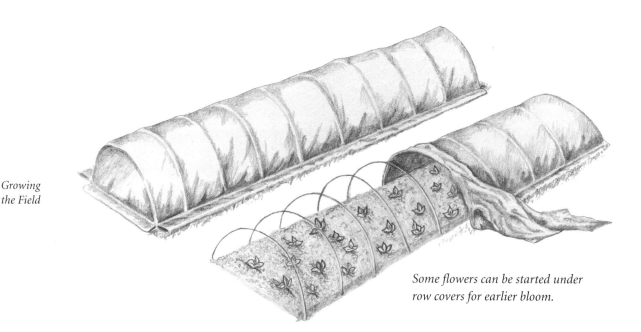

*Some flowers can be started under
row covers for earlier bloom.*

3. Next, you'll need hoops to erect over the plants. They don't have to be elaborate: We get a coil of no. 9 or no. 10 wire and cut it so that the circle becomes a U-shape. You can also use a 4-foot length of any kind of strong wire, bent into an arch. Push the wire hoops into the ground every 3 feet.

4. Finally, you'll need row cover to drape over the hoops. You can buy several types of row cover, including spun polypropylene, slitted clear plastic, or micropore plastic. Stretch the row cover over the hoops and anchor it to the ground, either by covering with soil, or with lengths of reinforcing rod or 2 x 4s. Be sure to get it well anchored, because if wind pulls it loose, the flapping row cover can damage the plants. To make it more secure, put another hoop on top of the plastic about every third hoop.

Once your tunnels are up, keep watch on the temperature. Remove the row cover once all danger of frost is past and daytime temperatures reach the upper 70s (Fahrenheit, or mid-20s Celsius). Keep the plants well watered with the drip tape or soaker hose.

FALL PLANTING

For many flowers, fall is the best time to plant because they need a period of cold before they can develop blooms. By planting them into the garden in fall, you can expect to get flowers in spring. If you wait until spring to plant them, in many cases you won't get flowers until the following spring.

There are a few cautions about fall planting, however. First, the term "fall planting," though commonly used, is actually a misnomer because most plants need to be in the ground well before the autumnal equinox on September 22.

They need time to develop roots and get well anchored in the soil before the weather turns cold. It's not so much the hard freezes of winter that you have to worry about; rather, it's the freeze-and-thaw cycle of autumn that causes the soil to expand and contract, actually heaving plants out of the ground if they aren't well rooted.

In general, plants should be in the ground six weeks before the average first freeze.

To help the plants get rooted quickly, they need a boost of phosphorus and potassium, which stimulate root growth. Bone meal and rock phosphate are good organic sources of phosphorus; greensand is a good source of potassium. Don't give your new plants nitrogen in the fall, because it stimulates top growth, and soft new growth is susceptible to winterkill.

Watering is a little tricky in fall: You want to provide enough water to feed the roots, but not so much that the foliage grows lush. Poke a finger into the soil to check its moisture. Water when the soil starts to dry out, but don't keep it constantly wet.

Finally, be sure to control insects on new fall plantings. These young plants still need their foliage in order to continue photosynthesizing, so avoid letting grasshoppers, beetles, or other herbivorous insects munch the tender leaves. You may need to shield your plants with row cover or shade cloth.

As you select fall transplants, keep in mind that when it comes to size, bigger is not necessarily better. Most commercial growers plant perennials grown seventy-two to a flat—that is, with a root ball about 1¼ inches square by 2 inches deep. Home gardeners should purchase larger plants, but you don't need to buy 1-gallon perennials. By planting in fall and taking good care of your smaller plants, you'll have big plants by spring anyway.

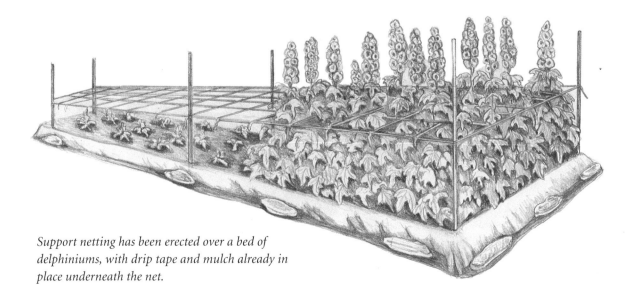

Support netting has been erected over a bed of delphiniums, with drip tape and mulch already in place underneath the net.

SUPPORTING FLOWERS

Many tall flowers can be irreparably damaged by wind unless you provide some support for them. In a small garden, you may choose to put small stakes or individual plant supports next to tall flowers. But if you're growing flowers by the row, you may want to consider supporting them with twine or with a special material called support netting.

Twine works fairly well in dense plantings of tall flowers such as larkspur or yarrow. All you have to do is place tall stakes at the four corners of the beds, and every 12 feet or so along the length of the bed; then run twine around the perimeter of the entire bed to prevent the plants from falling outward. The plants will hold one another up within the bed.

With shorter, more sparsely planted flowers that need support, you'll want to use support netting. The plastic mesh, with roughly 6-inch-square openings, is erected horizontally over the bed when plants are still small. As the flower stems shoot up, they grow right through the mesh. Some plants require two tiers of support netting, although most will do quite well with just one layer.

Before you can erect the support netting, you have to plant, lay drip hose, and mulch. Once the mesh is in place and the flowers begin to grow through it, you will not be able to get underneath with a hose or a hoe.

To erect the netting, you can make stakes with slots carved into them to hold the plastic mesh in place. Alternatively, you can use T-posts or even reinforcing rod pushed deeply into the ground. Both these types of metal bars have grooves to keep the support netting from slipping up or down. Several farm suppliers sell support netting, or you can buy it directly from the manufacturer. See appendix 2 for additional information.

WEEDING

The best time to weed is when the weed seeds have just germinated and are poking up less than an inch high. Of course, you're usually still busy planting when the weeds are that small, but if you can break away long enough to run a hoe down your beds, you'll be doing yourself a favor.

We have a couple of hoes that are indispensable in our market garden, and we're sure many a backyard gardener would benefit from them as well.

The most important is our wheel hoe. This nifty tool has a U-shaped hoe and a wheel at the end of a long handle with double handlebars. As the operator pushes, the hoe rolls along. Once you get up steam and start walking along at a fast pace, you'll be amazed at how quickly weeding is accomplished. We estimate that a wheel hoe makes us eight times more efficient than a hand-held hoe.

Naturally, there are times when you've let the weeds grow too long, or you haven't made your lines straight enough to use a wheel hoe, and only a hand-

The indispensable wheel hoe.

held hoe will do the job. It's useful to have an assortment of styles in your toolshed. For small weeds, we like the colinear hoe designed by Eliot Coleman, because it allows you to stand up straight. Stirrup hoes work well when the soil is dry and weeds are tiny and numerous. Warren hoes have triangular blades and are useful for cultivating close to plants. And when things have really gotten out of control, you'll need a basic American shank hoe to chop out those big roots.

WATERING

Flowers demand a regular supply of water. Some tolerate dry conditions better than others, but nearly all will look healthier and withstand stress better if they receive an inch of water per week.

The best way to water depends entirely on the size of your garden. If you have a small flower bed, you can probably water with a hose. I have a few beds right around my back door, and I actually enjoy standing around with a hose in the evening as the children play nearby. Besides being a calming activity, watering with a hose also helps cool off the yard much more than drip irrigation can.

There's both art and science involved in hand-watering a garden. In general, plants like a gentle spray that feels like rain; it washes the leaves clean and visibly invigorates the whole plant. The best time to deliver water from overhead is in the early evening, after the sun has gotten low in the sky, but before the stillness of night sets in. Watering at that hour gives plants time to dry off before it gets cool, and

Growing in the Field

also provides water for the roots during the night, when plants are actively growing.

To deliver an overhead shower, you can use a wand with a rose sprinkler, which should be held upward so that the water drops gently from above. You also can use a fan-shaped sprinkler on the end of the hose.

Some plants should not be watered from above, particularly in humid climates, because wet foliage can promote powdery mildew, rust, and other diseases. Zinnias, snapdragons, roses,

Keep a few different types of hoes to fit different situations. From the top are the American shank hoe, collinier hoe, Warren hoe, and stirrup hoe.

A Basic System for Drip Irrigation

You can irrigate up to a half-acre at a time with a garden hose attached to this relatively inexpensive drip system. Here's what you need:

- a filter, rated 150 mesh or greater
- a pressure regulator, from 8 to 15 psi
- a distribution ("header") line for transporting water across the end of the field to each row (usually a plastic lay-flat hose)
- drip tape to water each row
- feeder tubes (about ⅜-inch plastic tubing) to connect the lay-flat hose to the drip tape

To set up the system, first lay the drip tape down the beds. On a 4-foot-wide raised bed with up to four rows of plants, you'll need two lines of drip tape. On wider-spaced crops, you should use one line of drip tape for each row of crops.

Next, lay the header line across the end of the field. With an awl, punch a hole in the header line wherever it meets the lines of drip tape. Punch another hole in the drip tape, about 6 inches from the end, and connect the drip tape to the header line, using the thin feeder tubes. Seal each end of the drip tape by folding it under twice and holding it closed with a 2-inch collar cut from another piece of drip tape.

At the beginning of the header line, attach the filter and the pressure regulator. Then hook up the garden hose that will deliver the water from your faucet.

Every few weeks throughout the season, or whenever you detect a problem with the system, take off the collars holding the drip tape closed and flush out the system. Also, flush the filter frequently. ⌒

End of drip tape

and bee balm are examples of plants that are susceptible to moisture-caused diseases. When hand-watering these plants, use a wand with a rose sprinkler and water the soil right around the plant, rather than the plant itself.

Drip Irrigation

In dry climates and wherever water conservation is important, you should invest in a drip irrigation system. Drip irrigation delivers the water right to the base of the plants, and no moisture is lost from evaporation to the air.

For small gardens, you can purchase "leaky hose," which weeps water throughout its length. Lay the hose in the garden, winding it through the bed so that every plant comes within about 2 feet of the hose. You can cover the hose with mulch. But first, try watering the bed with the leaky hose to find out how long you need to leave it turned on in order to saturate the soil. In general, the soil should be evenly moist throughout its top 2 inches, and somewhat moist below that.

Larger growers can easily set up an inexpensive irrigation system with drip tape. Up to five acres can be irrigated with the system described in the box on page 54. That's a very rudimentary system, though, and you may want to invest in more sophisticated equipment, such as emitters that you insert to match your plant spacing.

PEST AND DISEASE CONTROL

As an organic grower, the most frequent question I am asked is what to do about pests and diseases. The answer may seem unsatisfactory to inexperienced growers, but here it is: Pests and diseases are best controlled by preventive measures such as soil fertility, appropriate irrigation, timing of plantings, and selection of varieties. Organic production is not a simple system. There is no magic bullet that will take care of all problems—often, there is not even a quick solution to a single problem.

The organic grower has to become knowledgeable about the garden ecosystem. That means learning the weeds, learning the insects, understanding what eats what and when, recognizing when plants are stressed, and knowing what they need in order to overcome stress. It means being an astute observer, and a willing researcher. Some of the answers may lie in books, but many will be available only by educated experimentation, or by trial and error.

Being an organic grower also means accepting the limitations of your ecosystem. You may have to accept that certain plants won't grow for you, because the insect or disease pressures are too great. Some people have a hard time accepting such limitations. Although they may willingly acknowledge that Southerners can't grow peonies, which require a certain amount of winter chilling time, they refuse to admit that Midwesterners can't grow asters because of the regionally widespread disease known as aster yellows.

Our nation's agricultural system conventionally takes the attitude that insects and diseases can be eradicated, but this philosophy has led to some drastic measures that harm the health of the environment as well as the health of the farmer. And for what? For the ability to grow one kind of plant, when there are so many others to choose from? Although research has provided us with many relatively benign methods of controlling pests and diseases, some of the so-called solutions come at just too high a price. Chemicals that solve one problem in the garden may lead to further problems elsewhere in the garden. Broad-spectrum pesticides kill the target pest, but they kill most of the other insects, too—including the beneficial ones that were keeping other pests in check.

An organic system is more holistic. The organic flower farmer chooses plants that grow well and that won't invite an inordinate amount of problems. The organic grower is close enough to the flowers to know what is attacking them; then the farmer finds a way to take care of that one problem, without affecting the rest of the ecosystem.

In general, there are three ways of approaching a pest problem: physical controls, biological controls, and chemical controls.

Physical Controls

Physical controls keep pests away from the crop. Here are the most commonly used products:

Row covers are thin, light plastic fabrics that can be draped over wire hoops set above plants, or even laid right on top of the plants. They are best used when plants are young, to prevent insects from damaging them. After the plants mature, row covers become impractical.

Sticky traps are pieces of cardboard covered with a tacky glue that will trap any insects that alight on them. They come in either yellow or blue, catering to the color preferences of certain insects. Thrips, for example, are most attracted to the color blue, so a blue sticky card for every 100 square feet in the flower garden will help reduce thrips. Most other insects prefer yellow, so you'll need one card every 50 square feet. You can also purchase yellow sticky tape to wrap around the perimeter of certain crops.

Some sticky traps come in boxes that contain a pheromone, or chemical sex attractant. The pest is lured into the box by its scent, and then gets stuck there on the glue. These lures are specific to the type of insect you're trying to control.

Biological Controls

Biological controls include predatory and parasitic insects, plus microbial organisms such as fungi, bacteria, and nematodes. These organisms target specific pests, and there are literally hundreds of them, so you need to consult a good supplier for suggestions about the best approach to your situation. Here are some of the more widely used biological remedies:

Bacillus thuringiensis is a species of bacteria with several strains that attack specific insects. *B.t. kurstaki* is used against the caterpillars of leaf-feeding moths, and dried-flower growers often employ it to prevent infestation by Indian meal moths.

Nosema locusta is a kind of protozoan that is mixed with bran bait and fed to grasshoppers. The grasshoppers die and are eaten by other grasshoppers, and so the protozoan is spread throughout the population.

Beneficial insects include ladybugs, lacewings, spined soldier beetles, and predatory mites. Many vegetable growers actively recruit beneficial insects by planting habitat- and food-providing plants for them. The most insect-friendly plants are flowers, particularly the umbelliferous flowers, such as Queen Anne's lace, dill, fennel, and cilantro. Researchers at Colorado State University recently named thirty plants that are most attractive to ladybugs, lacewings, parasitic wasps, syrphid flies, and tachnid flies, all beneficials that prey on pest insects. The cut-flower varieties found to be highly attractive to beneficials include *Anthemis tinctoria* (golden marguerite), *Astrantia major* (masterwort), *Veronica spicata* (veronica), *Achillea millefolium* and *A. filipendulina* (yarrow). You may already have many of these plants growing in your garden or meadow; if so, you're a step ahead in the search for beneficial insects. You also can purchase and release insects that are known to prey on the specific pests troubling your garden.

The "Sources and Resources" appendix includes names of companies that supply beneficial insects and other biological pest controls. Most suppliers are excellent sources of information about how many organisms you need, how and when to release them, and so forth. Be sure to seek advice before purchasing beneficials, including how to keep them in your garden. Many a grower has gone out and bought a bag of ladybugs, released them one day, and found them all gone the next. Before you release any kind of beneficial insect, you have to make sure that your garden is hospitable enough for the creatures to stay. If they don't find food or shelter immediately, they will move on.

Chemical Controls

Relax—these aren't as bad as they sound. Many naturally occurring chemicals are available to the organic grower for pest control. Most of them target just the pest and don't harm beneficial insects, and the active chemical agents all disappear within a day or two of being sprayed.

Insecticidal soap dissolves the membranes of soft-bodied insects, and affects only those that are sprayed directly. It is used on aphids, thrips, whiteflies, fungus gnats, flea beetles, mites, scales, slugs, and snails.

Horticultural oils are highly refined petroleum products that coat plants and smother many disease spores and insects. These oils can be mixed with baking soda to prevent powdery mildew and black spot. The recipe is 1 tablespoon baking soda, 2½ teaspoons summer oil, and 1 gallon of water. A weekly spray is needed to prevent the foliar (leaf-affecting) diseases.

Neem is a tropical-tree extract that kills more than seventy-five types of pests, but doesn't harm mammals, parasitic wasps, or predatory mites. It kills on contact, and can be used as a deterrent to feeding on flowers.

Pyrethrins are extracted from the pyrethrum plant (*Chrysanthemum coccineum*). Insects sprayed with pyrethrins are paralyzed and then die. Many pyrethrin formulations are made with piperonyl butoxide (PBO), which is forbidden under many organic certification agency standards. Check before you buy.

Garlic is the active ingredient in several pest-control products. It acts as a fungicide, discourages insects from feeding, and even repels bees. (This effect would be bad for a vegetable grower, who needs bees for pollination, but good for a flower grower, who doesn't want bees because flowers decline more quickly after pollination.)

Other botanical pesticides, including rotenone, ryania, and sabadilla, are sometimes used as last-resort controls by organic growers. However, their use is controversial because they are broad-spectrum insecticides, which means they kill all kinds of insects, including beneficial ones. Some organic certification agencies may not even allow their use. Consider such pesticides only if your crop is threatened and other controls have failed, and be careful in handling and storing them, because they are dangerous to humans, birds, fish, and pets. Also, be sparing in their application, so that you don't disrupt the balance of pests and predators in the rest of the garden.

It isn't possible for this book to describe all the pests that you might encounter in your flower garden. Fortunately, there are several excellent reference books to help you identify specific insects, learn their life cycles, and understand which strategy will control them best. You will find these books listed in the notes for this chapter, in appendix 2, and I recommend that you buy one before you need it. Then, keep alert in the garden. Identify insects to determine whether they might be a threat to your crop. Observe the level of damage, if any, and decide whether it's tolerable. The simple fact is that strong, healthy plants aren't likely to succumb to pests or diseases, so you should focus your energy on enabling them to grow well.

Hartland Flower Farm ⤳ Hartland, Vermont

*H*OWIE MYERS IS LOOKING FORWARD TO THE DAY WHEN HE CAN RETIRE FROM HIS law practice to become a full-time flower grower at his farm in Hartland, Vermont. But before he can make his living as a flower farmer, he says, he's got to plant another five thousand peony plants.

"Once we get the place in order, when the perennials are producing and we've got ten thousand peonies producing, then there's hope," Howie says.

Howie started growing flowers in 1991 at a farm in Tunbridge, Vermont, then moved to his current location near Hartland in 1994. He already has twenty acres of his new farm planted, mostly in perennials.

"I'm in a rural area, and there's no way in the world I could make any money trying to sell to florists or at farmers' markets," he says. "The direction I'm moving toward is having two to four major crops suitable for shipping all over, plus other crops to have in sufficient numbers to ship to Boston and Montreal throughout the season. I need to grow the kinds of things that have a reasonable profit potential, so I'm moving to high-end flowers, mostly high-end perennials. That's the vision that has been distilled over five years of hit and miss."

Howie's first big crop of the season is French tulips, which are pulled rather than cut, with the bulb intact, to provide the longest vase life. The tulips are shipped all over the country by overnight express. The next big crop is the peonies, which are cut in the bud and shipped immediately or held in cold storage for up to three weeks.

After the shipping season ends, Howie begins weekly truck deliveries of a wide array of other flowers. Some of his top crops include globeflower (*Trollius* spp.), Oriental lilies, larkspur, sunflowers, monkshood, phlox, bishop's weed (*Ammi majus*), Matsumoto asters, and lisianthus. His season begins in mid to late May and runs through the first frost, which can occur any time from September 10 to mid-October.

The fields at Hartland Flower Farm lie in a bowl-shaped valley surrounded by forested hills. Perennials are planted in raised beds that follow the contours of the gentle slopes. With most perennials, Howie uses a heavy black landscape fabric on the beds, with a thinner fabric on the paths. Before laying the polypropylene fabric in the field, he burns planting holes through it with a branding iron, using a template cut in plywood. Once the fabric is down and anchored to the soil with big wire staples, he plants into the open squares. Finally, to prevent weeds from germinating in the bit of soil that remains exposed, he surrounds the plants with a thick layer of mulch.

The post-harvest facilities at Hartland Flower Farm are excellent. An old barn has been converted into work space, where employees bunch the flowers and put them in perforated plastic sleeves bearing the Hartland Flower Farm logo. An addition to the barn houses a big walk-in cooler where flowers are kept until they're ready to go to market. In the space above the walk-in cooler is a screened room for drying flowers. Howie also owns his own refrigerated truck, with which he makes his wholesale deliveries.

Weeds are Howie's biggest frustration. He has a crew of five who spend most mornings, when the flowers are still too dewy to harvest, weeding by hand or with a tiller. Some crops, such as lisianthus, are grown on black plastic mulch. Even so, he says, weeds are a constant threat.

"My problem is that I'm an absentee farmer," he says. "I sit in my law office all day."

Frustrating as it is to try to run a farm while still working a city job, Howie knows that he will have a running start on the flower business when the time is right to quit his law practice. Within a few years, he hopes, he'll have refined his production system, be well established in his markets, and have all those peonies blooming. ❧

CHAPTER 5

The Dried-Flower Garden

ONCE YOU'VE EXPERIENCED THE BEAUTY AND USEFULNESS OF A FLOWER garden all summer, you'll mourn the coming of autumn. But if you've been looking ahead to the drab days of winter, you can preserve your garden's bounty for dried-flower bouquets, arrangements, wreaths, and other crafts. A dried-flower garden can be the same garden you've used all summer for fresh flowers, or you can specialize in flowers for preserving.

For the commercial grower, "drieds" can bring a welcome influx of cash at the end of the season. Many flowers that you've been harvesting all summer will be invigorated by the cooler weather of September. When the frost date gets closer, you can start harvesting those abundant flowers for drying, so that nothing goes to waste. A few baskets of drieds keeps your market stand looking colorful and attractive well into fall. And many growers find that the diminishing amount of farm work in fall gives them time to add value to their dried flowers by crafting with them.

Virtually any flower can be preserved, by one method or another. The easiest way of preserving flowers is to air-dry them, but this is effective only with certain species. Flowers also can be preserved with glycerine, which is taken up through the flower's stems, replacing water and leaving the blossom soft and lifelike.

To maximize hanging space, tie three 12-inch
lengths of string to wire or plastic clothes hangers.
Bunch harvested flowers with rubber bands. Slip one
bunch over each string and pull the string tight.
You can also hang bunches from individual nails in
rafters by their rubber bands. Or hang numerous
bunches on a piece of lath, then suspend the lath
between the rafters.

Small, thin-petaled flowers (such as pansies and violets) are best preserved by burying them in silica, which looks like sand and absorbs the water from the flowers. Finally, there's freeze-drying, which can preserve nearly anything, no matter how fleshy or moist, but which is available only from businesses that own the necessary but very expensive freeze-drying machines.

AIR DRYING

The only equipment you need for air-drying flowers is a warm, dark place with good air circulation. If your drying room is too bright, the flowers' colors will fade. Likewise, if the flowers aren't dried quickly, they will fade or turn brown. For most flowers, you can use any room that has low humidity. (Running a dehumidifier or small heater helps if your climate is humid.) A barn with a hayloft is an excellent place to dry flowers; a garage or garden shed works well, too, if you can open windows or run a fan to keep the air moving. Cellars are usually too damp for drying flowers, but they may be suitable in dry climates or during a dry summer. In many cases, small farmers use their greenhouses, provided that no plants are growing there in the summer, and either cover the entire structure with black plastic or black landscape fabric. Alternatively, they build a tent of black plastic inside the greenhouse. Larger commercial growers construct special buildings where they can apply heat to kiln-dry the flowers quickly.

Flowers should be picked at the peak of perfection if you intend them to be everlasting. (Why preserve a sad-looking flower? It will only get sadder.) The optimum time for picking a flower to dry is generally the same as the best time to pick it for fresh use. In the list of recommended cut flowers (appendix 1), you'll find guidance on the best harvest time for each recommended species.

Pick your flowers in the late morning, after the dew has dried but before they are subjected to the heat of the day. Make sure they are free of moisture, because mold will quickly cover wet plants hanging in a dark place. Gather the flowers into small bunches fastened with rubber bands. Then hang the bunches upside down in your chosen drying area.

Check the bunches every few days to see if they are dry. You'll be able to feel when the flowers are dry, but to be sure the entire plant is ready to be taken down, try bending one of the stems near the bottom, where it was covered by the rubber band. If the stem snaps, the flowers are ready. If it's still flexible, hang up the bunch again to dry some more. This is very important. There's nothing more disappointing than putting away bunches of flowers you thought had dried, only to find a few months later that a bit of remaining moisture has ruined the whole boxful.

Once the flowers have dried, wrap them in tissue paper or newspaper, and put them in boxes that can be sealed from the light. They should be stored in a dry, warm place until you're ready to use them.

Drying Upright

Some flowers keep their shape best if they are dried standing up rather than hanging upside down. To get them started, stand the flowers in an inch or two of water in a container that you have placed in a dry, dark place. The flowers will look like fresh-cut flowers for a few days, but will gradually dry after the water has been taken up from the vase. The list of recommended cut flowers (see appendix 1) mentions those that are best preserved in this way.

Some blossoms that are great for drying have stems that won't stay rigid no matter what you do. Helichrysum, more commonly known as straw-flower, is the prime example. If you want to use strawflowers for wreaths or in other projects where you will just glue on the blossoms, you can simply pinch the flowers off the plant before they are fully open and dry them in a shallow box or basket in your drying area. If, however, you want to use the blossoms in arrangements, you should insert a florist wire in place of each stem soon after you have cut the flowers. After you've pushed the wires into the bottom of the flowers, stand them upright in a can in your drying place. As the flower dries, it will shrink and tighten its grip on the wire.

PRESERVING WITH GLYCERINE

Flowers that get too brittle when air-dried often can be preserved with glycerine, a colorless and odorless syrupy liquid that is used in hand lotions and other cosmetics. The glycerine is taken up the stem like water, where it replaces the natural moisture in the flower. Flowers treated with glycerine retain a soft feel and won't shatter when handled. Glycerine is also the only way to preserve most leaves, and foliage can add a new dimension to your floral designs.

Statice (*Limonium sinuatum*) is one flower that can be easily air-dried, but is commonly preserved with glycerine for the floral industry because it retains a much more lifelike feel. Most preservers also combine floral dye with glycerine, for two reasons. First, watching the dye move up the stem lets you know when the process is complete. Second, dye gives the flower or stems a more vibrant color to match its

Helichrysum stems are too weak to hold up the flower heads when dry, so it is best to insert a florist wire into the base of the blossom as soon as it has been cut. As the flower dries, it will tighten onto the wire.

soft feel. Many popular dried plants, such as baby's breath (*Gypsophila paniculata*) and bunny-tail grass (*Lagurus ovatus*), are often dyed in designer colors when they're glycerinized. Statice is commonly dyed green to make the stems look fresh. (Except for occasional bleeding into white statice flowers, the dye won't show up in the blossoms.)

If you're using glycerine, pick flowers when they are fully mature, because immature or aging blooms will not take up the solution readily. Mix one part glycerine with two parts warm water. Use only an inch or so in the bucket, because you will have to replace the solution for each new batch. Stand the flowers in the bucket, in a dark place, and leave them in the solution for a week or so, until the top blossoms have a silky feel. When the glycerine has been absorbed throughout the flowers, take them out of the solution and hang them upside down in a warm, dry place to finish drying.

You also can preserve leaves by immersing them in glycerine solution; this process usually takes about the same amount of time as glycerinizing through the stem.

PRESERVING WITH SILICA

Some flowers that are too fragile to air-dry or glycerinize can be preserved in silica gel crystals, a desiccant. Silica crystals made for the purpose of flower drying have color indicators that turn pink as they absorb moisture. When the silica gets damp, it can be dried in a low oven (250 degrees Fahrenheit, or 120 degrees Celsius) for two to three hours, until the color indicator becomes blue again. With this technique, the crystals can be reused almost indefinitely. You can buy them at a wholesale florist supply outlet or at a craft shop.

To dry flowers using this method, put a couple of inches of silica gel crystals in an airtight plastic storage container. Lay the blossoms, face up, with stems removed, on top of the crystals. Make sure that the flowers aren't wet and aren't touching one another. Gently pour the silica crystals on top of the blossoms, burying them completely at least a half-inch deep. Close the container tightly and put it in a dark place. Check the flowers after two days to see if they have dried. Uncover them gently, using a paintbrush or cotton swab, as they will be fragile.

The trick to drying flowers in silica is in the timing. If you leave them in too long, they become brittle and may fall apart when you try to use them. If you don't leave them in long enough, they will quickly rehydrate and go limp when exposed to humid air. So check your containers every day after the first twenty-four hours and remove any blossoms that have dried. Most flowers will be sufficiently dry within two to four days.

Many crafters spray their silica-dried flowers with a type of polyurethane coating specially made for floral use. It's not what I would call an organic substance, though, so be careful to use it sparingly and in a well-ventilated place. If you live in a humid climate, it may become obvious to you that dried flowers

Place flowers blossom-up in a container and pour silica crystals over them. After a day or two, unearth them with a paintbrush.

need a protective coating in order to last, but in drier climes, you can probably forgo this step.

Store uncoated silica-dried flowers in another airtight container that has just a trace of crystals spread across the bottom to prevent reabsorption of water. Keep the container in the dark until you're ready to use the flowers, in order to prevent colors from fading.

Silica-dried flowers can be used flat, hot-glued to wreaths and swags. If you want to use these flowers in arrangements, you can glue them to a stiff wire that you then wrap with green floral tape to look like a stem.

Silica drying may seem like a lot of trouble, and it is. However, this method does produce beautiful results from flowers that otherwise would not dry well. I have used silica to dry lilies, fully opened roses, and pansies—none of which could be air-dried. A handful of these delicate, colorful blossoms can go a long way in crafting, and they will add a distinctive look to your creations. Even commercial growers who sell wreaths and other value-added products will find it advantageous to accent their crafts by preparing small runs of silica-dried flowers.

Commercial growers who don't have the time to silica-dry their own blossoms can purchase boxes of dried ones from floral wholesalers. One company in particular, Knud Nielsen, makes a gorgeous presentation of fragile flowers (such as dogwood and pansies) by resting them on excelsior in strong, plastic-wrapped boxes.

FREEZE-DRYING

Freeze-drying is a method of preserving flowers that leaves them looking nearly lifelike. As with any preservation method, freeze-drying removes the water from flowers, but it does so by taking the water from a liquid to a solid state, and then to a vapor. When done properly, there is little tissue damage, so freeze-drying produces truer color and flower shape than other preservation methods.

For a short time in the 1980s, there was a boom in the freeze-drying industry as many small-scale crafters, growers, and florists purchased freeze-drying machines with hopes of making a fortune. Prices for freeze-dried floral material were sky-high, and so was demand. Entrepreneurs penciled out the money they could make, and it looked like a great business opportunity.

Unfortunately, the freeze-drying business turned out to be a financial catastrophe for many small enterprises. Running a freeze-drying machine was more time-consuming and labor-intensive than expected; lack of service and frequent breakdowns put machines out of commission for long stretches of time. Moreover, some machines took much longer to complete a drying cycle than the owners had been led to believe. The result was that production—and revenue—often fell far below the levels predicted in the business plan. Some owners simply couldn't pay back the loan they had taken out on the $40,000-plus freeze-drying machine.

Still, many freeze-drying businesses are humming along profitably.

Freeze-dried flowers and vegetables, which can command up to $5 apiece retail, can be sold wholesale, direct to florists by mail-order and locally. Preserving wedding bouquets or other sentimental flowers has become a big business for some freeze-dried companies.

If you would like to purchase freeze-dried material for your own use, contact the International Freeze-Dry Floral Association, listed in appendix 2, "Sources and Resources." This group can give you a list of members in your area who sell to the public. And if you're interested in pursuing freeze-drying as a business opportunity, join the association and attend a conference before you invest your life savings. Members will give you the true scoop on the business.

The Dried-Flower Garden

A commercial freeze-drying machine for flowers.

CONTROLLING DRIED-FLOWER PESTS

Indian meal moths, the same kind that get into flour and other grains, often infest dried flowers, both in storage and when they're made up into an arrangement. Some growers put pheromone traps into boxes of stored flowers. The traps will attract only the males, however, and a few males will still find their way to females and mate. Consequently, pheromone traps are probably better used to monitor your flowers for the presence of the moths. In many commercial dried-flower operations, cardboard strips impregnated with insecticides are added to the stored flowers. (That's another good reason to grow your own!) There are several organic controls for meal moths; some are more appropriate to home gardeners, and others are best used by commercial growers.

- Put the flowers in the freezer for four to seven days. The larvae will be destroyed and your problem will be resolved. If you see meal moths flitting around your house in winter, you should suspect that there has been a hatch in your dried-flower arrangements. If it's well below freezing outside, move the arrangement to an unheated garage, porch, or shed for a few days to kill any remaining larvae. Swat the slow little moths inside your house so they can't reinfest the flowers when you bring them back inside.

- Shortly before harvest, you can spray the flowers with *Bacillus thuringiensis* (Bt), a type of bacteria that kills only certain species of caterpillars, including the larvae of the meal moth.

- Heat will dry out the moths and their larvae. Temperatures of just 105 to 110 degrees Fahrenheit (40 to 43 degrees Celsius), sustained for twenty-four hours, will kill all stages of the meal moth. Higher temperatures work faster; only twenty minutes is required at 150 degrees Fahrenheit (66 degrees Celsius). This is another advantage of kiln-drying flowers, as described in the profile of Wisconsin grower John Hurd (see page 73).

- Sorbic acid, a common food additive, also has been found to kill insects in stored products. It can be sprinkled in boxes or around buildings.

The life cycle of the Indian meal moth.

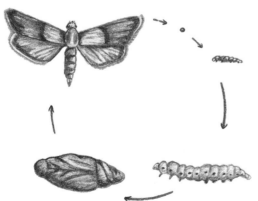

JAPANESE CROP BINDER

Grains and grasses are popular among dried-flower growers, but cutting the thin stems is a time-consuming task. Many growers in recent years have purchased a piece of Japanese rice-harvesting equipment called a crop binder to help with the job.

The crop binder is built like a walk-behind tiller, with a motor and transmission that propel it. As you walk down the crop row behind the machine, sickle bars on the front cut the crop at ground level; tines then lift the crop and move it into the machine, where a packer similar to a hay baler bundles it. When the bundle reaches a prescribed weight, a door is activated and the bundle is tied up, then ejected from the machine.

"They will go through a field as fast as you can walk," says Max Webster, whose company, Willamette Exporting, imports the machines from Japan. "They can eject fifteen to thirty bunches a minute."

Although these machines work best with grains and grasses, they also can be used with certain flowers such as gomphrena and larkspur, where the entire plant is harvested. At a cost of $7,000 to $10,000, they are designed only for commercial operations. ⌒

For more information, contact Willamette Exporting, 7330 S.W. 86th Avenue, Portland, OR 97223; 503-246-2671.

If you're drying grains as well as flowers, be aware that mice will view your drying shed as an all-day buffet. The first year I grew wheat for drying, I hung it in bundles from nails on the barn wall and was amazed to find that mice had figured out a way to walk up the walls to feast on the wheat. Afterward, I always hung my grains from wires suspended across the room. I half expected some tightrope artist to make its way across the wire to the wheat, but that hasn't happened yet.

COMMERCIAL DRIED-FLOWER PRODUCTION

Dried flowers, which seemed like a fad a decade ago, have settled into their status as a staple of the floral industry. Peak demand is seasonal, beginning in the fall and running through spring, but it's reliable. Marketing opportunities abound for dried flowers.

- Most market gardeners will find that drieds, particularly in mixed bouquets, sell well at farmers' markets during the summer, and can help extend the retail season well into the fall. Dried flowers can provide the critical mass that a grower needs to attract customers to the stand for other autumn crops, such as pumpkins and winter squash.

• Many larger farmers—particularly in prairie regions—have converted part of their acreage to dried flowers, and do a good business selling them wholesale. With a few dried products such as wheat, grasses, and some direct-seeded flowers, production isn't much different from regular row-crop farming. Harvest, post-harvest, and marketing are entirely new, however, so the farmer who wants to get into the dried-flower business can expect to increase his or her workload considerably.

• On-farm markets can increase sales with value-added dried products, including mixed bouquets, wreaths, and other crafts. Craft classes are potentially a good way to generate revenue on farms that can offer some kind of indoor workspace, such as a bright and clean barn.

• Some growers switch from farming to crafting in late summer, and make the rounds of autumn and Christmas craft fairs. Dried-flower crafts can prove quite profitable for growers who can convert a few dollars' worth of their own product into $60 wreaths. Labor is the one pitfall, however. Crafters who come up with designs that can be produced quickly will come out ahead. By contrast, elaborate, time-consuming crafts are likely to be money-losers once your own labor is taken into account.

TIPS FOR SELLING DRIEDS

Even simple bunches of dried flowers become value-added products when you wrap them in a square of florist paper and tie them with a piece of raffia or ribbon. A basket of dried-flower bouquets, attractively wrapped, will bring customers to your farmers' market stand and spur many impulse purchases. Remember to keep your drieds out of the sun to prevent them from fading, so that you can sell any leftovers the following week.

For direct sales, price your dried flowers higher than your fresh ones. If you make prices the same for fresh and dried flowers that are equally beautiful, you will cut into your fresh-flower sales. And try to sell most of your drieds direct to the final consumer: The markup on dried flowers at a florist or gift shop is substantial, which means that you can make a good profit by pricing yours competitively when selling to the consumer.

If you hope to sell to craft stores, florists, and gift shops, be prepared to accept low prices. These shop owners can purchase high-quality dried bouquets and arrangements at unbelievably low prices from wholesalers. You can find out prices a couple of ways. First, read the industry magazines listed in the "Sources and Resources" appendix. (You don't have to get a year's subscription; just order a sample issue.) Trade publications are filled with advertisements from dried-flower wholesalers. Some list prices in their ads, while others require you to send for a price list. With a handful of price lists, you will quickly get a sense of how much your flowers are worth.

Even more helpful are the gift-industry shows, where you will not only see competitors' prices and bunch sizes, but also preview designs that are coming into style. Gift shows are held frequently at the trade marts in most metropolitan areas. At these shows, manufacturers rent booths to display their product lines. It's expensive to register as a vendor, and you may want to attend a few shows as a buyer before you decide whether it would be worth the expense to rent a booth yourself. If you're unsure whether there is a gift show in a city near you, ask a few local gift-shop owners. If you explain that you want to become a dried-flower grower, they will surely tell you which shows are the best for you to attend. In addition, most trade publications run calendars listing the many national and international shows held in the biggest cities.

Finally, go to the floral wholesaler where you buy your supplies, and check

POPPIES

Poppies have become a mainstay in the dried-flower business because of their interesting pods. The most popular cultivar for dried use is 'Hens and Chicks', which has a large central pod surrounded by dozens of tiny pods. It is one of several beautiful and useful varieties in the species *Papaver somniferum*, or opium poppy.

Technically, it's illegal to grow *P. somniferum* because opium, an illegal drug, can be made from the sap of the plant. It's also illegal to possess "poppy straw," which includes any part of the plant other than the seeds.

Until recently, these laws had gone unnoticed by flower growers and dried-flower wholesalers, who were doing a booming business in poppies. But within the past few years, the Drug Enforcement Administration (DEA) of the United States Department of Justice has begun warning growers and wholesalers that cultivating or selling poppies is illegal. The DEA has even asked U.S. seed companies to voluntarily stop selling all varieties of *P. somniferum*.

Some seed companies, however, disagree with the DEA's attempts to eradicate *P. somniferum*. They argue that the species has great merit in both the landscape and in dried designs, and that people are not buying poppy seeds to make opium. As of this writing, the issue is unresolved, so check your current flower catalogs to find out whether *P. somniferum* is still available to gardeners.

If *P. somniferum* is unavailable, the next best poppy to grow for dried pods is the perennial Oriental poppy, which has fairly large pods, though not as large as those of the opium poppy. Several other poppies have interesting pods, but they are quite small. ❧

out the inventory of drieds for sale to florists. You'll get ideas for what to grow, as well as an understanding of the quality that florists expect. In general, your flowers are going to look a lot better than the wholesaler's; once you realize this, you can use it as a selling point.

Selling successfully at craft shows requires you to have a product line that stands out from the crowd. This is where your creativity comes into play. Look for innovative containers, or make your own. Don't read the same publications as everyone else—instead, browse the fresh-flower magazines to find ideas that translate to drieds. For example, a magazine for florists has featured inexpensive glass cylinders covered with twigs of pussy willow; these would make great containers for a dried arrangement. Don't rely on the motif that happens to be popular this year. (Remember all those pink and blue geese? They came and went shortly before the golden sunflowers.) Develop your own motif.

Crafters disagree about whether it's cheaper to grow all your own materials, or buy them. Keep track of the time you spend growing, harvesting, and drying your flowers, in order to decide whether you might be better off buying some or even all of your materials. Try buying some things that you can't grow, and selling them alongside or incorporated with your own product. For example, you may grow plenty of small, filler-type plants, but need a big, attention-getting flower for your bouquets. Buying dried roses or peonies might very well give your bouquets the crowning touch that puts them into a much higher price range. Just be sure you're marking up every purchased flower that you sell.

If you try to sell both fresh and dried flowers, you may meet yourself coming and going. Although the growing of each is the same, the marketing is quite different. Try to keep good records that will allow you to compare the profit margin on each type of product. Obviously, selling flowers fresh by the bunch is going to be far less labor-intensive than harvesting, drying, storing, and then crafting products. But you must also take into consideration the strength of each market: How much can you sell fresh? How much dried? In addition, you must consider the overall workload on your farm; for example, if your growing season is short and a September frost puts you out of the fresh-flower business, you may need a few months of dried-flower sales in order to make a profit.

Ultimately, the type of flowers you grow can't be determined solely by arithmetic—you need to take subjective factors into account, too. The most important one, in my opinion, is your own personal enjoyment. If you really love crafting with drieds, then by all means do it! You'll be happiest at work you enjoy, whether or not it's the most profitable approach. If, on the other hand, you don't really like to spend time working with drieds, why bother with it? The first few years that we grew flowers, I made wreaths to sell at farmers' markets. The wreaths were quite popular, and at $40 each, I made a profit. But I did not enjoy sitting up till midnight, crafting, after working outside all day. As soon as I got a good hold on the fresh-flower market, I stopped doing drieds altogether.

Avatar's World ❧ *Edgerton, Wisconsin*

J OHN HURD RETURNED TO SOUTHERN WISCONSIN AFTER COLLEGE TO TAKE OVER the farm that has been in his family for five generations.

He picked up where his father left off, growing row crops and raising Holsteins. But after a time, he realized that, much as he wanted to farm, conventional agriculture wasn't for him. He had no fondness for cattle and he felt isolated by the long hours he spent on a tractor.

In 1987, John looked around for farming alternatives and decided to try growing flowers, grasses, and grains for drying. Thus was born Avatar's World, wholesaler of a wide variety of dried materials for floral design and crafts. ("Avatar" is a Sanskrit word for the deity who returns to Earth in different clothing; John loosely interprets it to represent the nature spirits who oversee the growing of flowers.)

Today, John grows seven acres of flowers for the wholesale market. He maintains a display room on the farm, and employs four people year-round. He still raises five hundred acres of row crops, but his farm now has a completely different feel to him.

"When I thought about what I didn't like about farming, it was mostly that it was so isolated, that I didn't have people around me," he says. "This has brought people to work on the farm whom I see daily; the contact with people is important."

The market for dried flowers has grown steadily since John started in the business.

"Dried flowers have gone past the fad stage," he says. "The trend has lasted longer than three or four years. Even in the short time we've been doing it, I've seen a change in attitude. At first, I would take dried flowers to florists and they just weren't interested. Now, florists are the fastest-growing part of the market."

The demand for dried flowers lasts nearly all year long, he says. He ships about half his annual volume between August and November, the rest in winter and spring. Demand is strong in spring because that's the busiest time for florists, who are increasingly mixing drieds with fresh flowers; also, manufacturers of dried arrangements begin making their fall designs in March.

With such a long holding time between cutting and selling flowers, proper drying is critical. Hanging them in a shed just doesn't do the job. Too often, the flowers don't dry completely inside, and mold develops later. Or they dry too slowly, and lose color in the process.

John has determined that a better method of drying is a kiln where heated air is circulated and humidity is controlled. With forced warm air, flowers dry faster, staying fresher-looking and retaining shape and color better than air-dried flowers. John's kiln is a truck trailer, painted black and well-insulated. Outside, a propane-fired furnace blows air heated to 100 degrees Fahrenheit (38 degrees Celsius) through the trailer.

Most flowers need only a day or two to dry completely. They're a bit brittle when they're thoroughly dry, however, so they must be rehydrated slightly to keep them from shattering when handled. For some flowers, opening the kiln door at night will introduce enough humidity to rehydrate them. For others, John hoses down the kiln floor with water and lets the flowers absorb the moisture. For proper storage, the perfect moisture content of dried flowers is 15 to 20 percent. Meters used by farmers to test the moisture content of hay can also serve to monitor flowers.

John adds that his kiln now has a humidity level of 30 percent. If he were to build it over again, he would use misters to keep humidity at 50 percent, eliminating the need for the rehydration procedure.

The kiln has been a great advance for John's business in several ways. Not only does it dry flowers to perfection, creating a longer-lasting product, but it also takes the uncertainty out of drying times. Because John knows how long each flower takes in the kiln, he can schedule his harvest accordingly. For example, linum (flax) takes one day to dry, so when he plants linum, he plants three rows—just enough to fill the kiln. A few days later, he seeds another three rows that will be ready for harvest after the first batch has been dried and boxed. Every crop can be scheduled to bloom in quantities that fit the kiln and in a se-

quence that spaces out the harvest over the season.

The kiln also helps John determine what *not* to grow. He has discovered that the bloom time on delphiniums overlaps the drying time for peonies. Since he can't accommodate delphiniums in the kiln, John says, there's no sense in growing them.

John is probably best known in the flower world for his dried grains and grasses. He grows several kinds of wheat, plus rye, oats, broomcorn, flax, big and little quaking grass, northern sea-oats, fountain grass, giant feather grass, and canary grass. He harvests the grasses and grains with a Japanese rice harvester—a walk-behind machine, like a tiller, that cuts and bundles the stems.

Because he started as a "regular" farmer himself, John is often approached by farmers who tell him they want to get into flower growing to supplement their income. He always tells them, "Start small."

"They have to remember it takes as much time as starting a new business," he says. "It's not like adding one hundred head of cattle when you already have two hundred. There's a big learning curve with something this different. And there isn't always some place to sell your crop, as there is with corn. It always worries me when someone calls and says they're thinking of doing twenty-five acres of dried flowers. I know this thinking. I tell them to start with a quarter-acre total. They will soon find out that there's more work in ten acres of flowers than in one hundred acres of corn." ◃

Valencia Creek Farm ~ Aptos, California

WHEN CHRIS BANTHIEN AND HER PARTNER BUILT THEIR HOUSE ON A STEEP hillside near the Monterey Bay in Aptos, California, Chris knew she would have to specialize in flowers that could withstand hot sun, ocean fogs, and sandy soil.

She chose Mediterranean herbs as her main crop, and the choice proved an ideal match for her climate. Chris now grows about five acres of lavenders and ornamental oreganos, many of them little-known species and varieties that aren't grown commercially elsewhere in the United States. Her ornamental herbs, which can be used both fresh and dried, are sought out by floral wholesalers and customers at farmers' markets.

Chris grows a half-dozen varieties of lavender that are strikingly different from one another. The flowers of 'Provence', for example, are much lighter than the dark purple flowers of 'Hidcote', but the foliage is grayer than that of 'Grosso'. Fragrances vary, too, and Chris can tell in a breath which lavender she is handling.

Oreganos are another matter. The genus *Origanum* is large, and its many species cause confusion in the nomenclature. They range from short, shrubby plants with tiny pink flowers to tall, rangy plants with big, round bracts like hops. While only a few of the oreganos are used in cooking, nearly all of them are lovely fresh or dried. Chris grows about a dozen varieties, and finds that they cross-pollinate freely, resulting in hybrids that might be seen nowhere else.

Some of Chris's favorites include:

- *O. laevigatum* 'Hopley's Purple', which has tall purple stems and purple flowers.
- *O. dictamnus* 'Dittany of Crete', which produces small, hop-like bracts that are green when mature.
- *O. rotundifolium*, which has green, hop-like bracts up to an inch in diameter. The bracts are light green when dried.
- *O. rotundifolium* 'Kent Beauty', which looks like the preceding variety, but the bracts have a rose tint.

Even the common culinary oregano provides good flowers for drying. *O. vulgare*, subspecies *vulgare*, has pink flowers enclosed in purple bracts.

Although the California climate is perfect for growing herbs, the large deer population in the Aptos area makes Chris's enterprise a challenge. The deer didn't bother the herbs for years, but they have recently developed a taste for them, she says. Just before the oreganos bloom, the deer come through and browse on the tips, which ruins the stem. She has already erected a 7-foot deer fence around a few acres of perennials and hydrangeas, and expects that she will soon have to fence her entire production area to prevent deer damage.

When Chris started her business in 1989, she primarily was selling dried herbs to consumers at farmers' markets. But then a few wholesalers found out about her wonderful herbs, and by 1996, more than half of her revenue came from wholesaling. Although much of her production is now sold as fresh flowers, Chris still makes use of the spacious hilltop barn she built. She has devised a system to hang the herb bunches quickly and with plenty of air circulation. A wooden frame with wires stretched across it creates the gridwork. Plastic clothes-hangers are always standing ready, with a piece of string attached to the bottom bar of the hanger. As the bunches come in from the field, bound with rubber bands, the string is slipped up through the middle of the bunch, where the rubber band holds it in place.

Chris also grows a sprinkling of other herbs and flowers, most of them quite unusual for Northern California. She raises several varieties of ornamental wheat and triticale, a wheat-rye cross, for drying. She also grows curry plant (*Helichrysum petiolatum*). In her climate, this fuzzy-leaved plant, which is grown in windowboxes elsewhere in the country, grows to 7 feet tall and as big around. *Monarda citriodora* (lemon mint), with its whorls of purple flower bracts, and *Craspedia* (golden drumsticks) are also popular for her.

Until now, growing unusual plants has made for easy sales. Now, Chris says, "Everybody's growing oregano." Actually, only the common oregano has recently begun to appear on the wholesale fresh-flower market, but those occasional sightings have sounded a warning for Chris. Once a flower becomes readily available, the price drops and wholesalers aren't so eager to buy it. (Currently, wholesalers want Chris's product so badly they actually drive to her farm to pick it up!)

Her strategy for the future is to stay ahead of the competition by continually growing new varieties and unusual species on a trial basis, then taking them commercial as they prove themselves worthy. But she thinks that a commitment to quality is even more important than staying on the cutting edge.

"Attention to the details of cleanliness, uniformity of bunch sizes, and consistency of a beautiful product presentation go a long way in establishing loyalty between customers and the grower," she says. ✿

CHAPTER 6

Woody Ornamentals

SOME OF THE BEST PLANTS FOR EXTENDING YOUR SEASON AND FILLING out your bouquets are the woody ornamentals. "Woodies," as they are affectionately called by professional growers, are trees and shrubs that come back every year and form a hard, woodlike outer tissue on their stems and branches. Many parts of woodies—flowering branches, twigs, cones, pods, berries, and so on—are gaining wide usage in creative floral design.

For the home gardener, making use of woodies may be as simple as walking around the yard to see what kinds of plants are available. Some will be quite obvious; who hasn't forced a few stems of forsythia in late winter, or brought lilac blossoms inside in spring? Other possibilities may be hiding right under your nose, such as the glossy leaves of old-fashioned spirea that shine in a bouquet, or the pink catkins of a maple tree that hang gracefully in an arrangement. Once you have become attuned to the charms of woodies for cutting, you will be able to choose new plantings with an eye to their usefulness indoors as well as out.

For the commercial grower, woody ornamentals require a big capital investment, and several years before payback begins, so a great deal of research is advisable in order to determine which woodies are best for you. Ten years ago, the demand for woody ornamentals was an untapped market for cut-flower growers. Florists wanted tall flowering branches for hotel and other large-scale arrangements, and there was a strong interest in unusual seasonal materials, such as berries and bare twigs.

Although many growers have jumped into the business in recent years, and certain materials are now widely available, the production of woody ornamentals for cut flowers is still a new frontier. Even the most experienced growers say they rely on continual experimentation to find the best cultivars, harvest times, pricing, and markets. The market is out there, in other words, but you may have to develop it yourself.

BENEFITS OF WOODIES

Consider the many advantages of growing woody ornamentals. Most obviously, they are long-lasting perennials, which, once established, require less intensive care than annual flowers. And in most cases, woodies need to be pruned annually, so cutting branches for flowers is beneficial to the longevity of the plant. Most flowering shrubs, for example, should be pruned right after flowering anyway; cutting them just before they bloom won't hurt them.

In addition, there are varieties of woody ornamentals suited to nearly every climate, and many of them are quite specific, which limits competition from other areas of the country. Southern California growers can corner the market on tender Australian shrubs, such as proteas and leptospermum. But they can't grow lilacs or hollies, which need an extensive chilling period and thrive only in northern climates. Similarly, forsythias and flowering crab apples can only be grown where the winters are cold but not severe, and where there aren't late freezes.

Another benefit to cut-flower growers is that woody ornamentals can be used to extend the marketing season. Flowering branches can be forced for sale early in spring, which could help you get your foot in the door of the florist or wholesaler, and keep that door open for your summer cut-flower production. As fall comes on, there are plenty of plants with interesting bare branches, foliage, or berries that can be sold well into the winter.

CHOOSING VARIETIES

The primary woodies grown for the floral trade are boxwood, dogwood, forsythia, holly, hydrangea, jasmine, lilac, pussy willow, and corkscrew willow. Some are imported from the Netherlands, but an increasing number are being grown in the United States. And many, many other plants are grown in small quantities but are in greater demand every year, as floral styles change to incorporate more of these structural elements. For example, fruit tree blossoms are quite popular at present. Many of those available to the trade are actually prunings from real working orchards. Enterprising flower growers who already have the marketing connections have started working with orchardists to collect the branches as they are pruned in late winter. The flower growers then bring the prunings back to their own farms to force the blossoms for market.

To determine which plants would work for you, the first step is to spread out a variety of nursery catalogs and compile an inventory of prospects that are hardy in your area; also, get cultivar recommendations from your Cooperative Extension office. Unless your state has an expert in floriculture, you'll probably have to get your information from home-gardening and landscaping specialists. Your research should narrow your list to species that will survive not only your winters, but also your summers, rainfall, soils, and pests.

You may also find experimental material right on your own land. Forsythia, spirea, lilac, mock orange, and flowering quince are examples of common landscape shrubs that have value as cut flowers. Many native species (such as redbud, rhododendron, and dogwood) also have potential. Even common, unimproved varieties can give you information about vase life, forcing requirements, and microclimates on your land.

SPACING

If you plant a new shrub or tree as part of your landscape, follow the planting and spacing directions provided by the nursery. You will want to give the plant plenty of space if it is to serve as both a landscape specimen and a source of cut branches. Likewise, if you're a commercial grower who wants woodies to serve as both windbreaks and cutting material, you should give them plenty of space.

However, if you are planning to use your woodies only as cutting material, your spacing considerations are different from those of a landscape or windbreak planting. In some cases, you can plant shrubs or trees quite close together as a way of forcing them to grow vertically and produce long, straight stems. For example, butterfly bush (*Buddleia davidii*) should be given at least 5 feet of space if grown as a landscape plant. In a commercial bed, however, you can plant it as close as 18 inches from the next bush, since it will be cut back to the ground every year.

On the other hand, many species of woodies have no established recommendations for spacing, because few people are growing them commercially. You may have to figure these out yourself, species by species. One important consideration for spacing is how to keep the plants weeded when they are young. If you plant them into a cover crop such as clover, or into grass, be sure to leave enough space between rows to get your mower in. At the same time, try to envision the plant at the size it will be when fully grown, and leave enough room to get a truck or tractor through. Harvesting those big, heavy branches can be hard work, and you will not want to thrash through a jungle of your own making every time you bring the flowers in from the field.

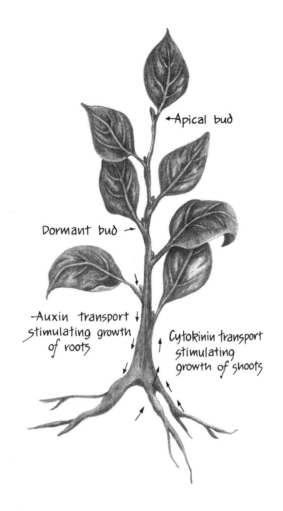

Apical bud

Dormant bud →

-Auxin transport
stimulating growth
of roots

Cytokinin transport
stimulating
growth of shoots

In a typical plant, the dominant apical bud prevents the development of the dormant buds or side shoots. Once the apical bud is removed by pruning or pinching, the other buds will develop.

PHYSIOLOGY OF WOODY PLANTS

You have to know a bit about the physiology of woody plants if you are to succeed in using them as cut flowers. Like all plants, the woodies grow most vigorously at the tip, or apex. The apex consists of a small dome of actively dividing cells, called the apical meristem, which produces hormones called auxins. Auxins, in turn, stimulate the growth of xylem, the woody transport system that carries water, minerals, and hormones from the roots to the tip of the plant. By producing auxins in the tip, the apex causes the xylem to be extended, thus ensuring a clear pathway for nutrients and hormones from the roots. These root hormones, or cytokinins, stimulate cell division in the plant. If they are being transported directly to the apex, the most active growth will occur there, in the bud.

When you remove that apical bud, however, the nutrients, water, and cytokinins continue to pass up through the stem, but are then diverted to the next tier of buds on the stem. In due course, these lateral buds develop into the leading shoots on the plant, causing it to branch.

The implication for the grower of trees and shrubs for cut-flowers is simple: If you prune the apical bud from the plant when it is small, it will branch low to the ground and produce long, usable stems. If you prune a larger plant, you must cut it back hard to get a flush of long stems. By pruning the growing tip from a plant that is already close to its mature height, you

Branches can be cut in late winter and put into buckets of floral preservative solution at about 50 degrees Fahrenheit. After a few weeks, the buckets can be moved to a bright, 75-degree room or greenhouse, and the branches will burst into bloom.

Branches should be cut low to the ground to stimulate tall new growth.

81

Forcing Blossoms

Most flowering shrubs have a specific chilling requirement, which you can usually find in reference books. Some peaches, for example, need two hundred hours at temperatures of 35 degrees Fahrenheit (2 degrees Celsius) before they can be forced to bloom. Although you can probably tell by looking at a branch whether it has buds on the old wood, there's no way to tell whether it has had a long enough dormancy. You can either wait till late winter (four to six weeks before the usual bloom time) to begin forcing, or cut earlier and keep the branches in a freezer to ensure adequate chilling.

When you are ready to force the blossoms, recut the stems cleanly at a 45-degree angle and slit any thick stems about an inch up from the end. Put the cut branches in warm water with floral preservative, and bring them into a warm, bright room. (Exposing them to direct sun will help the flowers develop good color.) Mist the branches regularly to keep them from drying out.

Commercial growers find that they get more blossoms with longer vase life by warming up the branches in stages, rather than bringing them immediately up to springtime temperatures. For example, start the branches in a cool greenhouse (50 degrees Fahrenheit, or 10 degrees Celsius) for two weeks, then move them to a warmer greenhouse (75 degrees Fahrenheit, or 24 degrees Celsius) to finish opening.

The late David F. Jenkins of Jenkins Wholesale Florist in Port Royal, Virginia, was one of the pioneers in growing and forcing woodies for their flowers. Jenkins would often take buds to the point where they were ready to open, then store them in a cooler to put blooming on hold. He found he could hold them that way for several weeks. Then, as orders arrived, he could move the branches back to the warm greenhouse to finish opening within a few days. During a lifetime of experimentation (his father had grown the first woodies for cutting when David was a child), Jenkins became intimately familiar with the chilling and forcing requirements of dozens of species. He was so comfortable with his understanding of how flowers bloom that he was able to provide plum blossoms for several presidential inaugurations. Imagine how critical the timing was on those orders! ❧

will create a network of short branches near the top, which will not provide good cutting material. The moral of this lesson is to be tough about pruning: Cut the plant back boldly, and you'll have plenty of good stems next year; cut it back timidly, and you'll ruin the plant for cutting next year.

WHEN TO HARVEST

Deciduous shrubs flower either on one-year-old wood or on the current season's growth. As a rule, those that flower on one-year-old growth are the spring- and early-summer–flowering shrubs. Their buds form the previous year and are ready to burst into bloom when warm weather arrives. The best time to prune these shrubs for overall plant health is just after they bloom, to ensure that new shoots will grow during the summer and produce blooms for next spring. Therefore, no harm is done to these plants by cutting them before they bloom (for forcing) or while they are blooming. As long as you cut the stems according to basic principles of sound pruning, your flower harvest will affect the plant no differently than an annual pruning. Be careful about cutting fall foliage or berries, however, as some of these plants have spent the summer producing next year's flower buds. If you take them in fall, you won't have flowers in spring.

Shrubs that flower on the current season's growth are generally those that flower in late summer or fall. These shrubs should be pruned in late winter, just as the buds begin to swell, to allow plenty of time for new growth. When you harvest them at their natural blooming time, you are in effect doing an early pruning. Assuming that the plants are hardy to your climate, they will sit dormant throughout fall and winter, and begin growing again in spring.

One important rule about harvesting any type of woody ornamental (or any plant, for that matter) is that you must leave at least one-third of the foliage on the plant when you cut. If you cut more than that while the plant is still growing, it will not be able to nourish the roots and it will die. Once the plant has gone dormant, it may be cut to the ground.

HARVEST AND POST-HARVEST

The woody stems of trees and shrubs take up water less easily than do the soft stems of herbaceous plants. To help your cut woodies take up water, you can increase the stem's surface area in contact with water. First, make your cut on a sharp diagonal, which has the added benefit of preventing the stem end from resting flat on the bottom of your container and getting plugged. You also should split the bottom of the stem about 1 to 4 inches, depending on the length of the stem. Old floral guides may tell you to crush the stem ends with a hammer, but this method has been discredited in favor of splitting them. Crushing the stems releases small particles of the plant into the water, which can cause the growth of bacteria and ultimately clog the stems.

Woody plants also require floral preservatives to increase water uptake and prevent the growth of bacteria. Preservatives are particularly important for

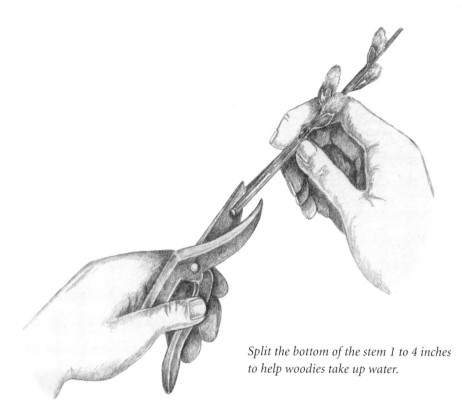

*Split the bottom of the stem 1 to 4 inches
to help woodies take up water.*

flowering branches that haven't fully opened, because the blossoms need the sugar in the preservative in order to continue opening. Homemade recipes will suffice, as long as they contain both sugar and an acidifier (see chapter 7).

SPECIFIC INSTRUCTIONS FOR WOODIES

In the list that follows, you will find an introduction to some of the most commonly grown woody ornamentals. These plants are frequently used in the floral trade, and they can be cultivated throughout most of North America. (Australian and other tender woodies grown in California for the floral industry are not included here.) This list is not intended to be exhaustive; rather, it aims to provide a few different examples of how woody plants can be handled to yield cut materials. Dozens of other plants, both cultivated and wild, can be used, and their harvest and post-harvest care will be similar to that of the plants listed here.

For many woody plants, there is only sketchy information about harvest and post-harvest because they have only recently been grown for cutting, and there is little experience on which to base recommendations. When lacking specific advice, experiment! If a stem wilts or fails to bloom under one set of conditions, try something else. Many plants will hold up well in the vase, as long as you can figure out what they really need. Use the map on page 158 to determine your hardiness zone.

Buddleia davidii—Butterfly Bush
See the list of recommended cut flowers in appendix 1.

Callicarpa americana—Beautyberry
These shrubby southern natives produce lovely rose or white berries all along the stems in fall. They produce on new growth, so you should cut them back nearly to the ground in late winter.

Cut long stems; place them immediately in hot water and floral preservative. After two hours, stand the stems in buckets without water for two days. The leaves then can be easily removed, leaving just the berried stems. At this point, return the stems to water. The berries last up to two weeks in a vase.

Caryopteris clandonensis—Bluebeard
The lacy blue flowers and small silvery leaves of *Caryopteris* make it an excellent shrub for cutting. It flowers in late summer, too, when it's useful for cooling down the hot colors of summer flowers. Although this shrub is reliably hardy only to Zone 6, I have had plants survive harsh winters here in Zone 5. It flowers on new growth, so it can be cut back in late winter.

Harvest when flowers are in full bloom, and place the stems in hot water.

Celastrus scandens—Bittersweet
Florists love the clusters of orange berries fresh or dried in fall. This plant should not be harvested from the wild, because it is becoming scarce. However, it is easy to cultivate, and growers in many parts of the country are planting it. Although only the female plants produce the fruits, male plants are needed to pollinate them.

Cercis canadensis—Redbud
This beautiful American native that lights up the spring woodlands throughout much of the United States has become a popular item with florists. It should be cut when half the buds on the stem are open. Floral preservative extends its vase life.

Chaenomeles speciosa—Flowering Quince
This big, boisterous shrub is smothered with bright coral flowers in early spring, shortly after forsythia blooms. Prune old wood to keep it flowering. Harvest the stems when buds are beginning to open; branches also can be cut in late winter and forced in a cool greenhouse.

Cornus sericea—Red Osier Dogwood
The smooth, bright red branches of red osier dogwood can be cut in late winter, when the color is most intense, and kept refrigerated in water for several months.

The new wood is the most colorful, so cut the plant back every year to encourage new growth. There are also yellow and orange cultivars.

Forsythia × *intermedia*—Forsythia

The yellow flowers of forsythia bloom in early spring on the previous season's growth. They can be forced by bringing them into the house six weeks before their normal bloom time. On a commercial scale, they can be cut in late November and held in a freezer at 29 degrees Fahrenheit (−2 degrees Celsius) for a month, then brought into a 50-degree (Fahrenheit, or 10 degrees Celsius) greenhouse, where they will bloom in three weeks. Forsythias also can be cut at their natural bloom time while the buds are still tight. Regular harvesting should keep the plants producing; old ones can be rejuvenated by cutting the oldest wood down to ground level just after flowering.

Hydrangea spp.—Hydrangeas

Several varieties of hydrangea can be grown for cut or dried flowers. *H. arborescens* (Zones 3–9), also known by the name of its chief cultivar, 'Annabelle', produces big white clusters of flowers that turn green, then brown. *H. macrophylla* (Zones 6–9), the big-leaved hydrangeas, produce the colorful clusters that are desirable as dried flowers. They do best in mild coastal climates, because their buds (which are formed on the previous year's growth) are easily damaged by winter warming and later frosts. Blue-flowering varieties will be pink in alkaline soil. *H. paniculata* (Zones 3–8) is widely grown for its conical white flower clusters (panicles) that later turn pink, then green, then brown. To dry them, stand the stems up in a dry container when the flowers are papery. The most common cultivar is *H. paniculata* 'Grandiflora', nicknamed "peegee" hydrangea.

Cut hydrangea stems when about half the flowers on the panicle are open. Split the stem ends about an inch.

Ilex spp.—Hollies

The red-berried, evergreen plant of Christmas fame is only one of many species of holly. One of the more popular species being planted now is *Ilex verticillata* (winterberry), a deciduous species (Zones 3–9) that covers the stems with red berries. Like all hollies, there are separate male and female plants, and you need to plant both in order to produce berries. Stems are harvested whenever the berries are mature; if the leaves haven't fallen, you'll need to pull them off.

Nandina domestica—Heavenly-Bamboo

Nandina is a wonderful plant for southern and coastal growers in Zones 6–9. The reddish, lacy foliage can be grown as a filler. It also offers white flowers in spring and red berries in winter.

Prunus spp.—Flowering Almonds, Plums, Cherries

This genus includes dozens of species and cultivars, some of them fruiting and some merely ornamental. Nearly all *Prunus* flowers can be forced in late winter; they can also be cut just as they begin to bloom.

Pyracantha spp.—Firethorns

These are grown for their fall berries. Dozens of cultivars have been developed, with fruit colors ranging from gold to orange to bright red. Cut the stems back hard to improve the next year's growth.

Salix spp.—Willows

The two willow species most important in the flower trade are pussy willow (*Salix discolor*) and curly willow (*S. matsudana*). They are easily propagated by softwood or hardwood cuttings, so you can quickly increase your stock from just a few plants. Root them in a soilless mix; then pot them until they're big enough to transplant to the field.

    The pussy willows can be cut in spring, just as the catkins are emerging, and can be held in preservative solution in a cooler for several weeks. Curly willow can be cut after the leaves have fallen and the contorted stems are most brightly colored. With both plants, if you cut the branches back to within 6 inches of the ground in late winter, you will have good stems the following year.

Syringa spp.—Lilacs

There are more than two thousand cultivars of the old-fashioned common lilac (*Syringa vulgaris*), and there are several additional species that can be grown as far south as Zone 8. (Consult your Cooperative Extension service for recommendations.) The blossoms can be forced six to eight weeks before their normal flowering time. When cutting them in bloom, cut early in the morning and remove all foliage except the two leaves below the panicle, or flower cluster. Place the stems in a warm preservative solution, and keep them in a cool place away from bright light. Immediately after flowering, thin the plants to allow air circulation. Old lilacs can be rejuvenated by cutting one-third of their old branches to the ground each spring.

Viburnum spp.—Viburnums

This genus includes 225 species, several of them excellent for cutting. Hardiness varies by species, but many can be grown in Zones 3–8. Among those grown for cutting are *V. carlesii* (Korean spice viburnum); *V.* × *burkwoodii* 'Mohawk' (Burkwood viburnum); *V.* × *carlcephalum* (snowball viburnum); *V. opulus* (European cranberry bush); *V. opulus* 'Roseum' (European snowball bush); and *V. plicatum* (double-file viburnum). Several of these can be forced, and all produce good blossoms. Many viburnums also produce ornamental berries and foliage in

Salix discolor *Pussy Willow*

fall. Be aware, however, that cutting in fall may reduce flowering in spring, as many varieties produce their buds on the previous year's growth.

Weigela florida—Weigela

The pink, red, or white flowers smother the arching branches of this old-fashioned shrub, which grows well in Zones 5–8. It blooms in early summer for several weeks. The vase life is less than a week, but weigela is so pretty that it's worth growing anyway.

Star Valley Flowers ∾ Soldiers Grove, Wisconsin

JOHN ZEHRER, THE SON OF A MINNESOTA DAIRY FARMER, BOUGHT A FARM IN southwestern Wisconsin in 1982 and began milking Jerseys. He realized, however, that the economics of the dairy business made for an uncertain future in farming.

So John started looking around for high-value crops to provide additional farm income. He had heard about a rising demand for curly willow, a twisted branch that is used in floral designs, and he thought it might grow well in his climate. He planted a few beds of curly willow beside his house, where it began to grow like a weed.

John realized that woody ornamentals might be the perfect crop for his hilly farm. He started investigating the other types of woodies used in the floral trade, and found a half-dozen plants that were in common use. His research gradually turned up more and more woody plants that weren't widely available to florists but had good potential as cut branches. And he found wholesale buyers who expressed interest in doing business with him.

The curly willow plantings were soon joined by a field of red osier dogwood, lilac, pussy willow, smoke tree, golden ninebark, witch hazel, spirea, and euonymus. The beds of new plants fanned across one hillside, then jumped to a second field, and then a third. John also started growing annual and perennial cut flowers because "I had to have something to finance my shrub habit," he says.

Today, the Jersey cows are gone, replaced by thirty-five acres of woody plants and ten acres of cut flowers. John's business, Star Valley Flowers, sells to wholesalers, to grocery stores, and at farmers' markets in Chicago; he also delivers to about thirty retail florists and several wholesalers in Minneapolis. His plant list includes dozens of species that provide cutting material nearly year-round. He and his crew of ten take a break only from mid-December to mid-January.

Bumping through his fields in a pickup truck, John points out the successes and failures of a decade of experimentation. Curly willow is still important in the floral industry, he says, "but everybody and his dog is growing it." The same is true of peonies, he finds. Barberry, though beautiful, is too thorny and is being eliminated from John's field. Peegee hydrangea grows well, but the flowers are turning brown before they color up, so John has erected a tent of shade cloth over the plants in an effort to save them.

One of his greatest hopes is for the five acres of bittersweet he planted recently. The vines are growing on strong trellises designed for grapes. Viburnums are another favorite. John has eight varieties, which provide a long season of flowers, foliage, and berries for cutting. *Viburnum trilobum* 'Wentworth', with red fall foliage and bright red berries, is one of his most successful.

Other crops John thinks have good potential include *Ilex verticillata* (winterberry), which sports bright red berries in winter; *Hamamelis mollis* (Chinese witchhazel), which bears fragrant yellow flowers in late winter; *Philadelphus coronarius* (mock orange), with four-petaled white flowers in late spring that are extremely fragrant; and *Euonymus bungeanus* (winterberry euonymous), grown for its pink-capped berries. To growers with acidic, sandy soils, John also recommends *Tamarix ramosissima* (tamarisk) for its long, pink plumes in midsummer.

When starting a new crop, John says, it's not cost-effective to buy big plants. Instead, he buys what are known in the nursery business as liners, or rooted cuttings, and grows them 4 inches apart in a well-drained, composted, and irrigated bed. To increase a small planting, he takes his own cuttings and roots them in his greenhouse before planting them into the nursery bed. The plants should be grown to a height of about 18 inches before they're ready to be set out in the field in their permanent location.

While the young plants are getting started, John also prepares his field. Ideally, he likes to begin field preparations a year in advance of planting. He seeds white Dutch clover and birdsfoot trefoil, both legumes that provide nitrogen to the soil and help choke out weeds. Once the clovers are established, he rents a tree planter from the local Farm Service Agency (formerly known as the Agricultural Stabilization and Conservation Service, or ASCS) office and makes short work of digging the holes.

John warns that the shrubs should be given plenty of space. When he started growing woodies, he planted most of them on a 4- by 4-foot grid. Many of those plants are now crushed together and spilling out into the pathways. Today, new plantings go in rows that are spaced 10 to 15 feet apart, with 4 feet between the plants in each row.

Although John's business evolved from his

own interests and from market demand, he finds now that it has gotten too big for his liking. His time is spent marketing on the phone and managing in the office, rather than farming in the field. "There's a certain amount of efficiency that comes out of a home-run business," he says. "But now, when I have ten people cutting, I'm hardly even out there."

So, as he moves into his second decade of selling flowers, John is considering his options. Maybe he'll eliminate the annual and perennial flowers, or reduce the number of markets he sells to. Or he might even just shorten his season. In any case, John will always have the thirty-five acres of shrubs flourishing on the hillsides around him. ❧

CHAPTER 7

Harvest and Post-Harvest

THIS IS THE MOST IMPORTANT CHAPTER OF THIS BOOK, BECAUSE HARVEST and post-harvest are the most important steps in the life of a cut flower. By now, you have spent months planning, planting, and nurturing your flowers. Your reward is a garden full of blooms that are beautiful to behold. But the moment is at hand when you will transform those garden flowers into cut flowers. Their success in the vase will be determined entirely by how you handle them from this time onward. And if you're in business, your financial success hinges on whether you do it right. This is no small matter.

When harvesting, you must learn to think like a flower, to empathize with the flower, to understand the physiological processes that are at work in this small miracle of nature. To do this, you need to call upon your basic knowledge of the biology of plants.

A flower is, technically, a plant's mechanism for reproducing. Its purpose is to attract pollinators. Once pollination has occurred, the flower fades and the seed begins to grow, starting the next generation.

Your job—cruel as it may sound—is to cut the flower in its prime, before it has had a chance to reproduce. Remember, once it has been visited by insects or shed its pollen to the wind, it has finished its work and is on its way to obsolescence. To ensure the best possible vase life, you must cut the flower at the perfect time.

TIMELINESS

The stages of flower development range from tight bud to full bloom. When should you cut your flowers? The perfect harvest stage varies for each species. That information, if it is known, appears in the recommended cut-flower list in appendix 1. For flowers that aren't listed, a rule of thumb is to cut just after the blossom has opened fully, and before it is showing pollen. Once you start to see a lot of loose pollen on the flower, it is beginning to senesce—a polite way of saying it is getting old and dying. A senescing flower will have a short vase life.

Some species can be cut in the bud stage and then bloomed in the vase, which gives you many more days of vase life. When selling to a wholesaler or to a retailer who won't be selling all the flowers within a day or two, cut as many in the bud stage as you can. Peonies, for a dramatic example, can be cut in the bud and held in a refrigerator for several months. Iris can be cut in the "pencil stage," when the flowers have emerged from the green sheath and are showing a pencil-thin streak of color. Lisianthus can be cut when the first flower on the stem is not quite fully opened; that flower and several smaller buds on the stem will open in the vase. If you use the proper floral preservative, a single stem of lisianthus can last up to a month!

In most species that have many small flowers on a stem, you can cut after the first few flowers open, and the rest will open in the vase. Delphinium,

Campanula persicifolia (peach-leaf bellflower) opens from the bottom to the top of the stem and can be cut when one or two flowers are open and several more are swollen and colored.

Harvest and Post-Harvest

Papaver orientale (Oriental poppy) can be cut in the advanced-bud stage, when the petals are ready to unfold as shown in the lower bud in this illustration. If cut in the tight bud stage, as shown by the bud at the top, the flower may not open.

larkspur, gladiolus, and snapdragon are examples of spike flowers that open from the bottom to the top; they should be harvested when just one-fourth to one-third of the lower flowers on the stem are open. Daisy-like flowers can usually be cut when the petals have begun to unfurl, but before they are fully open.

TIME OF DAY

The old debate still rages on: should flowers be cut in the morning or in the evening? Actually, there are advantages to each of these times. When you cut in the morning, the flowers are at their most turgid; they will be less likely to wilt,

CUTTING EARLY TO PREVENT INSECT DAMAGE

One of the tricks to growing flowers organically is to cut them before insects have a chance to destroy their beauty. I learned this the hard way during the first summer I grew sunflowers commercially. The guidelines I had received from various sources said that sunflowers should be cut when about one-fourth of the disc flowers—the tiny flowers in the brown center—were open. But by the time this happened, cucumber beetles had chewed holes in all the petals.

So I started to cut sooner. I harvested the sunflowers when the petals had just opened, and they held fine. But a few beetles were still getting their bites in, so I started cutting earlier and earlier, until I was cutting the flowers before the petals had even unfurled. The flowers eventually opened in buckets, were just as vibrant as those that bloomed outside, and were cosmetically perfect.

This trick works well with nearly all the composite flowers, which have large, flat outer petals subject to insect damage. Daisies, gloriosa daisies, rudbeckia, and gaillardia all can be cut early and bloomed indoors. Zinnias, although they are in the same family, aren't as attractive to insect pests and don't suffer the same kind of chewing damage, so it's best to cut them once their blooms fully open. I also have found that some sunflower cultivars are less receptive than others to cutting early, so I recommend that you experiment with a dozen or so of each type that you grow in order to find out just how early you can cut. On the other hand, most of the spike-type flowers (delphinium, larkspur, etc.) can be cut when just one or two flowers on the stem are open. The alphabetical listing of recommended cut flowers in appendix 1 gives specific instructions about the best time to harvest each type of flower, and there you will find many others that can be cut in the bud.

It's better to cut unopened flowers in the evening, when their stems are full of starches and sugars that will help them continue to open. You also should use floral preservative, which contains about 1 percent sugar. Some preservatives can be used at double strength to open buds; check the label. You can also make a bud-opening solution that contains 2 percent sugar by adding 5 ounces of sugar to 2 gallons of water. Leave the flowers in this solution in a cool place out of the sun, but not in a cooler, until the flowers open. ❧

and they will look their freshest. If, on the other hand, you cut in the evening, after the plants have been photosynthesizing all day, the stems will contain more carbohydrates, which will prolong their life in the vase. In either case, the ideal time is a relatively short window of opportunity. In the morning, you should wait until the dew has dried, because any moisture on the flowers in storage can lead to disease. Yet, you must finish harvesting before the sun gets too high and the temperature too hot. Similarly, if you cut in the evening, you should wait until the sun is low in the sky and the air has cooled. In a perfect world, flowers would be cut only when the temperature was below 80 degrees Fahrenheit (27 degrees Celsius). Few of us live in that perfect climate, though, so we choose the best cutting time from the options available.

I vote for the evening cutting because that is the most convenient time for me. If I'm transporting the flowers to a florist or making bouquets, I normally need to do those tasks in the morning. Regardless of when I cut flowers, before I handle them further, I want them to have some time to "condition," which means to take up water and recover from the shock of being cut. At the very least, flowers should receive an hour or two of rest time after cutting—before you remove them from water to make bouquets, or before you start jostling them by taking them to market.

CLEANLINESS

I can't say enough about the importance of sanitation for cut-flower growers. Dirty buckets or dirty clippers will introduce bacteria that will quickly plug the stems of your flowers and prevent them from taking up water. Without water, the flowers will soon wilt. You have to be scrupulously clean to ensure an adequate vase life for flowers.

Wash your buckets and vases carefully before each use, in a solution that contains a few drops of liquid detergent and a teaspoon of bleach for each gallon of water. Scrub your buckets and vases with a firm-bristled brush to remove any soil or dust clinging to the container. Rinse the containers thoroughly before you fill them with clean water. Wash your clippers in the same way, using bleach to sterilize them.

Large growers have industrial-sized washers for cleaning their buckets, but most of us small growers just use the kitchen sink or a utility tub in the barn.

TOOLS

All you need are clean containers and sharp clippers.

You can purchase buckets from a discount store or floral wholesaler, but most of the growers I know have discovered the treasure trove that lies behind the counter at supermarket bakeries and doughnut shops. All that gooey icing on doughnuts and sweet rolls comes from plastic food-grade buckets that are perfect for flower harvest. They come in 2-gallon, 3-gallon, and 5-gallon sizes. Fast-food places also are a good source for the 5-gallon size. Some national doughnut

Holding and Blooming Peonies

Because peonies bloom within a short period of time and then are done for the year, commercial peony growers extend the selling season by holding the peony buds in cold storage. When cut at the proper stage and held at the proper temperature, peonies can be kept for up to three months. The stored buds will readily bloom within a few hours when placed in water. Here's how it's done.

Cut the peonies when color is showing and the buds are soft all the way through, but before the petals have begun to open. Growers describe this as "the marshmallow stage" because the bud is about as soft as a marshmallow. You've got to hit this stage just right: if you cut too soon, the buds won't open in water, and if you cut too late, they will open and promptly drop their petals. Careful observation and a bit of experience will help you recognize the best time for cutting.

The marshmallow stage is short-lived, so you will have to check the peonies three or four times a day to catch all the buds at just the right time. If you miss a bud at 11 A.M., it will be too late to take at 3 P.M. Your biggest harvest will be in the evening; after warming up all day, the buds soften suddenly.

Peonies should be cut with about 16 to 18 inches of stem, leaving several leaves on each

stem. Never cut more than two-thirds of the plant; without some foliage left to continue photosynthesis, the plant will die.

When you cut the peonies, leave them dry and wrap them in bunches of ten in cellophane or vented plastic, with the stems exposed to air. Lay the flowers on their sides and place them in a cooler at 35 degrees Fahrenheit (2 degrees Celsius).

To bloom the peonies, cut off the bottom inch of stem and place the flowers upright in warm water that is at least 8 inches deep. The buds will open within a few hours, and the vase life of the flowers will be about a week. You can either bloom the peonies yourself before selling them, or sell them in bud with instructions for opening them. ∾

chains stick a big label on the side of the bucket; the label is difficult to remove and usually leaves an ugly stain. Other bakeries put the label on the lid, so the buckets stay clean and good-looking. Some bakeries clean their buckets, while others don't. Shop around for the best buckets—you'll find that they are out there in abundance.

My local supermarket sells buckets to me for 25 cents each. They are clean and sparkling white, and perfect for my small commercial operation. I like the 2-gallon size for most flowers, but I keep some of the larger sizes on hand for big flowers such as sunflowers. Some sunflower growers who harvest the entire 6-foot stem of single-stemmed varieties such as 'Sunbright' use 30-gallon plastic trash cans.

Tools growers use: Victorinox Flower Gatherers, top, and Felco pruners.

Any kind of flower container, whether bucket or vase, should be made of plastic or glass but *never* metal. Metals can react with the floral preservative and harm the flowers. You can still use those gorgeous French flower cans, though—just line them with a plastic container to prevent the water from coming in contact with the metal.

The clippers you use to cut flowers should be clean, to prevent the spread of bacteria onto the stems. They also need to be sharp in order to keep the stems from getting mashed, which can impede water uptake by the flower. A good pair of scissors will suffice for the home gardener. If you cut a lot of flowers, though, your work will go much faster if you buy a high-quality pair of pruners. I love my Felco no. 2 pruners, although they are quite expensive. They are comfortable to use, they cut through even woody stems, and they are sharp enough to cut through a dozen stems at once when preparing bouquets for market. I've also been impressed with the Victorinox Flower Gatherer. This ingenious little device has two spring steel bands that hold the flower between the blades after you have cut it, permitting you to cut and lift the flower from the bed with just one hand. It's especially useful for cutting tall, stiff flowers that are growing where you don't want to bend into the bed and risk knocking down adjoining flowers. This tool also helps when you're gathering a lot of flowers at one time, because you can cut with one hand and hold the bunch with the other.

THE BEST PEONIES

Peonies are the darlings of the spring flower world. Their soft colors and voluptuous blossoms make them useful for everything from casual bouquets to formal weddings. And there are hundreds of peony cultivars, ranging from early-blooming singles to late-blooming doubles, known as "bombs."

With so many gorgeous peony cultivars available, which are the best ones to plant for cutting? Several factors should guide you as you make your choices. The most important of these is bloom time. Does the cultivar you want bloom at a time when you will be able to sell or use the flowers? Another major consideration is vase life. In general, the best cut flowers last at least five days. Some peonies last much longer, but others have an unacceptably short vase life.

In 1995, Kansas State University Extension specialist Karen L.B. Gast tested twenty-nine peony cultivars to determine their vase life. Some scored much better than others. If six days is considered an acceptable vase life, all the white cultivars tested were acceptable, and all the red cultivars except 'Kansas' were acceptable. Among the pink cultivars, 'Wrinkles 'n' Crinkles' and 'Sarah Bernhardt' were unacceptable. The table lists the cultivars she tested, along with the number of days they lived in the vase. ∾

Harvest and Post-Harvest

Vase Life of Peony Flowers after Harvest

Cultivars	Vase Life (days)	Cultivars	Vase Life (days)	Cultivars	Vase Life (days)
Pink:		**White:**		**Red:**	
James Pillow	9.5	Festiva Supreme	8.6	David Harum	9.0
Mr. Ed	8.5	Dr. F.G. Brethour	8.3	Felix Supreme	8.5
Mrs. Franklin D.		Henry Sass	8.1	Karl Rosenfield	7.7
Roosevelt	8.3	Lois Kelsey	7.4	Felix Crouse	7.7
Raspberry Sundae	8.0	Festiva Maxima	7.3	Philippe Rivoire	7.6
Grace Batson	7.8			Shawnee Chief	6.9
Walter Faxon	7.3			Richard Carvel	6.8
Therese	7.2			Monsieur Martin	
Better Times	7.1			Cahuzac	6.6
Monsieur Jules Elie	6.4			Lora Dexheimer	6.5
Edulis Superba	6.3			Kansas	5.5
Reine Hortense	6.1				
Ozark Beauty	6.0				
Sarah Bernhardt	5.6				
Wrinkle 'n' Crinkles	5.5				

PRESERVATIVES

Commercial flower preservatives are unquestionably beneficial to cut flowers. They can extend vase life by several days; in some cases, flowers in preservative last twice as long as they do in plain water. An all-purpose floral preservative will contain these three basic ingredients:

- **Sugar.** The same stuff that you stir into your tea makes up the bulk of most commercial preservatives. It serves as food for the flowers, allowing them to continue to open. For most flowers, 1 to 2 percent sugar in the solution is adequate. For flowers that are cut in bud, a higher concentration of sugar may be needed. Gladiolus spikes, for example, may be treated with up to 20 percent sugar to get them to open. (For more about cutting early, see page 94.)

- **An acidifier.** Plants take up acidic water (pH 3.5–4.5) much faster than nonacidic water, so putting them immediately into water that has been acidified will prevent wilting blossoms and drooping necks. Citric acid, used in food, is commonly found in floral preservatives. Hydrating solutions, which are used to perk up stressed flowers, usually consist of citric acid and water. Alkaline water is not taken up well through the stems, so flowers may wilt if hard water is not acidified.

- **A biocide.** Sugar, soil, plant foliage, and other contaminants can cause bacteria to flourish in flower water. Bacteria plug the stems, preventing the uptake of water and leading to premature death of the flower. For this reason, preservatives have some kind of chemical that kills bacteria. Commonly used ingredients include 8–HQ salts, derived from coal tar, and the quaternary ammonium compounds, or QACs, which can irritate skin and mucous membranes. Chlorine, as in bleach, is also used.

Several other specialized types of flower treatments are used for particular situations. Their use is often referred to as "pulsing," which just means placing the cut stems in the special solution for a period from a few minutes to a few hours (a short pulse versus a long pulse). One special pretreatment is a hydrating solution to help plants take up water quickly. It consists of an acidifier such as citric acid. This solution often is used in hot climates where flowers wilt immediately after cutting, and it can be used to revive flowers that have been left out of the bucket too long. Another specialized pretreatment for flowers is silver thiosulfate (STS), which counteracts the effects of ethylene gas and greatly extends the vase life of some ethylene-sensitive flowers. However, silver is considered a heavy metal, and special disposal methods are required for most STS preservatives.

The exact nature of the ingredients in any floral preservative is considered a trade secret and is not revealed by the manufacturers on the label. However, you can get more details on the product by contacting the manufacturer and requesting its Material Safety Data Sheet (MSDS). The MSDS lists any hazardous ingredients contained in the product; explains the health, fire, and explosion hazards; and gives you emergency procedures to follow in case of a spill or leak. It also tells you how to handle the product and lets you know whether the ingredients are known to cause cancer, birth defects, or reproductive harm. I have read the MSDS on the preservative I use, and I feel comfortable with it. In general, I believe that floral preservatives need to be handled with care, but that they are safe when used properly.

Preservatives are a subject of dispute among organic growers. Some growers feel that the toxicity is so low as to be of no concern, and that the solution is taken up by the flower and therefore will not contaminate soil or groundwater. Other growers feel that they cannot in good conscience use preservatives, because of the toxic chemicals they may contain. Some people who use all-purpose floral preservatives still shun silver pretreatments because of the dangers associated with heavy metals, and because of disposal concerns. The organic certification agencies differ in their standards on floral preservatives. Most do not address the subject of flowers because the federal organic law (which at this writing has not yet taken effect)

FLOWER ENEMY NUMBER ONE: ETHYLENE

Ethylene is a gas naturally produced by flowers as they age. It is also produced by many other sources, and when flowers are exposed to extra ethylene, they age faster. Some flowers are particularly sensitive to ethylene, and will drop their petals or wilt almost immediately when exposed to it.

Sources of ethylene include ripening fruits and vegetables; exhaust from cars, trucks, tillers, and propane heaters; and smoke from cigarettes. You should try to keep all your flowers away from these sources of ethylene, but you must be especially conscientious with the flowers that are considered ethylene-sensitive. These include the following species:

Achillea (yarrow)
Aconitum (monkshood)
Alstroemeria
Anemone (windflower)
Antirrhinum (snapdragon)
Aquilegia (columbine)
Asclepias (butterfly weed)
Astilbe
Campanula (bellflower)
Celosia (cockscomb)
Centaurea (bachelor's button)
Consolida (larkspur)
Delphinium
Dianthus (sweet William)
Eremurus (desert-candle)
Gypsophila (baby's breath)
Lathyrus (sweet pea)
Lilium (lily)
Physostegia (obedient plant) ∾

HOMEMADE
FLORAL PRESERVATIVE

Over the years, people have experimented with all kinds of kitchen recipes for a floral preservative. Now that you know that a flower needs sugar, acidic water, and something to keep bacteria from growing, you can come up with your own ideas.

I myself have experimented with several homemade potions, including sugar, vinegar, lemon soda, bleach, and so on. I've even tested them under somewhat controlled conditions. Unfortunately, the homemade solutions haven't proven to be much better than plain tap water.

However, it never hurts to tell your customers something about how to prolong the vase life of their flowers. I slip a business-sized card into every bouquet sleeve with general instructions about flower care. Cleanliness is the most important message I want to get across; a New England grower told me once that she lectures her customers to "keep your vases as clean as your teacups," and I pass on that advice to my own customers. I also give them the best recipe I know for homemade floral preservative. Here's what the card says:

How to care for your cut flowers

When you get your flowers home, fill a vase halfway with tepid water. Cut 1 inch from the stems and strip any foliage that will be underwater in your chosen vase. Put the cut flowers immediately in the water. Bacteria will cause premature drooping of your flowers, so keep your vases as clean as your teacups. To prolong vase life, you can use this homemade flower food: To 24 ounces of water, add 1 teaspoon vinegar, 1 tablespoon sugar, and one crushed aspirin tablet. ❧

refers to food and fiber crops, but never mentions flowers. In Maine, certified organic growers may use floral preservatives as long as they let the consumer know; their labels can say, "Grown in accordance with organic standards; floral preservative added to the water." At least one manufacturer has tried to develop a flower food that contains all food-grade materials, but the results were disappointing. Vase life of flowers in the natural preservative wasn't much better than in plain tap water.

At present, the issue of whether to use floral preservatives remains largely a matter of personal opinion. Many people base their decision on how the flowers are being used. In the home, where you can change the water frequently, or run to the garden to cut more flowers, you don't really need preservatives. If you're selling at a farmers' market, you probably don't need preservatives; if you've followed all the other rules of flower hygiene, your customers will get five to seven days of vase life from their flowers, and will be back for more the following week. However, if you're selling to a florist or wholesaler, you probably should use a preservative because that's what is expected. If you choose not to use one, be sure to tell your customers so that they can add it themselves if they want. Or you could choose a middle ground, such as using a hydrating solution of citric acid and water to acidify hard water and increase vase life, but not using the preservative, which contains sugar and biocide.

WATER

Whether you choose to use a preservative or not, be aware that the quality of your water will have a great effect on the vase life of your flowers. *Alkaline* water (which is usually synonymous with hard water) does not move up the stems of cut flowers readily, so they may wilt prematurely. Salinity is another potential problem with tap water. You can run a few trials by comparing the vase life of flowers held in tap water against the same types of flowers held in *deionized* water. The results should reveal whether your tap water is reducing the quality of your flowers.

If you suspect that your tap water is harming your flowers, you should contact a floral preservative manufacturer and request a water test. (See appendix 2 for the names of several floral preservative companies.) Some companies will do the test for free, and others will charge a small fee of $10 to $15. After testing your water, the company will suggest ways to improve it. Several manufacturers make special formulas for alkaline water. Others will recommend that you increase the amount of preservative used. In extreme cases, you might be told that you need a deionization or reverse-osmosis system on your water line. In no case should you rush out and buy a water softener. Although hard water (which is high in calcium and magnesium) is often described as the source of vase life problems, it's actually the alkalinity associated with hardness that causes the trouble. Most water softeners take the hardness out by replacing calcium and magnesium with sodium. The sodium can be an even greater problem for the flowers.

Fluoride, which is often added to municipal water supplies to help prevent tooth decay, is another potential problem for flowers. Gladioli are particularly sensitive to fluoride, and may suffer leaf and tip burn from even low concentrations of fluoride. Fortunately, fluoride is highly unstable and will dissipate from water quickly, so you can leave your buckets of water standing at room temperature for several hours before picking glads into them.

HARVESTING

Cutting flowers quickly and efficiently is a skill you develop with experience. You need to cut the flower, strip the foliage from the lower part of the stem, and get the flower to the bucket. Most growers gather at least one bunch before making the trip to the bucket. Some even hire runners, who are usually teenagers, to carry the bunches from the harvester to the bucket. Some growers make their bunches in the field, as they cut them. Others carry the flowers loose in the bucket back to the work area and let them rest for a few hours before bunching them. Of course, you can skip this step if you're going to make bouquets, sell flowers by the stem at farmers' market, or sell the flowers to a florist who doesn't need to have them bunched.

If the weather has been dry and there is no soil clinging to the flower stems, you may be able to store the flowers in the same solution you used in the field. If there is soil on them, though, your flowers are at risk of bacterial contamination, so you should repack the flowers into clean solution.

In either case, be sure to strip away any foliage that will be underwater in the holding bucket. Stripping foliage for hours each day will leave your fingers raw if you try to do it with your bare hands. Find a pair of gloves that fit well and get used to wearing them. Or cut the fingers off a pair of rubber household gloves and cover just the fingers that get all the friction (that varies from one person to the next; I use the thumb, index finger, and middle finger on my right hand).

COOLING

Once the flowers are cut, you need to remove the field heat from them to ensure the best possible vase life. For the home gardener, bringing the freshly cut flowers into a cool house is usually all you need to cool them off. On a commercial scale, it's harder to reduce the field heat because the flowers are packed closely in the bucket and their sheer mass keeps them warm. When you start your flower business, you can get by with a cool porch or cellar for holding flowers for a few hours before using them. However, eventually you will want to get a refrigerator that can cool down to 34 degrees Fahrenheit (1 degree Celsius), the best temperature for holding most flowers. Not only does the cooler quickly remove field heat, increasing the flowers' vase life; it also gives you more options for when to cut and when to deliver. (For example, if storms are threatening, you can cut earlier than usual and store your flowers in the cooler.)

A walk-in cooler purchased new will cost many thousands of dollars, so be on the lookout for used ones. We bought our first cooler—an 8- by 10-foot walk-in model—for $300 at the auction of a defunct grocery store in a small town. Since then, two florists going out of business have offered to sell us display coolers. Keep your eye on the classified ads in local newspapers and in the floral industry publications listed in appendix 2. And check with restaurant supply companies and commercial heating/cooling contractors to see whether they know of any used coolers. Get your name out on the grapevine long before you absolutely need the cooler, but be ready to jump when one comes your way. If you expect to become a large-scale flower grower, you probably should buy a cooler made specifically for flowers. Floral coolers provide a relative humidity of 80% or greater, which preserves flowers that must be held in storage a long time.

You can also build your own cooler by creating a superinsulated box and installing a window-unit air conditioner. The directions for rigging the air conditioner to serve as a cooler are included in this chapter (see page 106). The cooler we are now using was built as a class project by students in an industrial design class at the local university. Their mission was to design a compact, inexpensive cooler that could be used to keep vegetables and flowers separate. (Vegetables and fruits emit ethylene gas, which hastens the decline of cut flowers.) The students created an 8- by 10- by 10-foot box with a dividing wall down the middle. Each side has its own door and its own air conditioner. The box is built into the corner of a shed, and the holes for the air conditioners are cut right through the

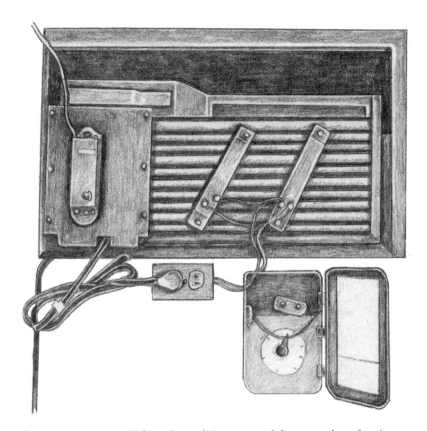

*An electrician can rig a window air conditioner to cool down nearly to freezing,
allowing you to turn an insulated box into an inexpensive flower cooler. The air
conditioner's normal switches must be disconnected and replaced with an industrial-
type thermostat. Then strip heaters must be mounted on the coils and hooked to a
timer that turns on the heaters intermittently to keep the coils from icing up.*

shed walls. We like the versatility of this cooler, because we can store vegetables
on both sides on the days we aren't cutting flowers, and vice versa.

TRANSPORTATION

To get your flowers to market, the absolute best form of transport is an air-conditioned cargo van. Second best is an air-conditioned family van with seats that
fold down or pull out. Next is a pickup truck with a camper shell.

The worst thing you can do to your flowers is haul them in the open bed of a
pickup: They just won't like the wind in their hair.

You can make a grid of 2 x 4s to hold your buckets upright and separate.
Florists' magazines also carry advertisements for a cut-to-order foam product in
which to nestle the buckets. I find that if I place the buckets bumper-to-bumper
and wedge them in with a length of 2 x 4, then make sure to corner carefully
when driving, they won't tip over.

TURN AN AIR CONDITIONER INTO A COOLER

A walk-in cooler can be a formidable expense for a small flower farm, even if you're fortunate enough to find a used unit. We sidestepped the problem on our farm by converting an old air conditioner into a refrigeration unit that would cool down to 34 degrees Fahrenheit (1 degree Celsius). Here's how we did it.

First we built an insulated box, divided into two equal compartments: one for vegetables and one for flowers. In one side of the cooler, which has about 140 cubic feet of interior space, we installed an eight-year-old, 11,000-Btu air conditioner. On the other side, we installed a two-year-old, 8,000-Btu air conditioner. The newer model was much more efficient, drawing 7.5 amps, while the older one drew 11.4 amps. Wiring and circuit breakers had to accommodate both air conditioners operating at the same time.

We disconnected the temperature switches on each air conditioner, and attached a new, industrial-style thermostat that would allow the temperature to be set to 34 degrees Fahrenheit (1 degree Celsius). The problem with a regular air conditioner is that setting the temperature so low would rapidly cause the coils to become a solid block of ice. To avoid this, we mounted strip heaters against the coils with a timer to alternately switch power from the air conditioner to the strip heaters, which melted the ice on the coils. Then power returned to the air conditioner, then back to the heaters, and so on, until the desired temperature was reached inside the box, and the thermostat switched off the air conditioner.

The smaller unit froze up during the hottest stretch of August, when temperatures reached 100 degrees Fahrenheit and humidity was very high. A refrigeration expert indicated that this happened, paradoxically, because the air conditioner was so efficient. The larger unit was not efficient enough to freeze its own coils. Setting the timer to allow more coil-heating time and shorter cooling time solved the problem. The recommended cycle time is twenty-four minutes of air conditioning followed by seven minutes of heating. (Incidentally, high heat and high humidity are conditions most likely to cause any cooler to freeze up.)

A qualified electrician should wire the air conditioner and heater coils.

Our cooler was based on a design by researchers at the United States Department of Agriculture. To obtain a copy of the USDA report, which includes an electrical diagram, request the October 1993 "Transportation Tip: The Portacooler," from Daniel P. Schofer, USDA Agricultural Marketing Service TMD, Marketing and Transportation Analysis, P.O. Box 96456, Washington, D.C. 20090–6456; 202-690-1303. ∾

Material List

- window-unit air conditioner, 115 volt
- 20-amp wall switch, with boxes and covers
- thermostat, 115 volt, 16 amp, with remote bulb
- standard junction box
- strip heaters, 150 watt, 8 inch, 115 volt
- insulated wire
- 1-hour cycle timer, SPDT, 115 volt, 20 amp

Sunny Dale Springs Peony Farm ～ Valley Center, Kansas

W HEN HAROLD FRYAR BOUGHT HIS FARM IN SOUTH-CENTRAL KANSAS IN 1953, one acre was planted in peonies. Harold and his wife, Glenna, knew nothing about peonies then, but they had 3,000 plants, so they decided to learn.

In the years since, the peony business has expanded into a family project for four generations of Harold's family. Today, about three acres of peonies are grown at Sunny Dale Springs Peony Farm in Valley Center, Kansas, by Harold's daughter Wilma Jackson, along with Wilma's children and their spouses, Randy and Debbie Jackson and Nancy and Keith Harimon. The great-grandchildren, now teenagers, also pitch in on the peony farm.

The family has found that the business they bought into so many years ago is rapidly disappearing, but that new markets for peonies are opening at the same time.

Peonies have had a long history as a commercial crop in the Midwest. Many farmers once kept a few acres in peonies, which they sold in full bloom as cemetery decorations on Memorial Day. But the Memorial Day tradition began to disappear as society became more mobile, with people often living far from the graves of their loved ones.

Fortunately, peonies have undergone a renaissance of popularity. They will keep for several months in cold storage, and they have been found to be excellent flowers for air-drying and freeze-drying. For Harold Fryar's descendants, this evolving market has meant a change in marketing and a change in work schedules.

The peony year begins in April, when all but the terminal buds on each stem must be pinched off to ensure that the remaining flower will grow large. Once that back-breaking task is done, the growers begin the long period of waiting and watching for the perfect moment to cut. Timing is crucial for peonies that are going to be kept in cold storage. They must be cut when the bud is soft all the way through ("when it feels like a marshmallow," Wilma says), but before the petals begin to open. Cut too soon, they won't open when brought out of storage. Cut too late, they will open and drop their petals immediately. The color of the bud, which changes as the flower develops, is another sign that growers get to know and understand.

Wilma says that if the peonies are ready at 11 A.M., cutting them at 3 P.M. will be too late. So she and the rest of the crew sweep through the fields three times a day, cutting those that are ready.

"Sometimes the atmosphere is just right and—pop!—they're blooming," Wilma says. She recalls one night when the family was returning home from a dinner out and saw the peonies shining in the moonlight. "I had everyone go change into their work clothes, and we picked them at night," she says.

Luckily, peony plants last for several generations. In fact, many of the original plants on the farm, probably seventy-five years old by now, have never been divided and are still producing prolifically. Wilma says

she has counted up to sixty buds on some of those old plants.

Neighboring farmers retiring from the peony business have sold their roots to Sunny Dale Springs. Wilma says the best roots are those with three or more eyes; they will be ready for harvest three years after planting. Smaller roots may need four years before the flowers can be cut.

Although the peonies are being cut for only two or three weeks in May, they do require some maintenance work. The biggest problem is with weeds. Wilma says the best weed control is well-timed cultivation, but she notes that even in years when the weeds got away from the family, the plants were unharmed. By September, when the plants begin to die back, the whole field can be mowed. Botrytis, a harmful fungus, is another common problem, particularly during rainy springs, so the plants are sprayed with sulfur as soon as they emerge from the ground. Frost protection, in the form of a sprinkler system, is another requirement for commercial peony growers. Sunny Dale Springs does not have sprinklers and has lost several crops over the years. One year, they harvested only three hundred dozen flowers, a tenth of their usual production.

Since all the action in the peony business occurs during the planting season for other crops, the family has found it difficult to expand into vegetables or other flowers. So far, the peonies have not provided a livelihood for anyone in the family. It is, for now, a fun project that unites the family and provides each member with some extra income. "We all get along great," Debbie Jackson says. "If we didn't, we wouldn't be doing this."

CHAPTER 8

Arranging Fresh Flowers

*F*OR MOST FLOWER GARDENERS, FLOWER ARRANGING IS SIMPLY A MATTER
of walking through the garden with shears and dropping the chosen flowers
into a favorite pitcher or vase. The result is usually fetching. But there will come
a time when you will want to display your flowers in a more formal manner.
Whether you are a backyard gardener or a commercial grower, once the word gets
out that you have a talent for flowers, you will invariably be asked to provide
them for parties, church services, weddings, and other events that require more
structured arrangements.

The mechanics of flower arranging are not difficult to learn; the tips in this
chapter plus a few hours of experimenting will give you a feel for what needs to
be done. The artistic aspect of arranging (more properly called designing) calls
for more time and consideration. A florist friend who has hired many designers
over the years tells me that you can't learn design; you must have a special talent
born of creativity and love for the flowers. Be that as it may, until you try, you
won't know whether you have the touch.

This chapter sets out the basics you need to know in order to get started in
flower arranging.

WHAT YOU NEED

The first thing you need when arranging flowers is patience. Especially when you're a novice, you can expect to have some false starts every time you begin an arrangement. You may have to arrange, rearrange, and then rearrange again before you achieve the look you like. So give yourself plenty of time—at least thirty to sixty minutes—whenever you sit down to work with flowers.

Gather all the materials you intend to use before you start: your flower shears or a sharp knife, already cleaned and disinfected; your container and a liner, if needed; floral foam; hot glue, floral tape, and wires; fresh floral preservative or water; and accessories, such as candles, that you might want to include in the design.

WHAT THE FLOWERS NEED

Your flowers should have several hours to condition before you start working with them. This means that after you have cut them, you should leave them in water or a preservative solution to recover and become turgid again. If you have a cool place such as a cellar or an air-conditioned room in which to leave them, so much the better. You need to get the field heat out of the flowers and have them actively taking up water through the stem before you remove them from their bucket.

Once you have removed the flowers from water, you should work quickly so that they aren't left lying on a table while you decide what to put where. As the stems dry, they will form a scar that prevents them from taking up water. So as soon as you're ready to put a flower in the arrangement, cut its stem again. Some flowers, such as roses and buddleia, should even be recut with their stems under water to prevent any air from plugging the stem.

CONTAINERS

Virtually anything that can hold water—or that can hold a plastic liner to hold the water—can be used as a container for a floral arrangement. In the pages that follow, you will see designs done in a cast-iron garden urn, clear glass vases, an antique silver tea box, clay pots, and a rattan basket. You can use bowls, coffee mugs, teapots, beer glasses, wooden boxes, candlesticks—whatever catches your fancy and complements your flowers. If the container isn't watertight, fit it with a plastic liner, either one that you purchase at a floral wholesaler or hobby shop, or one that you find in a kitchen cabinet, such as a cottage cheese or yogurt container.

Metal containers, though they may be watertight, should be lined, too. Never place flowers directly in a metal container, because the chemical interaction of preservative and metal can harm the flowers.

If your arrangement is going to be large, or if it's going to be moved around, you should attach the plastic liner to the outer container in order to prevent the arrangement from tipping out. You can either purchase a special kind of adhesive

Tools for Arranging Flowers

Going to a floral supply house for the first time can be somewhat overwhelming, as they are generally brimming with accessories, but the real work tools are gathered in a few small bins. It helps to know what you're looking for. Here are descriptions and pictures of the tools that will be most helpful to you as you begin to design with fresh flowers:

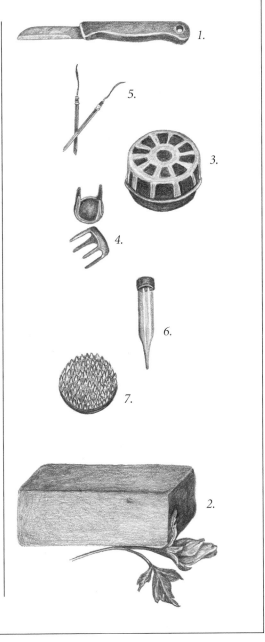

A knife (1), small and very sharp, makes clean, angled cuts in the flower stems.

Floral foam (2) is a water-absorbing foam for use with fresh flowers; there is also a dry foam for use with dried and silk flowers. Be sure to get the water-absorbing kind. From the wholesaler, you'll have to buy it by the case, which usually contains thirty-six bricks. (Each brick makes two medium-sized arrangements.) At a craft store, you can buy it by the brick.

Caged holders (3) are pieces of foam encased in plastic cages. They come in a variety of shapes, from small round cages for centerpieces to wreaths and easel containers for use in funeral work.

Anchor pins (4) are plastic devices that can be pushed into wet foam, to provide a flat, dry spot for gluing the foam to the container.

Wired picks (5) are green-dyed pieces of wood with thin wires at the top. They are used for holding ribbons or dried elements in wet foam.

Aqua picks or **Aqua tubes** (6) are little glass tubes that can be filled with water to hold individual flower stems. They are used when adding fresh elements to a dried design.

Pin frogs (7) are used to anchor stems in a container. ❧

clay from a floral supply house, or you can use hot glue or silicon caulk to hold the liner in place, if you don't mind leaving marks on the inside of the container.

FLORAL FOAM

Most florists use a highly absorbent foam to hold the stems in place in an arrangement. You will find floral foam at the wholesale floral supply house or at a hobby shop; the most common brand is Oasis. Be sure to purchase the water-absorbing type and not the dry foam, which is used for dried-flower arrangements. You can purchase floral foam in several different textures: soft for thin, delicate stems; medium for most flowers; and extra-firm for tall, thick-stemmed flowers.

Foam should be cut while it is still dry, with a sharp knife. Cut as big a piece as you can fit into your container, and make it about an inch taller than the rim. This extra height allows you to place flowers at different angles, so that they radiate and cascade from the container. You can also make the foam considerably taller than the container for a spectacularly full effect in large arrangements.

The foam will need to be attached to the container, again to prevent it from tipping out. You can attach it in one of three ways:

- Cut the foam so big that it gets wedged tightly into the container. This is the best strategy for relatively small arrangements, or for those done in containers that are meant to be reused, such as coffee mugs.

- Push an anchor pin into the bottom of a piece of wet foam; then attach the anchor pin to the container with adhesive clay or hot glue.

- Push the foam into the container; then tape across the rim. You can use special green florist tape, or nylon strapping tape for very large designs. This is especially important when the foam extends more than an inch or so above the rim of the container.

To get the foam full of water, soak it in a floral preservative solution or plain water. Standard foam should be soaked for fifteen to twenty minutes to ensure that it has absorbed all the water it can. There is also an instant foam, which requires only five minutes of submersion. Be sure to saturate the foam, because every flower stem must be in contact with water or the blooms will quickly wilt, ruining the arrangement. Remember, too, that the container must be kept filled with water, even when the foam seems moist. Otherwise, as soon as the foam begins to dry out, it will suck water from anyplace it can—including the stems of your flowers.

Floral foam should not be reused for commercial design work because of the danger that bacteria will be lurking within the stuff, ready to attack the next set of flowers placed in it. Also, most designs require so many flower stems that the foam will be riddled with holes and unable to hold flowers firmly if you try to reuse it for a new design. At home, though, where long-term survival and perfect stem placement aren't so critical, it seems a waste to throw out floral foam after only one arrangement. If it's not too severely perforated, let the used foam dry thoroughly; then add a little bleach to the soaking water next time. This should take care of any lingering bacteria.

OTHER WAYS TO ANCHOR FLOWERS

You don't need to use floral foam to create structure in an arrangement; there are several other mechanisms for holding the flowers where you want them.

- Marbles are perfect for achieving a design that looks somewhere between structured and dropped-in-a-vase. They're particularly nice in a glass vase. Just push the stems in at the angle you want them, and the marbles will hold them in place.

- Pin frogs are devices with upturned needles on a metal base. When you push the stems into the frog, the pins grab them and hold them tight.

- A grid of tape across the rim of your container can provide just enough separation of the stems to give you the look you want.

- A plastic-coated wire mesh netting, similar to chicken wire but more flexible, can be wadded into a ball and placed inside the container to hold

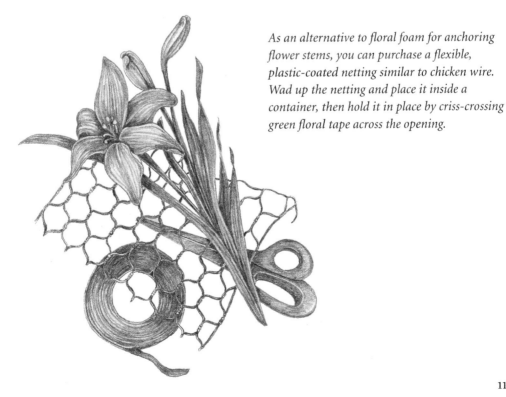

As an alternative to floral foam for anchoring flower stems, you can purchase a flexible, plastic-coated netting similar to chicken wire. Wad up the netting and place it inside a container, then hold it in place by criss-crossing green floral tape across the opening.

stems in place. This netting is also useful for covering a piece of floral foam when creating very tall arrangements, as it prevents heavy flowers or branches from ripping out of the foam.

• A sturdy branch or two used in the design can anchor flower stems, or several big stems can be crossed in the container to create a sort of grid for subsequent additions to the design.

PLACING THE FLOWERS

Start with the flowers that will create the outline of your design: first the tallest flowers, then those that form the sides. Next, fill in the front and back of the design. Don't forget to place some flowers and foliage quite low to the rim of the container, to conceal the mechanics (floral foam, tape, and so on). When placing flowers into floral foam, always recut the stems, and do it on a sharp angle to create a point that will slice into the foam readily. Flat stems usually mash the foam, and often the stem will bend slightly because of the resistance. You might not even notice this until a few hours later when the flower, unable to take up water, begins to droop.

Finally, if you're using foam, place flowers into the sides of the 1-inch lip of foam sticking up above the rim of the container. They will hide the foam, as well as give the design a fuller look. You can even place some stems angling down slightly, so that the flowers appear to spill out of the container.

COLOR AND TEXTURE

"There are no colors here that don't look good together," a florist once told me, when I asked how he selected colors from the dozens of buckets of garden flowers I had brought him. He would happily mingle orange and pink zinnias with red gomphrena—colors you would never think to mix in your clothing, but which looked cheerful and summery in a floral design. That bright look is so popular right now that you will even find brides choosing garden flowers in all colors. I recently provided yellow zinnias, gold rudbeckia, blue ageratum, and orange celosia for a wedding. I'm sure the final result was charming.

However, you may not always want to be bright and cheerful in your design. Let's consider some of the effects of color and texture that will help you achieve the look you want.

In general, the more similar the flower colors (that is, the closer they are on the color wheel), the quieter the final look will be. The farther apart on the color wheel, the more the arrangement will call out for attention. For example, an arrangement of purples and blues, which are adjacent on the color wheel, will be calm and soothing. But purple and gold, which are opposites on the color wheel, will look bold and even loud.

Variations in floral texture can have a similar effect on the finished arrangement. A big sunflower in a jug of small flowers will appear more startling than a big sunflower in a jug of big zinnias. It's the contrast in texture that makes the design call out for attention. Likewise, a vase of primarily small flowers will look quiet and refined. A variety of flower sizes and textures in an informal design will help accent the flowers without being too obvious.

LEARNING FROM DESIGNERS

One of the fringe benefits of my job as a flower grower is that I occasionally get to hang around the flower shop and watch the designers at work. I am always inspired by the creativity of good floral designers, and I've learned a great deal that has helped me as a grower. For example, I used to pass by snapdragons or larkspur that had a little bend in the stem. Then I found out that florists wire those long-stemmed flowers when using them in arrangements, to prevent the stems from flopping, so a minor twist in the stem won't matter anyway. In addition, really good designers like the little twists and turns nature provides, because these give the arrangement a fluid look. Now I'm a lot more relaxed about cutting flowers that look like they have come from a garden, not from a greenhouse.

I've also learned that flowers don't need to have 30-inch stems to be useful. In fact, most floral designs are much smaller, and the florists end up cutting the stems way down anyway. Besides, there's always a need for short-stemmed flowers that are placed low in the container to cover up the mechanics of floral foam or wire. Many materials besides what are technically considered cut flowers can be used: grasses, hostas, ivy, tree branches, shrub foliage, and so forth. I've learned to take along samples of anything that might be useful, and ask whether the florist wants to buy it. I've also had designers come out to my farm to stroll around and see what else they might want. As a result, I've sold things like basil from the vegetable field, spirea from an old hedge, and green wheat that was serving as a windbreak.

The more I watch these designers at work, the more my appreciation for my own flowers grows. I see how much more vibrant, more alive, my garden flowers are than the standard floral fare in the cooler. A basket of white glads and pink gerberas may be striking at first glance, but it quickly begins to look two-dimensional. A clay pot overflowing with a dozen colors of garden flowers is a delight to behold, and it demands further attention. In fact, sometimes it's hard for me to take my eyes off of such creations.

"I hope you realize what a joy it is to work with your flowers," a florist told me recently. After watching him work, I understand. ❧

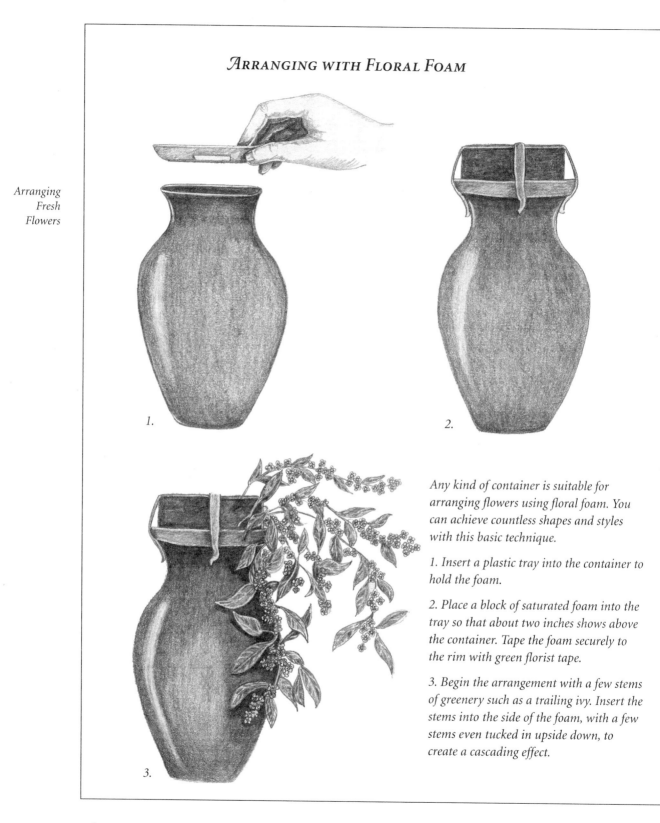

ARRANGING WITH FLORAL FOAM

1.

2.

3.

Any kind of container is suitable for arranging flowers using floral foam. You can achieve countless shapes and styles with this basic technique.

1. Insert a plastic tray into the container to hold the foam.

2. Place a block of saturated foam into the tray so that about two inches shows above the container. Tape the foam securely to the rim with green florist tape.

3. Begin the arrangement with a few stems of greenery such as a trailing ivy. Insert the stems into the side of the foam, with a few stems even tucked in upside down, to create a cascading effect.

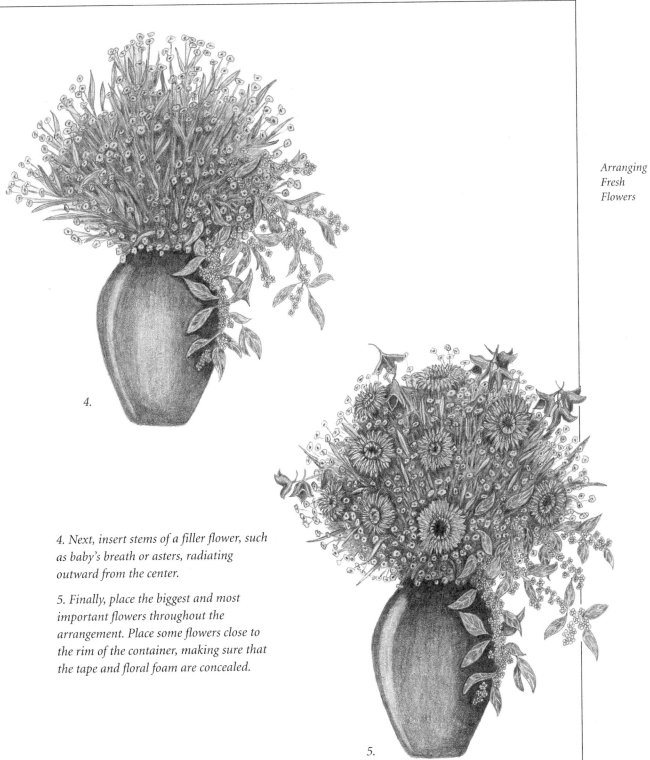

4.

*4. Next, insert stems of a filler flower, such
as baby's breath or asters, radiating
outward from the center.*

*5. Finally, place the biggest and most
important flowers throughout the
arrangement. Place some flowers close to
the rim of the container, making sure that
the tape and floral foam are concealed.*

5.

117

SIZE AND STYLE

There are aesthetic rules in flower arranging, but any good designer will tell you that rules are made to be broken. The chief rule is that the flowers should be two and a half times the height of the container. This principle is a good starting point, but don't let it limit your creativity. Sometimes, such as when you're doing a big arrangement to be seen from a distance, you may want to include a few branches or grasses or other elements that are much taller than the rule allows. Other times, such as when you're doing a centerpiece for your dining room table, you may want the flowers much shorter so they don't interfere with your guests' view of one another.

Styles of floral design are also the subject of rules that were made to be broken. If you were to attend floral school, you would learn all kinds of classifications for arrangements, from the spare look of *ikebana* (the Japanese style of flower arranging) to the lushness of Flemish designs. As you get more involved in flower arranging, you may want to take a more academic approach and try out distinctive, established styles. You'll find plenty of good books on floral design that can teach you various styles and their names. (See appendix 2 for a list of book sources.) As a beginner, though, your best bet may be to stick with the informal designs that really make garden flowers shine, whatever these designs might be called.

Country Essences Flowers ∾ *Watsonville, California*

*T*HE ROAD TO LINDA ARIETTA'S FARM PASSES THROUGH SOME OF THE MOST agriculturally productive land on Earth. Through the fertile vegetable and berry fields of Watsonville, California, then past acres of larkspur and sweet peas, the road climbs into the hills and ends in a garden that is dazzling beyond expectation.

Everything about Linda's farm speaks of a love of flowers. The house, a white Victorian with periwinkle-blue trim, is nearly engulfed by roses and hollyhocks. Inside, an extravagant bouquet brightens her kitchen table. Her

living room is a gallery of freeze-dried floral designs. In the courtyard between her house and workshop, flowers cascade from pots and hanging baskets; brilliant dahlias shine in a nearby garden; and casual bouquets decorate the patio tables. It's not hard to believe Linda when she says, "Flowers are my life."

Linda began dabbling in flowers more than twenty years ago, when she was a berry grower selling at farmers' markets. Year after year, she grew more and more flowers for farmers' market sales. In 1993, she decided to give up berry production and turn her attention entirely to flowers. She started Country Essences Flowers, a business that sells fresh and freeze-dried flowers, as well as floral designs. The company quickly took off, and now employs a staff of five designers and fifteen field workers who handle ten acres of flower production.

Country Essences markets flowers through a wide array of channels, clearly the result of enormous energy on the part of the boss. First are the fresh-flower sales: Linda and her employees sell at twenty-five farmers' markets per week, located from a half-hour to three hours away. At these markets, they primarily sell their own fresh flowers and berries from neighboring farms. Although Linda loves to make mixed bouquets, she says the labor costs make them unprofitable. Instead, she brings flowers to market in bunches, and will make bouquets to order on the spot.

Her next major marketing channel is the mail-order bouquet business. For several years, Country Essences has been shipping bouquets ordered through Smith & Hawken, the upscale garden retailer. The weekend before Mother's Day, Linda and her staff worked practically around the clock making seventeen hundred bouquets and boxing them up to send by overnight mail. She also produces several freeze-dried flower designs, such as wreaths, for mail-order retailers. Every season, she designs ten to twenty prototypes, from which the catalog companies select one or two.

Linda also supplies fresh flower arrangements to several hotels and corporations in San Francisco. She sells a large portion of her flowers to wholesalers. Increasingly, she has been sought out to do wedding flowers—a job she loves.

By freeze-drying flowers, Linda has opened a number of additional markets for Country Essences. Freeze-drying creates a long-lasting flower that looks much more lifelike than air-dried ones. Linda and her designers create permanent floral arrangements for sale by retail stores and through catalogs. Recently, she created a line of elegant Italianate designs for Neiman-Marcus department stores. She does a busy trade in freeze-drying bridal bouquets and other sentimental flowers.

Linda originated the idea of leasing freeze-dried floral arrangements to hotels and corporations. It's a good deal for her clients, because they can enjoy extravagant designs for about a third less than they would pay to buy them, and Linda will replace the flowers every three months. It's a good deal for Linda, because she gets more orders at the lower rental price, and because she can usually spruce up and reuse the arrangements.

"You need the catalog accounts for your bread and butter, but our love is the high-end art," she says. "Now we're doing a lot of corporate work. I can't stand to see an office without flowers. These people are sitting in these meetings that are so intense. Having one of our arrangements gives them a breath of fresh air—they can look up and see something organic."

Linda says she keeps on top of what's going on in the fields by walking them every morning before her workers arrive. The secret of her production success lies in continually planting over a long season. She purchases plugs, and points out, "We're constantly replanting. Every two weeks we plant larkspur, aster, sunflower, godetia, and more." Delphiniums are one of her specialties—she grows two acres of them. She also raises fragrant sweet peas; the first year she grew commercially, she planted so many sweet peas that she glutted the market and the price fell. Now she's growing a much smaller quantity.

Linda attributes her love of flowers to her childhood, growing up (in a house just down the hill from her farm) with a mother who loved to garden. Her mother's flowers, though, were off-limits for picking.

"I had this thing in my head that when I grow up, I'm going to have all the flowers I want to pick," she says. "I now have all the flowers I want to pick." ∾

CHAPTER 9

Going Commercial

A FARMER WHO WAS INTERVIEWING A CANDIDATE FOR A FIELD JOB ASKED her why she wanted to work with flowers. She responded that she found working with flowers so peaceful and therapeutic. "This isn't therapy," the farmer told her. "This is commercial floriculture."

That brief exchange illustrates the perception and the reality of flower farming. To an outsider, growing flowers for a living may seem idyllic. To the experienced grower, though, flower farming is like any other kind of farming—it entails hard work, long hours, physical discomfort, and frequently a high level of stress. Of course, like any kind of farming, it also offers personal freedom, the opportunity to work outdoors, a direct relationship between hard work and income, and the feeling of fulfillment that comes from producing something tangible. Growing flowers, rather than crops such as wheat or vegetables, has the added benefit of aesthetic enjoyment.

But flower farming isn't for everyone. I recently accepted an offer of harvesting help from a visiting friend. We went to the field in the evening, as the sun was getting low in the sky, and started harvesting a long bed of larkspur. I was enjoying myself immensely, appreciating the soft evening air and the intense blues and pinks of the larkspur, and the quiet reverie I always experience when focused on counting bunches. After about half an hour, my friend announced, "I could never be a farmer—all this bending and sweating." I was startled to realize that a task I found so enjoyable could be perceived as torture by someone else. It's a good thing she hadn't offered to set out a few thousand transplants or pull weeds on a hot afternoon.

Of course, if you're already a farmer or market gardener, you know about the work involved in commercial floriculture. You understand about muddy fields, hours spent bending, wet weeds rubbing against your legs in the morning, mosquitoes buzzing around your head in the evening, and so on. For you, growing flowers will be no more difficult than growing, say, cantaloupes in addition to watermelons.

But if you've never been a farmer before, perhaps you should take a hard look at whether you are truly cut out for the work. Gardening can be so pleasurable on

a small, relaxed scale. But once you have orders to fill, it can be just plain hard work. Many people launch into a market gardening business, thinking how great it would be to turn a gardening hobby into a livelihood. Then they realize that commercial production is much more arduous than they had expected, and they long for the days when they just puttered around in a flower bed for a few hours a week.

The work does grow on you, though. Even if the job seems difficult at first, experience does build efficiency. And once you've tasted the freedom of being your own boss, you may find it impossible to go back to working for someone else.

STARTING SMALL

When getting started in flower farming, it's a good idea to start small, and grow as you develop your markets. A half-acre (less than one-third the size of a football field) is a fairly ambitious start for one person working full-time. With a sixteen-week selling season, a decent growing year when most crops produce well, and markets for all you can harvest, you should be able to bring in at least $15,000 from a half-acre. I base this income prediction on my own experience and on that of other flower growers who have discussed their sales with me. This estimate is based on several assumptions about production and marketing. Here are the factors that will determine whether the $15,000 target figure can be achieved:

- **Space efficiency.** Flowers should be grown on raised beds, two to four rows per bed, with a 2-foot path between beds. Spacing between plants should be close, 9 to 12 inches in most cases.
- **Cultivar selection.** All cultivars should be tall, cutting types that are easily grown in the local climate.
- **Fertility.** Soil should be tested for general fertility, with amendments as recommended. Additional nutrients may be needed during the season.
- **Weed control.** Weeds can seriously reduce yield in flower crops, so it's important to keep the beds weeded.
- **Pest control.** Serious pest infestations can make flowers unsaleable, so appropriate pest control measures must be taken.
- **Irrigation.** Flowers need water, at least an inch per week, to yield according to expectations.
- **Harvest and post-harvest.** All flowers ready for harvest should be cut and handled so that there is no loss before marketing.
- **Marketing.** All flowers harvested must be sold.

Once you've satisfied these requirements, you should have no problem selling $15,000 worth of flowers from a half-acre. Whether you can sell $30,000 from a full acre will depend on whether you can find the market for them. Plenty of people do it; but, almost without exception, these one-acre-plus farmers started small.

DEVELOPING A MARKET

The next chapter will provide you with details about the many places where you can sell your flowers, with advice that will help you focus your efforts. A few words in general about marketing are in order at this point, though.

You will probably have to work hard the first couple of years to develop your own market. People are uncomfortable with the unfamiliar, and it often takes repeated exposure before they decide to buy. I know one flower farmer who tried to sell to florists when she started and was flatly turned down by each buyer she approached. But she kept going back, week after week, with whatever was new in her fields. "I wouldn't take no for an answer," she later told me. Slowly, the florists opened up to her. At first, it was just a few bunches of lilies that were more vibrant than the imports available on the wholesale market. Then, florists started to visualize ways to use the other unusual flowers she kept bringing in. As they came to realize that she was dependable and that her flowers were of a consistently high quality, a relationship developed that both the grower and the florist could count on. That farmer now sells all her flowers to florists.

The same sales psychology applies to the end (or retail) consumer, too. Growers who sell at farmers' markets may find their flower sales slow at first, because most customers go to the market to buy food. But shoppers will see the flowers, and the idea will stick in their minds. Perhaps they'll buy them the following week, or they'll pick up a bouquet the next time they want to take a small gift to a dinner party or to a sick friend.

Frankly, Americans are not completely at ease with fresh flowers, which they buy mainly as gifts rather than for their own use. As a result, flower consumption in the United States is only thirty stems per person annually, compared to eighty stems in Germany and one hundred fifty stems in the Netherlands, the two largest flower-consuming countries in the world. Our lower rate of consumption might be considered a liability in a flower business plan, but it can also be viewed as an opportunity. Obviously, many people in other countries find flowers well worth their money; the American entrepreneur has to consider what could be done to make flower buying more frequent among consumers here. In the Netherlands, flowers are for sale everywhere—in railway stations and airports, on street corners. And those flowers are much less expensive than the $30-a-dozen roses that Americans tend to think of when they think flowers.

I believe strongly that direct sales of field-grown flowers is a market that can be easily developed by small-scale producers. By selling at farmers' markets, through pick-your-owns, at roadside stands, from street carts, and from bucket shops in cities, small growers can make flowers available to average consumers, at an affordable price.

The trend among small farmers to sell flowers along with their produce has made some people in the floral industry feel threatened. In several cities, florists have convinced city officials that fresh flowers should be banned from farmers' markets on city property. As of this writing, no one has challenged those kinds of restrictions in court, but it seems inevitable that someone will. In the meantime, flower growers should be sensitive to the fact that some florists and floral wholesalers may view you as competition. You may sense hostility when you go to the wholesaler to buy supplies, and, if you're selling to florists, you don't want to brag about it to wholesalers. Likewise, your florist customers might be displeased to find that you're also selling at a farmers' market. The best policy is to remain discreet about your customers.

However, if you are ever confronted about "stealing" customers from someone in the floral industry, an argument can be made that your flower sales ultimately benefit everyone in the industry. When you sell directly to consumers, you help increase awareness of flowers, which has a ripple effect on other flower sales. If, for example, people get accustomed to having a country bouquet on the dining room table all summer long, they are more likely to go to a florist for a more formal arrangement for a party, or to buy flowers from the florist in winter. When you sell to retail florists, you are obviously providing something they can't get from the wholesalers—whether it be freshness, vase life, or uncommon varieties. Improvements in these areas will make customers happier, which will keep them coming back for more.

Competition is something you'll have to contend with in your own business, too. It's understandable why small growers feel nervous when they see a new grower selling flowers. But as you read the profiles of commercial growers sprinkled throughout this book, you'll see that there are many niches and many markets that can be explored. If you grow high-quality flowers consistently and price them appropriately, your business has an excellent chance of success.

PRICING

How do you set prices for flowers? That's one of the toughest problems confronting every direct-marketing farmer. Unfortunately, there are no easy answers because prices vary considerably, depending on a host of factors: supply, popularity, tradition, ease of cultivation, input costs, timing, the type of market, and so on. Prices also vary from one part of the country to another. So although I can't give you any definitive answers, I can provide some clues that will help you make more intelligent decisions about pricing.

To begin with, there are two approaches to setting prices. One is based on your cost of production; the other is based on the market. Let's look at the first model, the cost-of-production price.

Cost-of-Production Pricing

Tracking direct production costs is a fairly straightforward business. First, you add up all your farm-supply expenses, such as fertilizer, seeds, bulbs or plants, greenhouse utilities, flats, soil mix, floral preservative, buckets or boxes, rubber bands, bouquet sleeves, and so on. Next, add up labor costs for field work, harvesting, and delivery. For yourself, figure in the hourly wage you want to earn. ($20 an hour is approximately the equivalent of $35,000 a year for a forty-hour-a-week job, plus the self-employment taxes you must pay. If you need to earn your entire annual income from your flower business, your hourly wage during the growing season will have to be higher to compensate for the off-season.) For employees, include your share of taxes and benefits as well as their hourly wage. You should also add in your overhead costs, including depreciation on buildings and vehicles, insurance, taxes, business fees, dues and subscriptions, office supplies, bookkeeping, and utilities.

You're already keeping all this information for tax purposes; now you just need to apportion all these costs to each crop you grow. If you're growing an acre of liatris and an acre of peonies, it's an easy task. If you're growing sixty or seventy varieties, however, it's much more difficult. You may just want to lump certain kinds of crops together: all those that are direct-seeded go in one category; all those that are set out as transplants in another; and so on. Or you can simply look at your flower operation as a whole, and assign to it all flower production costs in a lump sum.

Once you've totaled your production expenses, you will know what each crop, or category of crop, is costing you to grow. To figure out how to price the crop, you also have to record your yields. For growers who sell everything by the bunch and record all sales on invoices, you've got all the information you need. Growers who sell mixed bunches, or through a pick-your-own system, need to be more deliberate about counting saleable stems of each crop. Divide your cost of production by the number of stems, and you will have figured the amount you need to charge for each stem in order to make your business viable.

Here's an example: Say you're spending twenty hours a week over a twenty-four-week season growing and selling flowers, for a total labor cost of $9,600 (24 weeks × 20 hours × $20/hour). You've figured your overall production costs to be $3,200. Your total production costs, then, are $12,800. Your yield is thirty thousand saleable stems. Divide $12,800 by 30,000 and you get roughly 43 cents per stem. Since most flowers are sold in bunches of ten, you know you need to charge an average of $4.30 per bunch. If you're averaging less per bunch, you're cutting into your salary and not making the comfortable, middle-class income that is the target in this equation. If you're averaging more per bunch, you're making a profit for your business and should probably be looking at expansion!

Market Pricing

The second approach to pricing is based on the broad market and factors beyond your control. You simply charge whatever the competition is charging, or whatever the market will bear. This is not as easy as it sounds, though, because it's difficult to find out the going rate. One clue is the United States Department of Agriculture (USDA) Federal-State Market News Service's ornamental crops report. These reports are issued from just a few cities in the United States, and usually include only the most common flowers. Many growers consider the reports flawed because the quoted prices fluctuate very little over the course of the year, whereas local prices are more volatile. Nevertheless, the reports do provide an idea of the relative value of different types of flowers. These reports can be purchased from the USDA by writing the address listed in the notes for this chapter, in appendix 2.

Many growers who sell to florists or wholesalers just depend on their customers to tell them the current prices. That strategy seems risky, and most growers who do it say that you've got to have a strong relationship with the buyer. The customer has to want you to do well, so that you'll be around in the future to keep supplying those beautiful flowers he or she has come to depend on. Other growers are flexible about pricing, starting out by quoting their most optimistic price, then coming down if the buyer hesitates. Some growers pick a price and stick to it all season; others vary the price according to supply.

Pricing is a constant process of trial and error at first. You must be on the watch for clues about pricing from many sources: the look on a customer's face; the number of flowers you sold last week; the number of flowers in the florist's cooler; the price reports from the USDA; the prices that florists are charging customers, which are often posted in the back of the shop; and so on. By being alert and using good judgement, you will eventually be able to figure out the market price. Chapter 10 provides additional information about pricing for various markets.

A Combined Pricing Approach

In a perfect world, the cost-of-production approach would be the only way to set prices, because it would reflect a fair compensation for the grower. In the real world, market forces dominate, and the commercial grower is going to have to bend to them. The smart grower, though, tries to incorporate both approaches into pricing. For example, if you know your cost of production and your target stem price, those numbers can help you decide what to grow. Let's say your target stem price is the 43 cents given in the earlier example. You know that a florist will pay only 20 cents per stem for daisies because that's the going wholesale price. So why grow a lot of daisies? Instead, you should be focusing on flowers that sell for 45 to 50 cents per stem.

Other factors in the cost-of-production model will vary, too, depending on the kind of flower business you are operating. One grower I know makes a profit on bouquets that average about 23 cents per stem, because she collects a lot of material from the hedgerows and pastures on her farm (no production costs other than harvest labor) and because she grows primarily direct-seeded flowers (very low production costs). Be aware that the equation can differ considerably from the 43-cent example and still result in a profitable flower business.

It may also turn out that you can't get the per-stem price you think you need in order to make a decent living. Let's say you've figured you need 45 cents per stem, but you are averaging only 30 cents per stem over the course of the season. You can look for places to cut your production costs, and you may in fact find that you are ordering more seed than you need, or hiring workers who are too slow, or a multitude of other factors. But you may also find out that you're running a pretty tight ship on production costs. Your next option for increasing profits, then, would be to find a new market for flowers that bloom on the days when you're not delivering to current accounts. In this way you can increase the quantity of stems sold without significantly increasing your production costs (though you'll still have to figure in the extra labor needed to pick and deliver for a new buyer).

If none of these options brings up your profit margin, however, you'll just have to face the fact that you are not going to be earning the income you had set as your goal in this equation. Many, many flower growers are happy to take a cut in income for the sake of doing work they love. They may decide they're satisfied earning $10 an hour rather than $20 an hour. The amount you need to make before you consider your business profitable is entirely up to you. And it will change over the years. Any new business takes a couple of years to get off the ground, so don't expect to make much of anything at first. As you become established, only you can decide if the hourly wage you're earning is worth your time.

The important thing to remember is that good records will help you succeed financially. The more detailed your records of costs and yield, the more you will be able to refine your production and marketing to maximize profits.

HOW MUCH TO PLANT?

When planting any crop, you need to know the average yield before you can determine how much to plant. For vegetable crops, it's easy; a host of USDA and state Cooperative Extension publications contain yield data. For flowers, though, there is little information on yield. The research that has been done tends to address only the major floral crops, such as snapdragons and statice. What information is available is compiled in Dr. Allan M. Armitage's book *Specialty Cut Flowers* (Timber Press, 1993). This book is highly technical, but it is essential reading for the serious commercial grower.

For the scores of minor flowers that you might want to plant, it's difficult to predict how many stems you will harvest. In the table on the opposite page, I have provided some guidelines, compiled from my own records for my Top Ten producing annuals in 1995. I recorded the amount I planted and added up the number of stems I sold of each flower. These figures are the basis of my "Half-Acre Flower Plan" (originally published by *Growing for Market*). With these quantities of flowers, plus a selection of other varieties, you should use a little under a half-acre and be able to sell at least $15,000 worth of flowers.

This information is by no means scientific, but it does give you a starting point for ordering seeds and plants. The table will help you understand how many stems you can expect from planting 1 ounce of seed, so you can determine whether you need to order ½-ounce or 4 ounces of a particular type of seed. In short, the table gives you a reference point on which to base your decision about how much to plant.

One other caution: These numbers were compiled in a year when I had virtually no crop failures, and weather conditions were as good as could be expected for my farm in Kansas. Weather can have a major impact on flower production, as it does on any type of crop. Just when you think a certain type of flower is guaranteed to thrive in your climate, some weird combination of circumstances might wipe it out altogether. This happened to me in the 1996 season: larkspur, one of my most dependable flowers, failed completely because of the combination of fall drought and record winter cold. Your weather may cause your yield to differ radically from the yields I'm reporting here; you may harvest far more or far fewer flowers than I did in 1995.

The best planting strategy for a beginning flower grower is to plant many different kinds of flowers in significant quantities. A packet of this and a packet of that just isn't going to work. Be extravagant in your planting—the worst that could happen is that you'll have more flowers than you need and they'll go unharvested. On the other hand, an overabundance of a certain flower could mean you'll succeed financially in spite of a couple of crop failures. Seeds are relatively cheap, so don't be afraid to plant more than you think you'll need.

THE TEN MOST PROFITABLE FLOWERS

Variety	Amount Planted	# Stems Sold	Sales
Zinnia 'Giant Dahlia Blue Point' or 'State Fair'	5 ounces of seeds	12,000	$4,800
Achillea millefolium and *A.* 'Coronation Gold'	240 plants	3,600	$1,800
Scabiosa	288 plants	2,600	$1,040
Larkspur 'Giant Imperial'	2 ounces of seed	2,000	$1,000
Ageratum "Blue Horizon'	288 plants	2,000	$1,000
Veronica 'Sightseeing'	100 plants	1,500	$750
Malva sylvestris zebrina	288 plants	800	$480
Salvia horminum	288 plants	1,200	$360
Snapdragon 'Rocket' mix	288 plants	600	$300
Verbena bonariensis	144 plants	750	$300
TOTAL SALES			**$11,830**

Adapted from "The Half-Acre Flower Plan," first published in Growing for Market *(Lawrence, Kans.: Fairplain Publications, 1995).*

SCHEDULING YOUR PLANTINGS

The biggest mistake made by beginning flower growers is to plant once and expect to harvest all season. Experienced professional growers know that they must plant nearly every week through the middle of the summer. Although there are a few plants that will flower for months, most have seasons, just as vegetables do. Some flowers like only cool weather and will bloom, in most parts of the country, only in spring and early summer. Some like it hot and won't start blooming until summer is in full swing. Many are daylength-dependent, which means they won't bloom, no matter when you plant them, until the amount of light each day is right for them.

Also keep in mind that most flowering plants have finished their work once they've produced seed. You can prolong their season by deadheading—that is, cutting off mature flowers so they won't have a chance to go to seed. The plant will then send up new stems to try again to fulfill its mission of producing seed.

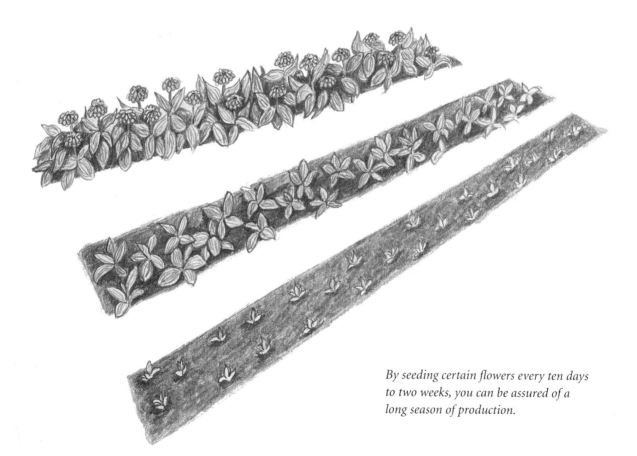

By seeding certain flowers every ten days to two weeks, you can be assured of a long season of production.

Once plants begin to look tired, and flower production begins to drop off, many growers just mow down the remaining stems. If the plants are fertilized and kept well watered, they will often send up a new flush of growth later in the season.

But, for many plants, the reruns aren't worth the wait. So commercial growers just plow down the finished crop and replant, or move onto new land that has been in a cover crop. By planting every few weeks for a month or more, you too can have a continuous supply of bright, fresh flowers.

Taking all these factors into account when scheduling your plantings requires a great deal of skill. In fact, it is probably the most intellectually challenging facet of flower growing, and therefore a skill that will be perfected only with experience. Unfortunately, you're going to have to figure out scheduling for yourself, because your climate will determine when specific plants bloom and for how long. Although the same flowers may be grown in many regions, the planting schedule in Texas will be quite different from the schedule in Vermont, or even Nebraska.

Some plants will not flower over a long season for various reasons. Daylength-dependent flowers, as noted earlier, will bloom when the days get long or short enough to suit them—no sooner, no later. For example, Mexican bush sage (*Salvia leucantha*) is a short-day plant and will flower only in the fall, and northern growers will find that frost kills this plant before the days get short enough to induce flowering. Perennials will

> ### ANNUALS
> ### THAT CAN BE PLANTED
> ### IN SUCCESSION
>
> *Ageratum* (flossflower)
> *Agrostemma* (corn cockle)
> *Ammi majus* (bishop's weed)
> *Centaurea cyanus* (bachelor's button)
> *Consolida* (larkspur)
> *Cosmos*
> *Euphorbia marginata* (snow-on-the mountain)
> *Gomphrena* (globe-amaranth)
> *Helianthus* (sunflower)
> *Helichrysum bracteatum* (strawflower)
> *Limonium sinuatum* (statice)
> *Nigella damascena* (love-in-a-mist)
> *Scabiosa atropurpurea* (pincushion flower)
> *Zinnia* ❧

bloom at the same time the second year, no matter when they were planted. Some plants are so dependent on the weather that they bloom only for a short period of time when the temperatures are right for them. (For instance, I have found that it's a waste of time to plant a second crop of snapdragons for harvest in July, because snaps have weak stems and poor flowers in the midsummer heat here in Kansas.)

In general, you can achieve staggered bloom times when you succession-plant those annual species that are not dependent on daylength or temperature, but rather bloom when the plant reaches a certain age. The box above lists some of the flowers that can be succession-planted.

You also can produce a longer season of bloom by planting different cultivars that flower at slightly different times. My main-crop larkspur is 'Giant Imperial', which usually flowers the first week of June. A bed of 'Early Bird' will come in ten days earlier, and though it's not as tall or strong as the main crop, it makes a solid contribution to my early-summer bouquets. Snapdragon cultivars can also be chosen for a longer season of bloom. As you start to grow commercial-scale quantities, you should ask your seed or plug company for recommendations about the best cultivars for your region.

Texas Specialty Cut Flowers ∿ Blanco, Texas

*P*AMELA AND FRANK ARNOSKY HAVE PROVED THAT YOU DON'T NEED A LOT OF money to start a flower business. By starting small, reinvesting their profits, and making financial sacrifices, they have bootstrapped their flower farm into a $100,000-a-year operation in just a few years.

"An enormous amount can be done without much money if people are willing to wait," Pamela says. "If you can move forward without being in too big a hurry, you can keep your expenses to a minimum."

The Arnoskys, who both attended graduate school in plant-related fields, got into the flower business in 1990 with $1,000 in savings and a $12,000 loan. They bought twelve acres of brushy land in the Texas hill country, put in a well, and built a 30- by 90-foot greenhouse. They grew bedding plants and poinsettias, and set themselves apart from the competition by doing it organically. Sales were good, so the second year they built a 20- by 90-foot cold frame, and the third year another one.

That spring, a group of local growers asked the Arnoskys if they would like to participate in a farmers' market that they were trying to start in Austin. Pamela and Frank didn't want to sell bedding plants at the market, because they didn't want to compete with their own customers at the garden centers. So they planted a quarter-acre of flowers in front of their house.

Summer came, and the farmers' market never materialized. The Arnoskys were left with a bountiful crop of cut flowers, so they got in their truck and started driving around Austin, looking for buyers.

"People were falling all over when they saw the stuff," Frank says. "That took us by surprise; we really hadn't known what to expect."

That first year, they sold everything to a flower shop downtown. The second year, they switched to Central Market, an upscale new supermarket in Austin. The demand for their "Texas Garden Bouquets" astonished them, and they scrambled to increase production to fill the orders.

Three years later, the Arnoskys have five acres of flowers and they are still struggling to stay ahead of the demand. A $1,000 delivery on Friday morning will be sold out by Friday night. Their biggest problem is deciding whether they want to get bigger, which means hiring employees and becoming managers, or whether they want to stay small and turn customers away.

The greenhouse plant business, meanwhile, has been abandoned. Their last crop of poinsettias was in December 1995, and Pamela and Frank now grow only five hundred flats of organic tomato transplants. They're building another greenhouse, however, as they expand their marketing season into winter by growing high-dollar flowers in cool greenhouses and their own transplants in a warm greenhouse.

Frank says the switch to cut flowers was somewhat scary, because bedding plants had been their bread and butter for many years. But the financial demands of the greenhouse business were just too stressful, he says.

"To make $18,000 net in the greenhouse, we had to make $96,000," he says. "We were having $10,000 bills for pots and soils and $5,000 bills for seeds and bulbs. We would stay awake at night worrying about how we were going to pay for supplies. It was exhausting to move that much material through here.

"Now, for $500 we get all the seeds we need. We work harder but we're less worried about money. It was really a matter of not wanting to be so caught up in the rat race."

The Arnoskys were fortunate to discover that they had good soil underneath the brush on their land. With about eight acres cleared, they devoted their time to building the fertility of their soil with cover crops and abundant quantities of compost. For three years, they did all their work with just a tiller; the fourth year, they bought a tractor. They still do without a cooler—instead, they wait until evening to cut their flowers, then leave them on a cool porch to condition overnight before making bouquets before dawn for delivery later in the morning.

Central Market continues to be the Arnoskys' biggest customer, and Pamela and Frank have definite ideas about how to keep their customer happy. First, they stress quality. They do whatever it takes in the field to produce strong, healthy flowers, including frequent boosts with an expensive organic fertilizer, irrigation, and the use of support netting to keep the flowers growing upright. They pick the flowers at the optimum stage for harvest, and only perfect flowers are used. They have figured out the best post-harvest procedures for their flowers, so some varieties get put in hydrating solution for a few hours, some get one kind of preservative, and some get another kind.

Pamela and Frank's bouquets are big and bold—a handful, rather than a set number of stems. They use clear plastic sleeves, with a packet of floral preservative tucked inside and labels on the outside that read "Texas Specialty Cut Flowers" and "Fresh from the Texas Hill Country." Bouquets are taken to the supermarket in clean, black plastic buckets that can be set right out on the display floor. The Arnoskys have a twice-a-week delivery schedule, and they keep to it. They deliver the flowers themselves, and they get cleaned up and dress well before leaving the farm so they can hang around talking with customers in the store. They work hard at creating an image of high quality and outstanding service.

Despite their long hours and their long production season, the Arnoskys love being flower farmers. "We're doing exactly what we wanted to do," Frank says. "We couldn't imagine doing anything else." ❧

'Tween Creeks Farm ∾ *Prague, Nebraska*

*B*ILLENE NEMEC BEGAN SELLING HER DRIED FLOWERS, HERBS, AND CRAFTS IN THE late 1980s at a fledgling farmers' market in Lincoln, Nebraska.

"We had ten vendors and we prayed for sixty people to come to market," she says.

She took over as market manager two years later and set out to develop the Lincoln market into a weekly event that would benefit growers, consumers, and the businesses near the market.

"I went out to every small town around here and encouraged growers to come to the Lincoln market," she says. "Whenever I saw a truck by the side of the road selling produce, I would stop and offer them a spot at the market."

At first, some of the vendors resented her efforts to bring in new growers. They worried that there would be too much competition for a limited number of customers. But Billene always believed that if the growers would come, the customers would follow.

She was right. In recent years, the market has had one hundred vendors and ten thousand customers each Saturday. It's not unusual for most growers to sell out, and several vendors make $1,000 a week there. Billene also thinks it's no coincidence that the Haymarket, the warehouse area where the market is held, has been resurrected as a trendy shopping and restaurant district.

"This has saved downtown," Billene says. "It has brought people down here who had never shopped downtown."

While the market has been expanding, so has Billene's business. The farmers' market that once provided most of her income now accounts for about half. She sells at craft shows in the fall and does an ever-increasing amount of custom work.

"I've had interior designers from Denver and Minneapolis order one-of-a-kind designs," she says. "A woman in California sends me swatches of fabric to design around." She also sells wholesale, and several buyers from the big cities have told her they triple the prices she charges.

Billene and her husband, Richard, bought and moved onto their land the one-room schoolhouse that Richard attended as a child. They live downstairs and have studio and retail space upstairs.

Down a hill from the schoolhouse is the half-acre garden where Billene grows some of the materials she uses in her dried-flower crafts. She grows the usual drieds, such as *Celosia cristata*, *Gomphrena globosa*, and *Helichrysum bracteatum*. She also grows marigolds and zinnias, which she dries by putting them in buckets with a small amount of water. As the water dries up, so do the flowers, but they keep their shape better than if they had been hung. She also makes extensive use of native materials, combing the prairie and roadsides of her farm for grasses, pods, twigs, flowers, and feathers. Hops, bittersweet, soapweed, false indigo, grains, and leaves of pear and apple trees all get collected for her unusual pieces.

Billene buys many of her materials, though, and has found that, even with purchased materials, her design work is more profitable that growing all her own flowers.

"Growing is so time-consuming," she says. "It's from five in the morning till ten at night. Then, when I find one or two days a week that I can design, I try to do twenty pieces a day."

She usually doesn't start designing till August, because dried-flower sales don't pick up until September. The rest of the summer, she and Richard sell vegetables, herbs, and edible flowers at the market. They are certified organic by OCIA (Organic Crop Improvement Association).

Although she has chosen to make craft shows a big part of her income, she doesn't really like them.

"It's nerve-wracking," she says. "The entry fees range from $10 to $175, so it can be a real gamble. At least at the farmers' market you have a following, and it's pretty much young, upwardly mobile people. At shows, you have so many variables: the weather, the age group that will come—you don't know who your competition is . . . I'm a people person, but some days I just don't feel like pushing my stuff."

A rule of thumb among crafters is that you need to have $1,000 worth of material for every $200 you hope to sell, she says. That usually calls for an incredible amount of time spent designing in the weeks leading up to a show.

Billene says she does the small shows in hopes of finding new customers who will come to her again and again. "They cost $10 or $15 to enter, and you can't buy advertising that cheap. You can put an ad in the paper that says dried-floral designs, but that doesn't really tell people anything. Here, they can see my designs; down the line is where I'll get my customers."

The Nemecs spent quite a bit of time cultivating customers. They give classes, both at the farm and elsewhere. They have been amazed at how little knowledge people have about growing and using herbs and flowers, and how eager they are to learn. "People are willing to travel two hundred miles to learn about the use of herbs," she says. Even in small, rural towns, Billene and Richard have found an eager market for herbs and organic produce.

People have asked her if she might be putting herself out of business by teaching people to grow and design with dried flowers. She doubts that will ever happen. "People take my classes so they can express themselves, not so they can copy my designs," she says. "One shouldn't ever be afraid of educating."

CHAPTER 10

Marketing Flowers

ON'T PLANT A CROP UNTIL YOU KNOW WHERE YOU'RE GOING TO SELL it." That's standard advice for anyone who is hoping to grow for market. But it's especially pertinent to the flower grower, because there are hundreds of types of flowers, and the types you choose to grow will depend entirely on where you expect to market them. Fresh flowers and dried flowers are two entirely different businesses, although they can mesh nicely and increase your income if you're well organized. Retail florists, wholesalers, gift shops, grocery stores, farmers' markets—all have different demands about varieties, colors, styles, time of harvest, method of delivery, and so on.

Figuring out what to grow means you have to do your market research before you order a single ounce of seeds. First, consider your own capabilities and limitations. How much land do you have? How much capital? What kinds of facilities and equipment can you afford? If you can work on your flower business only part-time, or only during certain months of the year, what are those times? What will those time restrictions mean about the kind of plants you'll be able to grow and harvest? What's the length of your outdoor growing season? When can you plant, and when will you consequently be ready to harvest? How well do these timing issues fit with your marketing opportunities?

Once you've honestly assessed your own situation, look into your community to see what kinds of markets look promising. Do you have several high-end florists in town or in a nearby city? Is there a wholesaler near enough to consider selling there? Is there a farmers' market? If so, is it inundated with flowers, or do you see an opening for a new flower vendor? Are you on a road that might be a good place for a pick-your-own operation? Are you near enough to air transportation that shipping nationwide is feasible? Does your community have summer tourist traffic? Are there gift shops that would sell dried flower bunches and crafts? How about fall craft shows or Christmas boutiques? Is there a progressive grocery store that would be interested in locally grown bouquets?

These are all questions that you need to consider as you research your market. The truth is, no one can tell you what will be the best market for your flowers. Every farm and every community combine to make a market environment that is unique. The factors that contribute to the success of any horticultural business form a complex web, much like a natural ecosystem, where everything is interrelated.

And although only you can figure out where your operation will fit into this business ecosystem, you can do it in an educated way by learning about the different marketing options for flowers. The sections that follow will detail the demands of the most common places to market flowers. As you begin to understand each type of business, you'll get a clearer vision of the path you should pursue.

RETAIL FLORISTS

A retail florist shop can be one of the most gratifying places to sell flowers. For one thing, florists are fellow flower-lovers. When you bring them buckets of well-grown, unusual flowers, your efforts will meet with heartfelt appreciation. That's a morale builder that will contribute to your job satisfaction. You'll also be pleased to learn that florists are probably going to pay you top dollar among your other market choices—if you find the right florist, that is.

Start your marketing with the most expensive shops in town—the places that do the society weddings and funerals, the country club arrangements, and the parties of the well-to-do. Those florists will be less price-conscious than the little mom-and-pop operations that sell baskets of carnations and chrysanthemums. The high-end florists also will be looking for the unusual, because they know that their sophisticated customers want something different. Not so long ago, the florist who wanted to do something different was limited to the exotic and even bizarre, such as proteas and bird-of-paradise (*Strelitzia* spp.). But the growth of the specialty cut-flower industry has opened the door for new flower designs that are lush, colorful, and romantic.

Put yourself in the place of the high-end florists. They have access to a standard menu of varieties from the wholesaler. Beyond the usual carnations, chrysanthemums, and roses, the flowers most available to florists are alstroemeria, aster, gerbera daisy, gladiolus, gypsophila (baby's breath), Dutch iris, liatris (blazing star), and statice (*Limonium sinuatum*). In recent years, California and Dutch growers have begun supplying a more diverse menu of specialty flowers such as larkspur, delphinium, stock, dianthus, freesia, lily, Queen Anne's lace, snapdragon, sunflower, and waxflower (*Chamelaucium* spp.). The flowers are usually nice-looking, if somewhat rumpled from being shipped in boxes, but the selection doesn't change much. The florist uses these standards to make baskets, centerpieces, bridal bouquets, sympathy tributes (arrangements to place on a casket or around it), altar arrangements, and so on. The shape changes, but often the flowers vary only a little.

Then, one fine day in early summer, you walk into the back room of the florist shop with buckets of unusual, fragrant flowers, cut just the evening before. If you've entered the right shop, the florist is going to sit up and pay attention. More important, he or she will buy from you and order more. Once you've gotten the proverbial foot in the door, you can start to work with the florist to accommodate his or her color preferences and busiest seasons.

Most big florists have walk-in coolers with glass fronts that also serve as display space. Humidity in floral coolers is kept at 80–90 percent to keep flowers looking their best as long as possible. For short-term storage on a flower farm, however, the lower humidity found in a produce cooler or homemade cooler is acceptable.

Aim High For Success

In 1990, my husband and I had been market gardening for several years, primarily selling gourmet vegetables to restaurants and at farmers' markets. I had begun growing an array of flowers for bouquets at farmers' markets, and one June day I decided that my flowers were so beautiful—there must be a market for them in the floral industry.

I made up several big bouquets of larkspur, *Salvia horminum*, baby's breath, painted daisies, and other intense pink and blue flowers, and I started driving around Topeka, Kansas, in my pickup truck. At the time, I didn't know anyone else who was selling to florists, and there were no books or magazine articles to give me advice, so I was pretty much operating in the dark about whom to approach, how much to charge, and so on.

The first two places I stopped were high-volume florists—but also among the cheapest in town. At the first shop, the woman behind the counter told me the buyer wasn't in. When I offered to leave the flowers for him, she declined and told me I'd just have to come again—but, no, she didn't know when to catch him. At the second shop, I asked for the buyer, and the clerk suspiciously asked me what I wanted. When I told her I wanted to know if he would be interested in buying my flowers, she replied, "I doubt it." At the third shop, I got a flat rejection: "We don't use those kinds of flowers," the designer told me.

Well, I was crushed; I wanted to get in my truck and retreat to the farm. But as I drove away from these disappointments, I passed the most expensive florist shop in town, and some celestial hand pulled my car into the parking lot. Without even letting myself stop to think about it, I entered through the leaded glass front doors with a bucket of flowers in each arm.

A stylish man was working at a counter. After a long moment, he looked up. Then he said, very slowly: "Ahhh! Where did you get those?" The appreciation—reverence even—in his voice told me I had found the right place.

That was the beginning of a relationship that continues today. David Porterfield, the owner of the shop, bought those first flowers on the spot, and he has bought practically every flower I have taken him ever since.

My flower production has quadrupled since that first year. I'm currently growing a little over a half-acre of cut flowers. My strategy is to hit the market as early as I can in spring and to sell as much as I can during June, the busiest month for florists. I grow both annuals and perennials that fit my marketing strategy. In July, my gardens hit their peak production, with both the early flowers (such as larkspur) and the summer flowers (such as zinnia) blooming together. Luckily, there's enough demand to keep me busy all month.

Because our farm is certified organic, I don't use herbicides or pesticides on the flowers. By August, though, grasshoppers, heat, and drought are causing trouble in my garden. I used to fret about that, and I exerted an incredible amount of energy trying to keep the flowers looking good in the midst of those assaults. After many years of being frustrated, I have now resigned myself to the fact that August problems are part of my climatic limitations, just as May rains limit Vermont farmers and September frosts limit Minnesota farmers. Rather than sit around the farm watching the flowers go downhill in August, we go to the beach. Then we start again in September, planting larkspur and other fall-seeded annuals, perennials, and bulbs, in anticipation of the next year's crop.

David Porterfield and his staff love working with garden flowers, because of their freshness, vibrancy, and continually changing look over the course of the season. Over the years, they have taken to referring to me as "our flower grower," and they have developed a reputation among their customers for the garden look of their designs. People who want flowers that look fresh and natural know to call Porterfield's. My flowers have been used at the governor's mansion, the country clubs, the most expensive houses in town, and at the funerals of the area's most prominent citizens.

"When I started using garden flowers, I wasn't sure they would be commercially acceptable," David says. "I was a little concerned that people wouldn't want to buy them because they could grow them in their own yards. But, as it turns out, people love to get these flowers!" ᴄᴡ

Marketing
Flowers

Planning for Holidays

For most American florists, the busiest times of the year cluster around the traditional flower holidays early in the year, including Valentine's Day, Easter, and Mother's Day, and around the November to January holidays, including Thanksgiving and Christmas. The May–June wedding season is another busy time.

Greenhouse growers schedule their crops around these seasons. If you're growing only in the field, in most parts of the country you're going to miss almost all of these holidays. Mother's Day is probably going to be pretty uncertain for you, too, but you may be able to schedule a few crops that you can sell in large volume for that holiday. Dutch iris, bearded iris, late tulips, and peonies may be in bloom in your area. Keep tabs on when flowers bloom, not just in your gardens, but in local municipal gardens, at universities, or in botanical gardens. In fact, you can call the horticulturists at such institutions and ask what's blooming in mid-May. You may learn of some early-blooming perennials or woody plants that would make good cut flowers.

Weddings create a huge demand for summer flowers, and you can capitalize on it by growing early-blooming varieties in pinks, whites, lavenders, and light blues. In recent years, there has been a trend toward brighter flowers for weddings, but the majority of weddings will still use a lot of white and pastels.

In most areas of the country, garden flowers hit their peak in July and August. Unfortunately, July and August are the slowest months for most florists because weddings are fewer, people are out of town on vacation, universities and colleges are closed, and it's often just too hot to entertain. In addition, the sight of outdoor flower beds in full bloom may diminish the demand for indoor flowers. Of course, the big events in life—illnesses, deaths, marriages, anniversaries, births, marital quarrels—don't take holidays, so there will continue to be a certain demand for flowers.

In some communities, however, midsummer is the *best* time for flower sales. If you live in an area attractive to tourists, you may have a great midsummer market for your flowers. Growers on Long Island, New York, or Nantucket, Massachusetts, find plenty of customers during this time of year because of the annual influx of high-income summer residents. If there's some kind of event or institution that keeps the locals busy in midsummer, flower demand will be high. In the horse country of Kentucky, for example, florists remain busy during the summer because of the high-society events associated with horse racing.

Get to know the community where you plan to sell, to find out whether people with lots of disposable income leave for the summer or stay and entertain. It can mean the difference between selling flowers and composting them.

Pricing for Retail Florists

Don't go to a florist and ask, "How much will you give me for these flowers?"— this makes you look unprofessional. Furthermore, letting your customer set the price will plant a seed of doubt in your mind about whether you're getting a fair price or whether the florist is taking advantage of you. It's far better to ask for what *you* consider a fair price. If your price is genuinely too high, the florist will quickly let you know; if it's too low, you'll eventually figure that out on your own as you increase your familiarity with your local market.

But how do you determine what's a fair price? You can use the cost-of-production model described in the previous chapter (see page 125). Basing prices on your costs of production, however, would require the full support of your customers in instances where your price is higher than the price of your competition. Realistically, most growers are subject to the whims of the marketplace. You may find you need to charge $1 per stem for your delphiniums because you had to buy the expensive perennial plants, and you had to support them with two layers of netting to protect them from your spring winds. But if the florist can get delphiniums from California at 50 cents per stem, don't expect to get $1 for yours. On the other hand, growing sunflowers may be a simple matter of pushing seeds into the ground and letting the summer sun and rain do the rest. Perhaps you need only 35 cents per stem to make a profit, but the florist may be accustomed to paying 75 cents per stem for Dutch sunflowers. What are you going to do? Obviously, you're going to get as much for each crop as the market will bear, hoping that your no-profit and high-profit sales will even out over the course of the season, and that you will make a profit overall. Then, when you review your records in the off-season, you can determine which varieties were profitable and which were not. Maybe you'll decide to leave delphiniums to the California growers.

The USDA's Market News Service publishes prices of cut flowers in a few cities across the country. You'll find the main address listed in appendix 2. The prices are most relevant to people selling to florists, because they are based on the prices that wholesalers are charging their retail customers. I have used these reports to guide me for many years, without receiving complaints from florists. You'll notice that I said I use the reports to *guide* me rather than to determine my prices. I still take my own production costs into account, and will often charge less than the reports suggest, as long as it keeps me in line with my own target stem price.

The USDA reports are useful in helping you know the general value of one variety in comparison to another. They also tell you where specific varieties are being grown during the year, which has an effect on their price and could give you a marketing window if you're able to produce such flowers in a season when the only product available is coming from the Netherlands or Zimbabwe. If you've got delphiniums and snapdragons, charge your customers the prices quoted in the USDA report. If your customers grumble, you can argue that the wholesalers' delphiniums and snaps came from the Netherlands many days ago, and that yours are fresher and will last much longer. If this argument doesn't persuade them, you can always agree to a lower price—but at least you'll be certain it's a fair price.

WHOLESALE FLORISTS

A wholesale florist will pay you less than a retail florist, but wholesaling can be an attractive market for several reasons:

- If you grow a large crop of a flower that's ready for harvest all at once—lilies or peonies, for example—you may have far more production at one time than you can sell retail.

- Selling to a wholesaler minimizes the amount of time you spend taking orders from and delivering to numerous florists. Many growers just don't want to spend a lot of time talking on the phone and driving around the city; they'd rather take a lower price and spend more time in their fields.

- If you're located in a rural area with little in the way of a retail market, wholesaling may be your only option. You may find that the only way to sell flowers is to ship them out of your area.

- Wholesalers may purchase a wide variety of products, from flowering branches in early spring to dried flowers, gourds, and ornamental corn in fall. They also can order enough of a specialty item to make it worth your trip, whereas orders from a retail florist are likely to be so small as to make a delivery inefficient. For this reason, you might experiment with unusual items such as branches of currant tomatoes or red peppers, and see if the wholesaler can take a sufficient quantity to make your effort worthwhile. Don't expect the wholesaler to be on the cutting edge, though. He or she is busy just satisfying demand from customers and probably won't devote a lot of energy to creating demand for a new product—that's your job.

If any of the above is reason enough for you to want to sell wholesale, go into this business armed with the knowledge that you have a great deal to offer the wholesale florist. Dealing with a local grower can be extremely beneficial to the wholesaler, so don't undermine your own worth just because you're a small farmer. If you grow beautiful flowers, get started secure in the confidence that you have a valuable product and service to sell.

There's nothing mysterious about the wholesale florist business, but you need to know a bit about how wholesalers operate so that you can figure out how best to fit in. Many wholesalers are regional or national chains. Denver Wholesale Florist, for example, has eight branches in cities across the country. Most big cities have numerous wholesale houses, which are basically intermediaries, buying flowers directly from growers or importers and reselling them to the retail florists in their area. Most smaller cities also have wholesalers who supply the flower shops in every town in the area.

Flowers can be the only crop on a farm, or they can be part of a market garden. Ornamental oreganos and lavenders are grown by the acre at Valencia Creek Farm in California (above). At the author's garden in Kansas, bachelor's buttons are interplanted with vegetables (left).

Flowers from the Homeless Garden Project in Santa Cruz (top left) are sold directly to consumers. At Coburn's Flower Farm in Carmel Valley, California (top right), shade-loving perennials such as coral-bells are sold to local retailers. The bells-of-Ireland grown on a large scale at Dos Osos Multifloro in California (bottom) will be shipped to wholesalers nationwide.

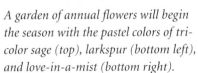

A garden of annual flowers will begin the season with the pastel colors of tri-color sage (top), larkspur (bottom left), and love-in-a-mist (bottom right).

By midsummer, a bolder palette of colors takes over the gardens, with Zinnia 'Blue Point' mix (top left), Rudbeckia 'Indian Summer' (top right), and sunflowers, such as the single 'Sunbright' (lower left) and the fully double 'Goldburst' (lower right).

(Top left photo: Mike Yoder; bottom right: Frank Arnosky)

On a commercial scale, flowers such as larkspur should be planted in straight rows for easier weeding. These fields show three essential ingredients of a successful commercial planting: straight rows for weeding, support net for wind protection, and yellow sticky cards to monitor for insect pests (above).

*Opposite page:
Larkspur should
be harvested for
fresh use when
about one-third of
the flowers are
open (top right).
For drying, let all
the flowers on the
stem open before
cutting and
hanging them
(bottom right).*

*Left:
Seed of many
varieties,
including Zinnia
'Blue Point' (at
left) can be
purchased as
separate colors to
suit local
preferences or
occasions. For
example, the pink
and white zinnias
will find a ready
market during the
June wedding
season, while
orange might be
in greater demand
as a fall crop.*
(Photo: Mike Yoder)

Karen Pendleton hangs statice and sunflowers in the grain bin that she uses as a drying shed on her Kansas farm (top).
Many organic flower growers use heavy black polypropylene landscape fabric for weed control on perennials (bottom).
(Top photo: Jim Patrico)

Black paper mulch and plastic mesh support netting will keep flowers weed-free and growing straight up, as with the snapdragon transplants (top left) and the pincushion flower (bottom). Most customers, though, don't object to the occasional twisted stem, provided it is as poetic as this larkspur (top right).

(Bottom photo: Mike Yoder)

To sell flowers, show them at their best. Some types, such as statice (above), are most eye-catching when they are massed. A few delphiniums and sunflowers in a vase at Country Essences Farm in California show customers how easy it is to create a stunning arrangement. At a farmers' market, bunches of flowers wrapped in florist paper and vases of garden roses spread across a table emphasize the exquisite colors and forms.

Shifra Levine of Sweet Meadow
Bouquets and Herbs in Vermont
is among a growing number of
farmers who sell flowers by
subscription. Shifra has thirty
customers who pay $18 per week
to have a bouquet delivered to
their door every week during the
growing season (above).
Displays should be informative as
well as beautiful. At this farmers'
market, informative and
interesting labels with clearly
marked prices help customers get
accustomed to buying flowers
(right).

The harvest from a single day in July provides the material for a diverse array of designs, from elegant to casual. Inexpensive glass vases direct all the attention to the flowers in these two arrangements. Blue Lisianthus 'Echo' and white Buddleia are left to speak for themselves (top). A ginger jar overflows with Cosmos 'Versailles', Zinnia 'Blue Point', Celosia 'Chief' and 'Forest Fire', and Rudbeckia 'Indian Summer' (right). Note the bows tied at the water line on both vases.

A clay pot radiates a profusion of summer flowers, including rudbeckia, snapdragons, Celosia 'Flamingo Feather', golden asters, nigella, and zinnias (left). Notice the sheet moss tucked into the saucer.

In another clay pot, the designer achieves a more natural look by letting all the flowers stand upright, as though they are still growing in the garden (right). A red honeysuckle climbs a branch of curly willow. Other flowers include a coral phlox, purple hybrid delphinium, blue belladonna delphinium, rudbeckia, zinnia, and yellow statice sinuata.

This long, low basket of summer flowers would be a lovely table centerpiece. It contains 'Sunbright' and 'Autumn Beauty' sunflowers, Celosia 'Forest Fire' and 'Chief', Echinacea 'Magnus', and Ageratum 'Blue Horizon'. Several fronds of ornamental grasses are attached to the floral foam at both ends, making loops across the top of the arrangement (top).

A garden urn brimming with zinnias, cosmos, blue salvia, and perovskia is accented with two small sheaves of wheat (right). The wheat was dried while still green, and it has been left that color for this arrangement. It will turn golden if it is exposed to sunlight.

Even the most common flowers can be made elegant with the right container and a gauzy ribbon. A small silver tea box holds a miniature arrangement of pink 'Sunbow' zinnias, purple gomphrena, rose statice sinuata, and pink yarrow.

ABOUT THE DESIGNERS

The floral arrangements on these pages were designed by David Porterfield and Mark Lamantia of Porterfield's Flowers in Topeka, Kansas.

David has been in the flower business since 1965, when his father opened Porterfield's. He now runs the business and remains an active designer. He has been on the Board of Directors of the American Institute of Floral Design, and was the design director for *Florist's Review* magazine. In 1976 he decorated the Statue of Liberty for the nation's bicentennial, using one hundred thousand roses, and he later worked on President Reagan's inaugural. He travels widely, doing the flowers for special events and giving workshops for other designers.

Mark has worked at Porterfield's since 1973 as a designer. He also teaches floral design at a local vocational school.

Arrangement photos: Mike Yoder

Many wholesalers also sell floral supplies, such as foam, ribbons, baskets, vases, preservatives, balloons, and the assortment of novelty items used to dress up flowers in most shops. As a market gardener who sells products to the public—and pays sales taxes, if applicable—you are eligible to shop at the wholesale florist. The store manager will probably ask you to fill out some forms and provide a tax number (or whatever document your state uses) to prove that you're a reseller. After that, you'll be treated like any florist, free to browse through the merchandise and buy whatever you want, although many items are sold only in large quantities. Going on a shopping trip is a good way to see the facility, meet the people who work there, and determine whether your product might be welcome.

The wholesaler's day begins early in the morning, ordering flowers, tracking down shipments, and calling florists to take orders for that day's deliveries. The pace is frenetic until noon, by which time most of the orders have left the warehouse and the employees have a chance to sit back and take stock.

Don't call a wholesaler in the morning, especially when you're making your first contact. You're likely to get a brusque response, which might give you the mistaken idea that the wholesaler doesn't want to do business with you. Start your business association by calling the wholesale house and asking whoever answers the phone for the name of the main buyer. Don't get into a conversation at this time; just get a name for future contacts. Then, write a letter to that person to introduce yourself and your product. Don't be afraid to talk about yourself, to tell about your experience. Tell the buyer where you're located; give full details about what you grow and when it will be available. You can mail or fax this letter.

A week or so later, in the afternoon, call the buyer, mention your preceding letter, and have a sales pitch ready. Friday afternoon generally is the calmest time to approach a wholesaler. You should have reached this point of contact about a month before you expect to start harvesting your flowers. Then, when the crop is ready, you should call again to discuss specific quantities and delivery dates.

Although preselling is the best deal for everyone, don't worry if you find yourself unexpectedly looking for a wholesale buyer of a crop that's ready at that moment. Wholesalers do make spur-of-the-moment purchases, especially if the price is right.

Because your flowers will go through extra handling at a wholesaler, it is particularly important to use proper post-harvest handling procedures. These include using clean, disinfected buckets and floral preservatives. If you're going to sell to a local wholesaler, you can deliver your flowers in the buckets you used for harvest. This is one of the benefits a wholesaler will see in buying locally. Usually flowers arrive dry in boxes after a few days in transit, and the wholesaler recuts the stems and puts them in buckets of preservative. Then, when a florist places an order, the flowers are taken out of the water, wrapped in newspaper, and again placed in boxes for delivery. Your flowers, which have never been out of water, are obviously going to have a better vase life. As long as your buckets are clean, don't worry about their style—many wholesale houses use the same 5-gallon icing or pickle buckets you can buy from the doughnut shop or fast-food place.

The wholesale florist is also going to benefit from your proximity because your product is probably going to be cheaper, even if you get the same prices that the big commercial growers in California or Colombia are getting. That's because those commercial grower-shippers add a box charge and freight charge, which the wholesaler must pay.

And how should you set prices? As always, that's the grower's hardest task. You need to follow the market reports and look for an inside source such as a retail florist who can tip you off to the going prices. (You'll get 40 to 60 percent less than the price being charged to the retail florist.) Don't try to undercut the competition on price—that's always a bad policy. Offer better quality, and ask for a price that pays your costs and a fair return, and you can hold your head up about taking customers away from your competitors. Whatever you do, don't ask the wholesaler how much he'll give you.

Wholesalers also are interested in local sources of flowers that don't ship well, such as cosmos and sweet peas. But don't expect wholesalers to tell you what to grow.

SHIPPING FLOWERS

If you can't sell all your flowers locally, you may want to consider selling regionally or even nationally. In that case, you will have to learn how to ship. Flower packaging is not standard throughout the industry. California growers use boxes that usually are either 44 or 48 inches long, but can be of other lengths. Width and depth vary, too, but most boxes are flat—about 8 inches deep—and about 20 inches wide. The top of the box usually slips over the bottom. You can probably get some castoffs from a florist or wholesaler, and take the samples to a box company to be reproduced and printed with your farm's name.

You should use plastic sleeves around each bunch to protect the blossoms. The sleeves can be purchased from the wholesaler, or by mail from one of the suppliers listed in appendix 2 (see the notes for chapters 7 and 8). Flowers should be packed with frozen gel ice packs, wrapped in newspaper. Bunches should be attached to the box with a cleat so that they won't shift in transit, damaging the blossoms.

Test your packaging by boxing your flowers, handling the boxes roughly, then letting them sit around for a day or two. Then open the box, recut the stems, and place the flowers in water to see if they revive. You may find that you're cutting at the wrong stage, or that the kind of flowers you grow don't ship well. Be sure to do this research carefully and thoroughly, since you will lose customers and money quickly if you ship flowers that arrive dead.

The most difficult task for a grower-shipper is finding reliable transportation for your product. Flower growers constantly complain about carriers mistreating their flowers, but these problems vary from place to place, and you will have to find out by trial and error who handles yours best. You should check with airlines, bus companies, Amtrak, UPS, private couriers, and freight companies to find out who is capable of keeping your flowers cool and getting them where you want them to go.

Once you have the logistics of shipping worked out, it's time to contact wholesalers in the areas where you want to market. Your target customers may be determined by transportation: Find out what cities are served fastest by the carriers available to you; then contact the wholesalers there.

To get names of potential customers, you can go to the public library and look up wholesale florists in the Yellow Pages of telephone directories for the cities you're interested in shipping to.

To launch your business relationship with these distant wholesalers, use the same procedure as for selling to local wholesalers, and follow up by faxing price lists when your crop is nearly ready. With luck, you'll get orders faxed back to you. If not, you will have to call the wholesalers to solicit orders.

If you're dealing with a wholesaler that has branches in other cities, you may be able to sell large quantities that the main warehouse will then put on a truck to their other outlets.

SUPERMARKETS

A bouquet business at a busy supermarket can be a good option for selling flowers. The main disadvantage is the time you will have to spend making the bouquets. At first, you can probably figure on one hour of assembly for each hour you've spent cutting, although you will get faster over time. You also will need to put your bouquets in plastic sleeves to protect them from damage when customers pull them out of the buckets to inspect them.

When you first approach a supermarket, find out if they have a floral department manager. In many smaller stores, the produce manager handles flowers. Call ahead for an appointment, and bring several buckets of samples along to show the manager. Be prepared to talk prices, signage, and delivery and payment schedules. Also, find out where to bring the flowers; some big stores have strict schedules for their loading docks, and you need to be there on time or you'll lose the sale.

You can arrange to sell your flowers either on consignment or outright to the floral buyer. In larger stores, the buyer will probably purchase the flowers outright. Smaller stores, or those not accustomed to selling flowers, may want to accept them on a consignment basis. In either case, it benefits you to ensure that your flowers are handled correctly once they are in the store. There's nothing more discouraging than selling flowers to a store and seeing them still there a week later, wilted and pathetic, with your farm's name on them.

In a supermarket, handling can be crucial. The ethylene gas emitted by many fruits and vegetables will cause your flowers to die prematurely, so make sure that the bouquets aren't being displayed next to the bananas or apples. You may find that you have to educate the supermarket staff about such matters as keeping the flowers from ethylene sources and keeping water in the buckets. Pay attention, too, to the kind of sign that the store puts up over your flowers. I once had a supermarket call my garden flowers "wildflowers" on a sign. In a town with a high degree of ecological sensitivity, people get upset about harvesting plants from the wild, and I'm sure that sign hurt sales. Suggest to the staff that your flowers be labeled "fresh, local flowers" and that your farm's name be used to identify them. You might even offer to supply a sign with a photo of you and information about your farm.

If you sell on consignment, you can check the flowers every couple of days, change the water, and replace bouquets as needed. You will have to provide the buckets, stands, and signs. Professional-looking displays can be purchased from floral wholesalers.

The prices you will get for your bouquets will probably be about half of what the store can charge, so take a realistic look at them. If they are head and shoulders above the carnations-and-statice bouquets that sell for $3.99, you can expect that the store will sell yours for $5.99, so you should ask for $3. Some stores will try to mark up more than 100 percent, and you should protest if they set the price too high, because sales will suffer. You want to sell flowers, and lots of them, so appropriate pricing is essential.

BOUQUET-MAKERS

A fairly recent phenomenon in the United States is the local bouquet-maker. Most of the bouquets you see in supermarkets are put together in foreign countries or in the cities where they first enter the United States, such as Miami. But there are some bouquet-makers who are setting up shop in other cities and are selling to supermarkets. Many of these bouquet-makers are willing to buy bouquets or bunches from local growers and distribute them to supermarkets. For growers who live far from the city or who don't have time to make a lot of stops, selling to a bouquet-maker can be ideal because large quantities can be sold in one place. However, your prices will be low, because both the bouquet-maker and the supermarket will have to mark up the flowers.

INVOICING AND GETTING PAID

When selling to florists, wholesalers, supermarkets, or bouquet-makers, you must prepare an invoice to ensure that you will get paid. You can purchase invoice books at office-supply stores; to make bookkeeping easier, get the kind that is numbered and has a duplicate copy that remains attached to the book after you tear out the original. Have a rubber stamp or labels made with your name, address, and phone number. Make sure the top line is the same as the name on your checking account, because that's how the person who pays you is going to write out the check. (If the checks are made out to your farm or business name, the bank may require you to open a separate business account, which is often more expensive than a personal checking account.)

Some businesses will write you a check when you deliver the flowers, and that, of course, is the best possible payment system for you. But in most cases, you will have to present an invoice when you deliver the flowers and have it signed by the person who receives them. Leave the original with the customer and keep the duplicate for your records. When you first establish a relationship with a customer, ask about the standard procedure for paying vendors. If you sense that there is some flexibility about payment, try to get paid weekly. But don't be surprised if you're told that invoices are paid once or twice a month. Try to accept the standard payment schedule to make it easy for the customer to buy from you. Once you have agreed on a payment schedule, write it on the invoices: "Net 30 days" means you expect payment within 30 days of the invoice date.

After that, it's up to you to keep tabs on payments. When you get a check in the mail, verify the amount against the duplicate invoices in your invoice book, and note the date of payment. If any invoices are skipped, call immediately to alert the customer to the problem. If a customer is regularly late in sending payment, don't be shy about asking for more timely checks. If you get excuses about the customer's cash flow problems, be careful with that account. You might end up losing money if you continue to sell there. Sadly, the small farmer who most needs to get paid is often the last one to receive a check, because he or she has very little leverage over the customer. By keeping track of your finances, you can stop delivering to delinquent accounts before your losses become too great.

FARMERS' MARKETS

A farmers' market can be a wonderful place to sell flowers, or a terrible place to sell flowers. It's wonderful when there aren't a lot of other flower growers and when you have a big crowd early in the morning. It's terrible when the weather is hot and the sun on the parking lot wilts your flowers in their buckets. Nothing looks sadder than droopy flowers.

Display is all-important at a farmers' market. Make as big a splash visually as you possibly can. Take as many flowers as you can possibly cut. You may not sell them all, but you will have the color and the critical mass to attract customers to your stand. Keep in mind that flowers diminish in their appeal as their quantity dwindles, even if the remaining ones are still quite beautiful. Try it yourself: Keep track of how quickly the first half of your flowers sell,

Display stands in various configurations can be purchased from floral suppliers.

149

then see how much longer it takes to sell the second half. We know of several growers who bring to market every floral element they can find, whether they expect to sell it or not, simply to create visual impact. That includes tall stalks of sunflowers; bunches of dried flowers; buckets of cattails, cornstalks, wildflowers, and grasses; and so on.

Mass your buckets where they will be most visible, raising them up off the ground so customers don't have to stoop to inspect them. Use clean, attractive buckets and clean shelving or tables to display your product, under an umbrella or canopy for shade. Use plastic sleeves on your bouquets and bunches, or keep a clear space on a table with a stack of florist paper, butcher paper, or even old newspapers on which you can smartly wrap up your customer's selection. Use attractive signs that are visible from a few yards away to let customers know your prices. Finally, identify the flowers whenever possible to save your customers the embarrassment of not recognizing a bachelor's button or lily.

Farmers' markets provide you with a great way to educate and inspire your customers. You want them to be happy with their flowers so they'll come back next week, so give them good instructions on how to handle the flowers.

Most farmers'-market sellers make bouquets before coming to market. Some, though, have good luck assembling bouquets on the spot. One grower I know has customers gathered around who watch him making bouquets, so he's as theatrical as possible about it. If your market is a busy one, you may have to hire one

bouquet-maker and one money-taker to staff your stand. When there is a lull, making bouquets is a good way to use that time.

Pricing is a touchy matter for the farmers'-market seller, and I think it helps to experiment a bit with your pricing structure. At some markets, a $6 mixed bouquet may be widely perceived as being too expensive, whereas a $4 bouquet seems reasonable. However, you may make more money by selling fewer bouquets. Let's say you price your bouquets at $4 and you sell twenty-five of them, for $100. If you price them at $6, you may sell only eighteen bouquets, but you will still make more money ($108) with less work. Try it both ways and see how you make the most money.

SUBSCRIPTION PROGRAMS

Community Supported Agriculture (CSA) is a new kind of relationship between farmers and consumers. In its purest form, consumers pay a lump sum before the growing season begins, in order to help finance a farm's operating costs. In return, they get a share of whatever produce is being harvested from the farm each week. A variation on this theme is the subscription program, where customers sign up at the beginning of the season to take one bag per week of whatever is produced, paying as they go.

Many of these CSA and subscription programs include cut flowers as a component. In some cases, they're covered in the price of the share. In many CSAs, though, flowers are considered an option, with an additional fee charged to people who sign up for flowers. You really have to know your members in order to accurately judge whether they would welcome flowers, or whether they would consider them a waste of their membership money. If you are just starting a CSA, decide which way you would prefer to handle flowers, then start out that way. People often will protest if you add flowers later, but not even notice if flowers are always part of the package from the day they sign up.

I sell about $100 worth of flowers per week through our subscription program, which offers a pay-as-you-go bag of vegetables every week for three hundred customers. I take bouquets or bunches of zinnias (depending on how pressed for time we are) to the store that serves as our distribution center. As people pick up their bags of produce, they can also pick up a bouquet and have it billed to their account. I think this system is a really good way to market flowers, because the customers don't have to hand over any money on the spot. The flowers are simply added to the bill, to be paid later—the perfect impulse purchase.

Growers also are experimenting with flowers-only subscription programs in which people sign up to have a bouquet dropped off each week at their home or office. Normally, it's hard to turn a profit on home deliveries because of the time involved in delivering. But if you can sign up ten or twelve customers at a single institution, such as a college or hospital, you can make such a system work. I know a flower grower near a tourist town who sells one bouquet per week to a large number of merchants in the downtown shopping area.

PICK-YOUR-OWNS

Many farm markets that offer pick-your-own (PYO) berries, pumpkins, or other crops have recently added cut flowers to the mix. Flowers are certainly a natural component of any kind of on-farm market or roadside stand. If you're already paying for liability insurance coverage that allows people go out into the fields to pick produce, you might as well let them pick flowers, too.

When setting up a PYO, your biggest consideration is access. You have to provide weed-free flower beds with plenty of room to maneuver between them. Nobody wants to wade through weeds or mud to cut flowers, and you'll increase your liability risk if you don't maintain wide, clear paths.

You also have to price flowers in a way that is easily understood by the consumer—for example, all the 25-cent flowers in one section, all the 50-cent flowers in another. Those flowers that are expensive and/or easily damaged in the field can be picked in advance and placed in buckets near the checkout stand, so that customers can add a special flower to their bouquets at the last minute. For example, you probably don't want customers cutting their own lilies because they might cut too much foliage, which means that your costly lily bulb won't survive. Try to imagine all the ways customers could ruin your flowers; then make plans to avoid those problems. In any case, you'll find out quickly enough what changes need to be made.

The equipment you'll need is minimal: some kind of containers with water, and some inexpensive kitchen scissors. When the customer returns the container full of flowers to the checkout, wrap the flowers in newspaper, butcher paper, or waxed florist paper.

Pendleton's Kaw Valley Country Market ∾ Lawrence, Kansas

Karen Pendleton's flower business started as a supplement to her family's pick-your-own (PYO) asparagus farm. But in the ten years since then, flowers have become one of the top crops at Pendleton's Kaw Valley Country Market in Lawrence, Kansas.

Karen now grows five acres of flowers and markets them through nearly every channel available to the flower grower, with a season that spans all but a few months of the year. Florists, farmers' markets, wholesalers, craft shows, on-farm market, weddings—Karen does it all.

Karen and her husband, John, were traditional farmers when they first decided to try their hand at the asparagus PYO. Their twenty acres of asparagus attracted thousands of customers to their farm every spring, and they soon realized they had a ready market for whatever else they wanted to grow.

"People would come here and buy $10 worth of asparagus and, as they were handing me a $20 bill, would ask, 'What else can I buy?'" Karen says. "I knew we could get the other $10 if we had more products."

Peonies were a likely choice for that first expansion because they bloom at the same time as the asparagus harvest, which runs roughly from late April to Memorial Day. The

JIM PATRICO

Pendletons expanded their business in several other directions, adding more products to be sold during the short asparagus season: They grew hydroponic tomatoes and bedding plants for spring sales; they created several of their own value-added products, such as blue corn chips and pickled asparagus; they planted rhubarb and spring vegetables.

Once the Pendletons had developed the variety they needed to increase sales during asparagus season, they expanded the length of their marketing season. Flowers have become one of their trademarks. Karen has increased production of fresh materials to make bouquets all summer long, selling most of them at farmers' markets and some to florists and wholesalers. She also grows large quantities of flowers for drying; she sells some of her drieds throughout the summer, but most of the material is put aside for design work.

Beginning in midsummer, Karen starts building her inventory of arrangements to take to regional craft shows in autumn. Her designs are immediately recognizable for their lush styling and intense colors. Deep pink peonies, purple statice, and golden sunflowers are among her signatures. Most of her designs are bold and extravagant—overflowing baskets, big wreaths, long garlands.

In 1990, Karen and three other dried-flower crafters in her area formed a marketing cooperative they call Friendship Gardens. The women attend craft shows together and take turns staffing the booths. They collaborate on wreath-making workshops and they hold a sale of Christmas crafts and gifts each winter at Karen's barn. Karen says the cooperative works, in part, because each woman has a distinctive design style. One woman works in the pale colors of prairie wildflowers, while another does miniature arrangements. Rather than competing with one another, Karen believes, the different styles create a lively booth that attracts more customers.

Karen has recently expanded into the market that many flower growers consider the final frontier: weddings. "I put it off as long as I possibly could," Karen says, "because I'd heard horror stories about brides' mothers." A few friends convinced her to do their weddings, however, and Karen learned that "the best way to advertise for weddings is to do a wedding." Within two years of her first wedding, she was doing one nearly every weekend of the summer.

Karen has been called upon to do everything from supplying a few buckets of fresh flowers to full-service floral work, including bridal bouquets, boutonnieres, altar flowers, and headpieces. The wedding flowers, she says, have ranged in price from $35 to $3,500. But she makes it clear to everyone who seeks her services that her flowers will not be the standard wedding fare—they will be the bold, natural flowers of her Kansas garden.

"If they want only flowers I don't grow, there's no reason for them to come to me, and I have been very upfront about telling a few people they should go to a florist," she says. "I'm not trying to take business away from florists. I'm trying to offer what florists don't."

Because of their bloom time, peonies have long been used to decorate graves on Memorial Day, and some florists seem to be stuck with that image of them. Karen's own customers, though, have been telling her a different story: Peonies have caught the hearts of a younger generation of women, who love their soft colors and fragrance. And Karen is the only person in her area growing enough peonies to outfit a wedding.

Although she hesitated about weddings for many years, Karen is now glad she has taken the leap. At one recent wedding, the father of the bride watched her hand out bouquets to bridesmaids and fuss over the headpiece of the bride, and he put into words what she had been thinking herself about this new venture.

"You must have the best job in the world," he told her. "You're taking people on the happiest day of their lives and making them happier." ↶

Land's Sake Community Farm ∾ Weston, Massachusetts

*I*N ONE OF THE MOST DESIRABLE SUBURBS OF BOSTON, WHERE MANY HOUSES SELL for half a million dollars, a thirty-six-acre piece of land stands untouched by development, set aside for organic farming.

The land, known as the Case Farm, is owned by the Town of Weston and is farmed by Land's Sake, a nonprofit conservation organization. The workers on the farm include dozens of middle-school students, who grow and harvest vegetables, berries, and herbs for an on-farm stand and for homeless shelters and food pantries in Boston.

Here, on the edge of the farm, is one of the first pick-your-own (PYO) flower farms in the United States. It was created in 1985, when field-grown flowers were just becoming popular with small farmers. It still attracts thousands of customers, who love to wander through the extensive beds of annuals and perennials in pursuit of their own bouquets.

The one-acre flower field borders a busy road, where its rich tapestry catches the eye of passing motorists and pulls customers into the farm stand's parking lot.

"The flowers are highly visible; they add a lot of color; and they make the farm a lot more festive," says Tom Gumbart, director of Land's Sake. "Because we're organic, we have a lot of families with young children who come out to pick because they know it's safe."

The PYO flowers also are a good revenue producer, Tom says. The acre of flowers generates about $10,000 in sales annually, with much higher potential. Although some flowers are cut every day for bouquets sold at the farm stand, most of the harvesting is done by the customers themselves.

Regular customers can purchase a "picking pass" that allows them to come to the flower garden whenever they want and pick all they want. Others can pick and pay by the stem. Easy, prolific annuals such as cosmos and calendula cost 15 cents per stem. Larger annuals such as snapdragons cost 25 cents per stem. Big, dramatic flowers that produce only one or two stems per season, such as certain sunflowers, delphiniums, foxglove, and gladioli, cost $1 per stem.

Erica Gorn, the farm manager, says that customers who want to pick their own flowers are given an inexpensive pair of kitchen shears (she recommends tying an orange tag to them so they can be found in the field if the customer drops them) and a 1-gallon plastic jug with the spout cut off. If she senses that customers have never cut flowers before, she will take them to the field and show them how to do it; she explains that every node on the stem is a future flower, so customers will understand that they shouldn't cut the plants back too severely.

Although children and inexperienced pickers can damage the gardens, particularly in spring when plants are young, Tom says the philosophy at the Land's Sake farm is to keep rules to a minimum so that community members can experience the farm for themselves. "We ask them not to trample things and not to cut flowers at the base, but that's about all," he says.

Many customers are interested in flowers that they can dry themselves for wreaths and arrangements, so the garden contains big plantings of gomphrena, celosia, statice, baby's breath, and lavender.

Tom says weeds are the biggest problem in the organic PYO flower garden. Customers don't want to have to push through weeds to cut flowers, so it's important to keep the beds and paths weed-free. However, tilling between beds to keep weeds out doesn't work in the PYO because this technique leaves muddy paths in wet weather. Many flower customers are people stopping on their way home from work, still dressed in good clothes. Grass paths, mulch, and frequent hand-weeding are the best solutions the farmers have hit upon so far.

Land's Sake also performs other land-conservation activities in Weston, including management of 1,500 acres of forest and 65 miles of recreational trails and fire roads. In addition, the organization conducts extensive environmental-education programs in the schools, including a project at the Weston Middle School in which students take part in maple sugaring, from tapping out to selling syrup at "sugaring off."

But flowers, in the minds of many Land's Sake members, have a particular relevance to the conservation organization's mission.

"What we ought to be trying to do in the suburbs is show how beautiful small-scale farming can be," says Brian Donahue, who helped build the PYO flower field more than a decade ago. "This flower garden provides a really good example."

For more information, contact Land's Sake, P.O. Box 306, Weston, MA 02193. ⌒

Parting Words

THE FIRST YEAR THAT MY HUSBAND AND I GREW FOR MARKET, AN EXPERIenced grower came to our farm to help us plant. He worked with us all day, providing expert advice as well as physical labor. We were overwhelmed by his generosity, thanked him profusely, and asked what we could do to repay him.

"Nothing. This is a pleasure for me," he said. "It gives me a chance to remember the excitement I felt when I was just starting out."

I understand now exactly what he meant. The optimism, anticipation, and adrenaline of those early years as a flower grower have come flooding back to me as I've written this book. I know that many of you who are reading this are experiencing those same feelings of excitement about your own venture into flower farming. I know that you're heading into one of the most intense, happy, worried, interesting periods of your lives. I wish you well, and would like to part with just a few words of advice about the nontechnical aspects of the business.

First, approach your new business with pure intentions, to provide a quality product while making your own livelihood. Don't start a flower business thinking that you're going to take customers away from an established grower, or from the florist or the supermarket. Try to develop the market. Promote your flowers as an alternative to balloons or candy. Go at it with the idea that you can sell flowers to people who have never bought flowers before. Seek a niche that hasn't been filled in your community.

Second, don't view other small farmers as your competition—think of them as your allies. In this big world of international conglomerates and global trade, we small-scale, sustainable farmers need to stand together. We have more in common than we have dividing us. We need to be looking at marketing cooperatives and information-sharing so that we all can prosper. Maybe we'll even find our friends within the business.

Finally, be persistent. Realize that any new business takes time to establish, and that you won't learn everything from this book or from your first growing season, or even from your first five growing seasons. Enjoy the steep learning curve that lies ahead for you. Don't be discouraged by your mistakes, but vow to learn from them. Be grateful that you have found work that will keep you intellectually challenged, probably for the rest of your life. If you really do love flowers, and you find joy in growing and selling them, you will succeed.

THE USDA PLANT HARDINESS MAP

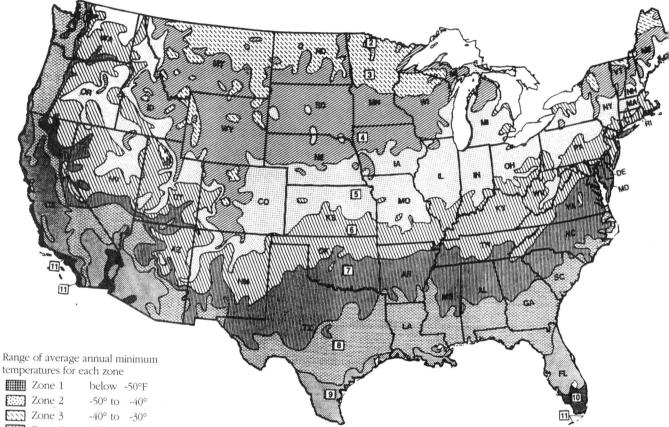

Range of average annual minimum
temperatures for each zone

	Zone 1	below -50°F
	Zone 2	-50° to -40°
	Zone 3	-40° to -30°
	Zone 4	-30° to -20°
	Zone 5	-20° to -10°
	Zone 6	-10° to 0°
	Zone 7	0° to 10°
	Zone 8	10° to 20°
	Zone 9	20° to 30°
	Zone 10	30° to 40°
	Zone 11	Above 40°

Recommended Cut Flowers

THE FOLLOWING SECTION INCLUDES ONE HUNDRED GENERA OF FLOWERS THAT are recognized as good fresh or dried cut flowers. These are the tried-and-true performers. Cultivars are named in some cases, but new ones are introduced annually, so you should use a comprehensive seed catalog along with this list.

Each entry begins with the botanical name of the plant, which I've used because common names often differ regionally and can be confusing. Also, I believe that if you're going to be a flower expert, you should know the real name of the plants you're growing. That's especially true for commercial growers: Florists and wholesalers respect the grower who sounds like an expert, and they appreciate learning Latin names that they in turn can teach their customers. In most cases, the genus name is all that is used in conversation. The pronunciation of the genus name follows in parentheses so you won't have to feel self-conscious about using the Latin. When two pronunciations are widely used, both are given. The common name of the plant follows its botanical name.

Next in order comes the classification of the plant as an annual, biennial, or perennial. Annuals flower the first season, then die. Biennials flower the second season, then die. Perennials will regrow every year from their roots, in the USDA hardiness zones listed (see map opposite). Some perennials may be grown as annuals, and that will be noted in the narrative. Some annuals may appear to be coming back every year, but they are actually self-seeding.

Most annuals do not tolerate frost, and should be planted when the weather is thoroughly settled in spring. Hardy annuals, however, can take a light frost, and can be planted a few weeks before the frost-free date; many can even be seeded in the fall and left to overwinter. This category usually includes the self-seeding types.

The following entries also state the plant's height when fully grown. Stem length is usually about the same height, but exceptions will be noted in the text.

The narrative for each plant gives you general information and advice about how to grow and harvest it. Vase life is provided where it is known; in many cases, though, no data on vase life are available. In general, the flowers in this list are considered good cut flowers because they last at least five days and longer with careful handling. Comments about drying pertain only to air-drying. As was noted in chapter 5, nearly every plant can be preserved, either by air-drying or by some other method.

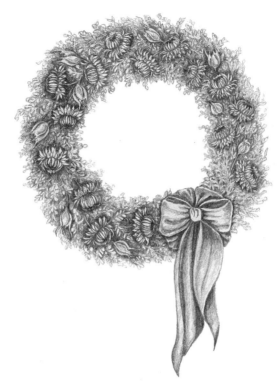

ACHILLEA (ah-kil-LEE-ah), Yarrow

Perennial, Zones 3–9 ⤳ 24–48 inches

There are several species and many cultivars in the yarrow family. Those good for cutting include *A. filipendula, A. millefolium,* and *A. ptarmica.*

The first, *A. filipendula,* is a 4-foot-tall, fern-leaved yarrow with bright gold, flat flowers that can get as big as 4 inches across. It will air-dry beautifully, holding both color and shape, and makes an excellent addition to autumnal wreaths and arrangements. It also is commonly used in the floral trade as a fresh flower. Vase life is seven to twelve days. 'Gold Plate', 'Coronation Gold', and 'Parker's Variety' are all good choices.

A. filipendula can be started from seed or as plants spaced 12 inches apart. Plants can go up to five years before they need to be divided.

Harvest when you can see pollen on the flowers. This is important, particularly for drying. Flowers that are picked before they are fully open will quickly droop in the vase and the cluster will lose its flat, round look when dried. If picked at the right time, they will last more than a week in water.

A. millefolium includes the common roadside white yarrow and its many cultivated cousins in colors that range from bright cherry red to palest pinks and lavenders to earthy peaches and terra-cottas. Highly rated cultivars include 'Fire King', 'Lilac Beauty', 'Rosea', 'Rosy Red', 'Moonshine', and 'Peach Blossom'. They grow 24 to 30 inches tall.

Some cultivars are available as seed. Other cultivars must be purchased as plants, but they will proliferate so rapidly that you will have hundreds of divisions within a few years. They should be planted about 12 inches apart, but will form such a thick mat that you will have to divide them every two or three years.

Like the gold yarrow, *A. millefolium* should be harvested when all flowers in the inflorescence are open and pollen is visible. Vase life is only four or five days. The plants can be air-dried by hanging them upside down.

A. ptarmica is about 20 inches tall and has clusters of small flowers that are used as filler in arrangements. 'The Pearl' and 'Perry's White' are good cultivars. Vase life is five to eight days.

ACONITUM (ak-ah-NY-tum), Monkshood

Perennial, Zones 2–6 ∾ *24–36 inches*

All species of this plant are extremely poisonous. Don't grow it where children can get their hands on it, as even the foliage is toxic. The blue flowers look a bit like delphinium except for the sepal shaped like a hood (which gives the plant its common name). It does best in cool, moist climates, and flowers in late summer.

Aconitum is extremely difficult to grow from seeds, so start with plants spaced 2 feet apart. Harvest when the first two or three flowers on the spike have opened. Vase life is seven to ten days in preservative.

AGAPANTHUS (ag-ah-PAN-thus), Lily-of-the-Nile

Tender Perennial ∾ *24–36 inches*

Agapanthus, with its balls of blue or white flowers, is widely grown on the West Coast in Zones 9 and 10. Elsewhere, it is not hardy. It is a beautiful flower, but its main drawback is that individual florets die and need to be picked off to keep the flower looking good. Harvest when several florets are fully open; the buds will continue to open in the vase for more than a week.

AGASTACHE (AG-uh-stash), Hyssop

Perennial, Zones 5–9 ∾ *36 inches*

There are several *Agastache* species that can be grown as cut flowers, but there appears to be some confusion about this genus, as seed companies have affixed various names to the species. *A. foeniculum*, anise hyssop, is also known as *A. anisata*. It has a nice fragrance and makes a good filler for mixed or herb bouquets, even though the colors are not very bright. You can buy the blue- and white-flowered strains separately. It is easily started from seed.

Two other species that are hardy only in Zones 7 through 10 but can be grown as annuals elsewhere are *A. cana* and *A. barberi*. Both have pink flowers and a lemony fragrance. *A. cana* is 3 feet tall; *A. barberi* 5 feet tall.

AGERATUM HOUSTONIANUM (aj-er-AY-tum, ah-jer-AH-tum), Flossflower

Annual ⌒ *18–24 inches*

In the early part of the century, florists routinely used tall ageratums. The long-stemmed types all but disappeared for a while as breeders focused on the dwarf bedding types that have become so commonplace along the edges of flower beds. Fortunately, the tall types are back, and they're a big hit with flower arrangers. 'Blue Horizon' is an intense medium blue that looks great with the hot colors of summer flowers. 'Florist's White' is a new introduction with the same clusters of fuzzy buttons in pure white.

Ageratum should be started in the greenhouse about two months before your frost-free date. The seed needs light in order to germinate, so cover it with just barely enough vermiculite to keep it moist. Germinate at 80 to 85°F (27 to 29°C); then grow on the seedlings at 60 to 65°F (16 to 18°C). The young plants are very susceptible to cold damage, so don't let them get hit by blasts from open doors or windows in cold weather.

Plant outside when all danger of frost is past; space plants 12 inches apart. Harvest when flowers are just beginning to open and they will keep for a week or more in the vase.

AGROSTEMMA (ag-roh-STEM-ah), Corn Cockle

Annual ⌒ *36 inches*

The silky, speckled rose blooms of agrostemma grow in sprays on thin, willowy stems. It is a charming flower planted in masses in a cottage-garden setting. Agrostemma is lovely in bouquets, although the small stems make it time-consuming to pick. It is best grown in places with cool summers, but you can raise a crop in warmer areas by planting in early spring.

Direct-seed in fall or early spring; space 6 to 9 inches apart. The plants will self-seed.

ALCHEMILLA MOLLIS (al-kem-MILL-ah), Lady's-Mantle

Perennial, Zones 3–7 ⌒ *18 inches*

Flower arrangers rave about the fluffy clouds of lime-green flowers on this plant. Unfortunately, it can be grown well only in cool climates. Start with plants and space them 12 inches apart. Cut when most flowers are fully open. It also can be air-dried.

ALLIUM (AL-ee-um)

Perennial ∾ 12–36 inches

Several species of *Allium* make good choices for cutting and drying. All are grown from bulbs, which multiply rapidly and are easily divided for propagation.

A. aflatunense 'Purple Sensation' is 24 to 36 inches tall, with 4-inch purple balls of flowers and strappy foliage. Bulbs should be planted 2 to 3 inches apart and 4 inches deep. *A. giganteum* grows a foot taller and its flowers measure 5 inches across. *A. sphaerocephalon,* known as drumstick chives, is 24 inches tall, with 2-inch flower heads that start out green and mature to purple. The foliage is thin, like chives. Bulbs can be planted 1 inch apart and 4 inches deep. Vase life is ten to fourteen days.

A. schoenoprasum is the common chive, which flowers early in spring, and makes a good edible flower or addition to herb bouquets. The cultivar 'Forescate' is taller and pinker and considerably more showy in the perennial bed. *A. tuberosum,* garlic chive, has flat clusters of white, star-shaped flowers in late summer on stiff stems. It makes a good cut flower and lasts seven to ten days.

AMARANTHUS (am-uh-RAN-thus), Amaranth

Annual ∾ 36–60 inches

The amaranths are a large genus that includes plants used for food, foliage, and flowers. Direct-sow them after danger of frost, or start them in the greenhouse with germination temperatures of 75 to 80°F (24 to 27°C) and grow them on for six or seven weeks at 65°F (18°C).

A. caudatus, known as love-lies-bleeding, bears long, fuzzy red ropes on 3-foot plants. For fresh use, harvest when at least three-fourths of the dangling flowers are open. For drying, let the seed begin to set; flowers should feel firm. The dangling flowers can be dried by standing them in a can and letting them drape naturally. *A. hypochondriacus* is grown for its bushy, upright spikes of red or green. Amaranth is popular with European gardeners and floral arrangers, so expect to see new ornamental cultivars of this age-old American native plant. Vase life of most varieties is seven to ten days.

AMMI MAJUS (AM-ee), Bishop's Weed, False Queen Anne's Lace

Annual ∾ 24–36 inches

This popular florist filler looks like an elegant cousin to the wild Queen Anne's lace *(Daucus carota)*. It gives bouquets an airy look, and the big, flat clusters of flowers provide contrast in shape. The twisting stems also add interest to arrangements.

Ammi requires alternating day and night temperatures, so it's best to direct-seed it into the field in fall or early spring. If you want to start it in the greenhouse

Recommended Cut Flowers

to get a jump on the season, chill the seed at 40 to 45°F (4 to 7°C) for two weeks before sowing. Daytime temperatures can be in the 80s (high 20s C), but nighttime temperatures in the 50s (10s C) will ensure the best germination rate, so do not bottom heat the seedlings at night.

Transplant or thin the plants to a spacing of 9 to 12 inches apart. The plants don't mind cold, so we often transplant them to the field under plastic tunnels a full month before the frost-free date. Ammi can get very tall and is susceptible to wind damage; most commercial growers therefore use one tier of support netting.

The flowers should be harvested when nearly all the florets are open, but before they start to shed pollen. Vase life is five to eight days. Harvesting too soon will cause them to wilt quickly. Because of the short window of opportunity, these are good flowers to sell locally. Note that the sap from the cut stems, combined with sun, can cause painful contact dermatitis in some people.

AMMOBIUM ALATUM (ah-MOE-bee-um), Winged Everlasting

Annual ∾ *12–30 inches*

Ammobium are tiny, pure white strawflowers with wide yellow centers when fully open. They are one of the few pure white everlastings, and their small size makes them unusual. But they shrink quite a bit when dried, and their stems are often too weak to hold up the heads, so you have to dry quite a few and use them in bunches to have any impact. They are not much to look at in the garden, but they will self-seed if put off in a patch by themselves. They're not a good choice for most commercial growers because of the time needed to harvest them.

A new cultivar, 'Bikini', is more compact and uniform than the species form. The variety 'Grandiflorum' has larger flowers.

Start seeds indoors six weeks before the last expected frost, or direct-seed after the frost-free date. Transplant or thin to 9 inches. In the South, ammobium can be sown in fall.

Harvest when flowers are half-open; they will continue to open as they dry. (If you wait to harvest until the flowers are fully open, the yellow centers will turn brown.) Hang the flowers upside down and dry them quickly for best color retention.

Ammobium also can be used fresh as a filler, and will last more than a week in the vase.

ANEMONE (ah-NEM-oh-nee), Windflower

Perennial, Zones 5–10 ∾ *8–36 inches*

There are several species of anemones that can be grown for cut flowers: *A. coronaria*, poppy anemone, is hardy in Zones 6 through 9, is 8 to 15 inches tall, and is grown from tubers. *A. japonica*, Japanese anemone, is hardy in Zones 5 through 9 and may be grown from seed. The thick stems and bright colors of *A.*

japonica make it popular with florists. It prefers cool weather. Harvest when blossoms are just beginning to open. The vase life of most species is short—about four to six days.

ANTIRRHINUM (an-ti-RYE-num), Snapdragon

Annual ❧ *18–30 inches*

Snapdragons are an important commercial floriculture crop, but most of the ones you see at the florist are grown in greenhouses under carefully controlled conditions to provide long, straight stems. Many people, some florists included, prefer the more casual look of field-grown snaps. They are easy to grow and prolific, and they come in a wonderful mix of colors, from pale pastels to clear brights. I consider them indispensable for the market and home cutting garden.

My favorites for cutting are the 'Rocket' series because of their tall stems. Home gardeners who hope to get some landscape value from snaps might prefer the shorter 'Liberty' series.

Snapdragons should be started indoors at 65 to 70°F (18 to 21°C) or purchased as plugs. Never allow the seedlings to become rootbound, and transplant them to the field at five to six weeks. Snaps are quite tolerant of cool weather, and can be transplanted a month before the frost-free date and protected with row cover. Space them 9 to 12 inches apart.

Snapdragons can get knocked down easily by wind, so it's a good idea to use one layer of support netting. Snaps quickly twist their tips upward, so if they're lying on their sides for even a short time, their stems will develop a nasty bend. The same is true after cutting—leaning the flowers against the side of a half-empty bucket will cause the tips to bend upward. Keep them straight at all times if you want straight stems.

Snapdragons should be harvested when one- to two-thirds of the florets are open. Pollination by insects causes the florets to drop off almost immediately, so if you have a lot of bees, you may prefer to harvest when the first few buds are showing color, then leave the cuttings indoors in floral preservative to bloom. Snaps are highly ethylene-sensitive, so keep them away from vegetables, fruits, cigarettes, and exhaust fumes. Flowers will last up to eight days in the vase.

AQUILEGIA (ack-wi-LEE-gee-ah), Columbine

Perennial, Zones 3–9 ❧ *24–36 inches*

Many cultivars of the wildflower columbine have been bred for use in the perennial bed and as cut flowers. 'McKana Hybrids' are large, long-spurred blossoms with tall stems. The newer 'Songbird' series are shorter, but with lovely pastel pink or blue and white flowers. The 'Barlow' series have double, spurless flowers that hardly look like columbines at all, but have their own charm.

Aquilegia are easily started from seed for flowering the following year, or you can buy plants. Harvest when flowers are more than half-open.

ARMERIA (ar-MEER-ee-ah), Thrift

Perennial, Zones 4–8 ⌇ *12–18 inches*

Though armeria is short, its stiff stems and bright pink ball-shaped flowerheads make it a favorite with flower arrangers. To start from seed, soak the seeds for six to eight hours, then germinate at 70°F (21°C). Space plants 12 inches apart. Cut when the blossom is fully colored. Armeria can be air-dried by hanging.

ASCLEPIAS (as-KLEE-pee-as), Butterfly Weed

Perennial, Zones 3–8 ⌇ *24–36 inches*

Several species are available to the cut-flower grower. *A. tuberosa* is the native butterfly weed with bright orange, yellow, or red flowers. *A. incarnata,* known as swamp milkweed, has flowers of dusty pink, red, or white. *A. curassavica* is a fall-blooming red flower.

A recent introduction of *A. curassavica,* 'Silky Gold', has pale orange flowers and long stems. It is hardy only to Zone 8, but blooms the first year from seed, so it can be grown as an annual.

Stems should be placed in hot water (120°F, 50°C) for one minute immediately after harvest to stop bleeding of milky sap. Vase life is ten to fourteen days.

ASTER (AS-ter)

Perennial, Zones 3–7 ⌇ *12–36 inches*

Three species of the perennial asters make good cut flowers. They are *Aster ericoides* (September aster); *Aster novae-angliae* (New England aster); and *Aster novi-belgii* (New York aster or Michaelmas daisy). All three have small, daisy like blooms arranged in sprays on the stem. *A. ericoides* 'Monte Casino' is widely grown in the floral trade as a filler. Colors of the others range from white to purple to hot pink. Hybrids of these species are also increasingly popular as cut flowers. Now widely available to florists is the hybrid *Aster × Solidago,* which is a hybrid of the aster and the goldenrod. The sprays of small, yellow flowers are used as a filler.

All the perennial asters flower in late summer or fall. Start with plants and give them plenty of space—12 to 24 inches. Cut when at least two to four flowers are open. Vase life is five to seven days in water.

Note that the perennial asters are not to be confused with the annual China asters (see *Callistephus chinensis*). ·

ASTILBE × ARENDSII (uh-STILL-bee), False Goat's-Beard

Perennial, Zones 4–8 ⌁ 24–48 inches

Astilbes are lovely plants that provide good color even in full shade. Their plumes can be white to red, and every shade of pink in between. They need plenty of water and do best in cool summers. Start with plants.

Harvest for fresh-flower use when one-half to three-fourths of the flowers on the plume are open. To prolong vase life, put freshly cut stems into hot water (130°F, 54°C), then let it cool to room temperature. If you use floral preservative in the vase, the flowers should last up to twelve days.

Astilbes also can be dried by standing them in a vase with just an inch or two of water and allowing the vase to dry out. For drying, harvest when the flowers are completely open.

ASTRANTIA (as-TRAN-she-ah, as-TRAN-tee-a), Masterwort

Perennial, Zones 4–6 ⌁ 24–28 inches

Starry flowers of pink or greenish white look like buttons surrounded by paper collars. They grow only in areas with cool nights. Seeds are difficult to start, so buy plants and space them 12 inches apart. Harvest when the top flowers are fully open; if you harvest too soon, they will wilt.

BUDDLEIA DAVIDII (bud-LEE-ah, BUD-lee-ah), Butterfly Bush

Perennial, Zones 5–8 ⌁ 5–10 feet

Although this is a woody shrub, I've included it here because it was listed as a favorite cut flower by growers in several regions (see chapter 1). These lovely bushes are an example of a plant that blooms on the current season's growth. They will grow to an astonishing size in one summer from small plants. You can start with rooted cuttings, thirty-six to the flat, and plant them 18 inches apart. When the first inflorescences bloom, be sure to cut them with long stems, leaving just a few nodes at the base of the plant. New stems will emerge from near the ground to provide you with a supply of long stems throughout the summer. Cut alternating branches, being sure to leave at least one-third of the plant intact. In most places, buddleia will die back in winter. Cut it in late winter to within 6 inches of the ground.

For the best cut flowers, harvest when half the flowers on the spike are open, but before the flowers that opened first begin to fade. Drop the stems immediately into hot (100°F, 38°C) water and let the water cool. If the stems aren't turgid, recut and put them in hot water again. With proper conditioning, the flowers will last five to eight days. (White flowers discolor quickly, and the darker purples seem to last longest.) Flowers also can be dried, and they remain fragrant.

CALENDULA (ka-LEN-djew-lah), Pot-Marigold

Annual ∾ 18 inches

Calendulas produce bright yellow, gold, and orange flowers in cool weather. In hot climates, they burn out by July. The petals are edible, and are usually sprinkled like confetti on salads or soups. For cutting, grow a tall variety like 'Prince'. Harvest when fully open. Because calendula tolerates cold weather, you can grow both a spring and fall crop.

CALLISTEPHUS CHINENSIS (kal-LIS-te-fus), China Aster

Annual ∾ 12–36 inches

The annual asters have long been grown as a florist's crop, but they have normally been grown under cloth in the field or in cloth-covered greenhouses. That's because they are highly susceptible to aster yellows, a virus that causes many plants in the aster family to become deformed and turn green to yellow in color. Aster yellows is transmitted by leafhoppers, so if you live in an area where leafhoppers are a problem, you might as well forget about asters. (Call your Cooperative Extension agent to find out if aster yellows is common in your area.)

However, if you can grow asters, you have a wide array of cultivars to choose from. Either buy a mixture or select the size and colors you want. Start the seeds indoors and transplant to the field after danger of frost. Flowers should be harvested when they're about half-open.

In the best circumstances, vase life is only about five days, and aster stems often droop even before the flowers wilt, which results in a shorter vase life. (Commercial growers treat them with silver thiosulfate to increase vase life, but this is not acceptable for organic growers.)

CAMPANULA (kam-PAN-yew-luh), Bellflower

Perennial, Zones 3–6 ∾ 18–30 inches

There are several species of *Campanula* that make great cut flowers as well as good plants for the perennial border. The best are *C. glomerata*, which has clusters of tiny violet flowers; *C. persicifolia*, with 2-inch bells of blue or white; and *C. pyramidalis*, with 5-foot-tall spikes. Seed is tiny, but can be started in the greenhouse, or you can buy plants. Harvest when one to two flowers on the stem are open. Vase life is one week in water, or longer with preservative.

CARTHAMUS TINCTORIUS (KAR-tha-mus), Safflower

Hardy Annual ∾ 36 inches

Thistle-like flowers in orange, yellow, or white are grown for fresh or dried use. The species has thorny leaves that make them difficult to cut, but newer introductions are supposed to be thornless. Plants are difficult to transplant, so direct-seed them after danger of frost. Thin to 12 inches apart. Cut for fresh use when the petals on the majority of buds on the stem are beginning to open. The foliage will wilt before the flowers. Vase life is one week. For dried flowers, let the blossoms open fully, then hang to dry.

CELOSIA ARGENTEA (sel-OH-she-ah)
Annual ⤳ 24–36 inches

Three varieties are great for cutting: *cristata* are the cockscomb (crested) types; *plumosa* are the feathery types; *spicata* are the relatively new wheat celosias.

All can be started indoors, but they tend to be susceptible to damping-off disease, so don't let them get too cool and moist. They also can be direct-seeded after danger of frost has passed. Plants get big, so give them 12 to 18 inches of space.

All three types of celosia will flower from midsummer until frost, and all will last at least a week in the vase. Harvest the crested types when they're fully open; the plumed types can be harvested when the plumes are 90 percent open. If you let celosias grow for a month after they've started flowering, the blooms will become immense. Some growers report cockscomb flowers as large as 8 inches across and 14 inches long.

All varieties can be air-dried by hanging them upside down (remove the foliage first), although the cockscomb types are the most popular for arrangements and wreaths. The wheat celosias become very fragile when dried and must be handled carefully to prevent them from shattering.

CENTAUREA CYANUS (sen-TAW-ree-uh, sen-taw-REE-uh), Cornflower, Bachelor's Button
Annual ⤳ 24–48 inches

The silvery rosettes of centaurea are some of the earliest plants to appear in the garden, having self-seeded from the previous year. They are beautiful in a mass (be careful you don't get mesmerized by them swaying in the breeze), and they make charming cut flowers. However, they are labor-intensive to cut and command a low price, so many commercial growers have decided not to raise them.

In Zones 5–10, you can sow the seed in the garden in fall for the next year's crop. Or you can start seeding early in spring and plant several times for a longer period of bloom.

Harvest when one-quarter to one-half the flowers are open. The vase life is one week. Bechelor's button can be air-dried.

C. moschata, sweet sultan, also can be grown for cutting. It has a sweet fragrance and puffy flowers of pink and white. Treat it the same as bachelor's button.

CENTAUREA MACROCEPHALA

Perennial, Zones 3–7 ∼ *2–4 feet*

Four-inch golden blooms, similar to thistles in shape, top this big-leaved plant. It is easily grown from seed, or you can purchase plants. For fresh flowers, cut when the blooms are one-half to three-quarters open. For drying, cut when the yellow petals are still just a tuft at the top of the flower. Vase life is one week.

CHRYSANTHEMUM LEUCANTHEMUM (kris-ANTH-e-mum), Shasta Daisy

Perennial, Zones 4–9 ∼ *24 inches*

Shasta daisies have a yellow center and pure white petals, and no matter how commonplace they may be, they still are the epitome of freshness. They can be used in colorful mixed bouquets, sold by the bunch, or made into all-white arrangements. If you have native daisies in your pastures or meadows, try moving a few plants into the garden and watch how much bigger the flowers grow. Seeds are started easily, or you can buy plants. Grow several cultivars to extend the daisy season. Space them 12 inches apart. Harvest when the petals are half open. Vase life is seven to ten days.

CHRYSANTHEMUM PARTHENIUM, Feverfew

Perennial, Zones 6–9 ∼ *12–18 inches*

Taxonomists have been renaming many of the plants formerly known as *Chrysanthemum,* so you may find feverfew now listed as *Tanacetum parthenium.* Small, fully double white or yellow flowers are used as a filler. Several new pure white cultivars are advertised as "florist strain," but they are tender and should be grown as annuals. Vase life is seven to ten days.

CLARKIA AMOENA (CLARK-ee-ah), Satinflower

Annual ∼ *36 inches*

This Rocky Mountain native requires cool weather in order to bloom well. The 2-inch ruffled flowers are available in a number of colors. Clarkia can be started indoors or direct-seeded in early spring.

This plant is considered by some authorities to be the same as godetia, which is an important commercial cut flower (see Godetia later in this list).

CLEOME (klee-OH-me), Spiderflower

Annual ⮔ 48–72 inches

Cleome, an old-fashioned flower, has recently begun to gain acceptance as a cut flower. It is a short-lived one, though, and therefore only good for local markets. Even after it drops its petals, the big balls retain their shape and add an airy touch to bouquets. It can be started indoors or seeded directly after danger of frost.

CONSOLIDA AMBIGUA (con-SOL-i-dah), Larkspur

Annual ⮔ 48–60 inches

Larkspur is one of the most important cut flowers for small- and large-scale commercial growers. It is a staple in florists' shops, widely used as a dried flower, easily grown, and a prolific bloomer. In short, it is a flower that you *must* plant.

Larkspur needs a period of vernalization, or exposure to cold, of at least six weeks below 55°F (13°C). In the South, in coastal California, and northward through Zone 5, seeds are planted directly into the field in the fall. Farther north, seed should be sown as early in spring as the ground can be worked. (Many northern growers also start the seed indoors and plant out small plugs. However, be aware that flowering will not occur until that six-week cold period has been fulfilled, so you must grow the plugs in a 50°F (10°C) greenhouse or a cold frame for two months.)

When direct-seeding larkspur, you can use a push seeder. Be sure to plant in straight lines to make weeding easier. The plants will form a rosette while the weather remains cool; then the stems will shoot up as the weather warms and days lengthen.

For fresh flowers, harvest when about one-third of the flowers on the stem are open. Put them immediately in water; floral preservative will greatly enhance the vase life of larkspur. For dried flowers, harvest when all flowers are open. Bunch and hang them upside down to dry in a warm, dark place.

COREOPSIS TINCTORIA (kor-ee-OP-sis), Calliopsis

Annual ⮔ 30–48 inches

Calliopsis produces 1-inch daisylike flowers of gold with a red center that make an excellent filler in mixed bouquets. It can be planted anytime in spring. Direct-seed or start with transplants spaced 8 inches apart. Plants need good drainage. In some locations, calliopsis gets so tall that it needs to be grown with support to prevent it from toppling over in a wind.

There seems to be some confusion in the seed trade between the tall species and a dwarf cultivar. Be sure you're getting the tall one.

COSMOS BIPINNATUS (KOZ-mos)

Annual ᑎ 36–60 inches

The pink, rose, and white daisylike flowers of cosmos are favorites of local flower growers because they are easily grown, produce lots of flowers, and are charming in bouquets. However, they do not have a long vase life, so they are best grown for local markets.

Seeds can be started in the greenhouse or sown directly into the field. Cosmos is a quantitative short-day plant, which means it flowers best under short-daylength conditions but will flower even during long days if the plant is mature enough. The significance for the grower is this: If you direct-seed cosmos in spring after danger of frost, the plants will flower only sparsely during the long days of summer, but then will really take off as the daylength drops below about fourteen hours of light per day. However, if you start your plants in the greenhouse, they will be mature enough by midsummer that they will flower even under the long days. Take your pick, or grow some each way to promote a long season of cosmos bloom. 'Sensation' is the tall, airy-looking mix of pink, rose, and white. Newer cultivars with stronger stems include 'Versailles' and 'Imperial' mixes, which are as tall as 'Sensation', and the 24-inch 'Sonata' series. Another nice one is 'Seashells', which has tubular petals.

Harvest cosmos when the petals on the first flower are just beginning to open. Cut a long stem, regardless of the number of unopened buds on it, because the plant will branch below the cut and produce many more long stems.

CROCOSMIA (kro-KOZ-mee-uh), Montbretia

Perennial, Zones 5–9 ᑎ 24–48 inches

Crocosmia are grown from corms and should be hardy as far north as Zone 5. (I'm in Zone 5, however, and recently lost a big bed of them to an unusually cold and dry winter.) They make a striking cut flower. The thin spikes bear upward-facing flowers in bold shades of red and orange.

They should be purchased as corms, and planted 6 inches apart when the weather warms. They will need to be divided every four years or so.

Harvest when the first few flowers are showing color or just beginning to open. They'll last seven to ten days in preservative. Alternatively, they may be air-dried upside down. The pods in fall are also attractive and may be sold to florists.

CYNOGLOSSUM AMABILE (sin-oh-GLOSS-um), Chinese Forget-Me-Not

Annual ᑎ 24–30 inches

The lovely soft blue of cynoglossum is so unusual it makes this plant worth growing. New cultivars are also available in pink and white. It's a great addition to bouquets, but you may find some resistance from florists because the spent blossoms drop their petals. New flowers open to replace the dropped ones, but some people don't like having petals showering on their tables. Other people don't mind at all, though, so you'll have to find out whether it will work for your customers.

Seed can be started indoors or outdoors as soon as the soil can be worked. Harvest the flowers as soon as a few are open.

DAHLIA (DAHL-yah)

Tender Perennial ∽ *24–48 inches*

Recommended Cut Flowers

Dahlias are grown from tubers that must be lifted after the first frost in fall and replanted in spring everywhere except Zones 7 through 10. A huge number of cultivars is available, from small, delicate pompons to doubles as big as dinner plates. The American Dahlia Society recognizes twelve different groups, based on flower structure.

Dahlias can be started either from purchased tubers or from seed, and many will bloom the first year from seed. Plant them out in the field after the weather has warmed, and give each plant about 2 feet of space. Tall dahlias need to be supported; many growers use wire tomato cages or three bamboo stakes surrounded by twine. To keep the tubers over the winter, dig the clumps and let them dry thoroughly, then put in boxes and cover with dry peat moss or sawdust. Store at 40–50°F (4–10°C).

Dahlias are one of the few flowers that cannot be cut in the bud—they simply won't open. Wait until they are fully open before cutting them, and they will last five to seven days in floral preservative. To dry, cut just before they are fully open, and hang them upside down.

DELPHINIUM (del-FIN-ee-um)

Perennial, Zones 2–7 ∽ *36–48 inches*

Delphiniums are standard fare in the floral trade. Florists can get two types: the Belladonna hybrids, which have smaller, more open flowers and an airy appearance; and the Wrexham hybrids, which have double, closely spaced columns of flowers on taller stems. They are commercially grown in both greenhouse and field, and are available to florists year-round.

You should think hard about whether delphiniums fit into your plans. If you live in a cool, moist climate, you should be able to grow them easily, so they could be a good choice. If your climate is less hospitable, however, you may not earn enough money to make them worthwhile.

Delphiniums will flower the first year from seed if they have had enough cold weather, so fall planting is generally recommended. Either start the seed in the greenhouse in summer for fall transplanting, or buy plants in fall. The tall hybrids will need to be supported in windy areas. Belladonna types are shorter and don't need support in most locations.

Harvest delphiniums when one-fourth of the flowers are open. Vase life is about a week. They are highly ethylene-sensitive, though, so keep them away from cigarettes, fruits, and vegetables. For dried flowers, harvest when nearly all the flowers are open and hang the stems upside down in a warm, dark place.

DIANTHUS BARBATUS (die-AN-thus), Sweet William

Biennial, Zones 3–7 ⤳ 12–24 inches

Dianthus is a huge genus of flowers with about eighteen species, most of which are called pinks. Only a few species and several more hybrids are tall enough for cutting. By far the most important species in the floral trade is the carnation *(Dianthus caryophyllus)*. It is so commonplace and inexpensive, however, that most small growers won't find it profitable to grow.

A better choice is *D. barbatus,* or sweet William. The faintly sweet-smelling flowers are arranged in tight clusters. Colors include red, pink, rose, purple, white, and bicolors. Sweet William flowers the second season after planting on stems about 15 to 24 inches long. It prefers cool weather, and will flower only in spring in hot climates.

Flowers should be harvested when about one-fourth of blossoms in the inflorescence are open. They will open more slowly inside than outside once the weather heats up, so you can cut more than you need and store them in water if they all start to bloom at once. Vase life is seven to fourteen days.

Dianthus
barbatus
Sweet William

DIGITALIS (dij-i-TAH-lis), Foxglove

Biennial, Zones 4–7 ⤳ 36–48 inches

These towering spikes of bell-shaped blooms make dramatic cut flowers, but all parts of the plant are poisonous, so be careful if you have youngsters in your gardens. Foxglove can be grown from seed or plants, and will flower the second year. Cut when about one-third to one-half the flowers are open.

ECHINACEA (eck-i-NAY-see-uh), Coneflower

Perennial, Zones 3–8 ⤳ 30–36 inches

The droopy prairie wildflowers that are coveted for their medicinally useful roots (*E. angustifolia* and *E. pallida*) are cousins to the more glamorous *E. purpurea*, which is a great cut flower. Several cultivars, including 'Magnus' and 'Bright Star', have been bred to form bright pink petals that don't droop. There are also a couple of white cultivars. Besides their bright color and interesting central disc, these echinaceas also offer the benefit of blooming for several months, from mid-summer until fall.

Start them from seed or buy plants. They aren't particularly demanding about fertility or water, although they do perform better and longer when coddled a little bit. Harvest the flowers when the petals have just started to unfurl, and they should last at least a week in preservative. For dried material, harvest older flowers and pluck the petals off them. Then hang the brown discs to dry.

ECHINOPS (EK-i-nops), Globe-Thistle

Perennial, Zones 3–8 36–60 inches

Globular, spiky violet-blue flowers are valued both fresh and dried. Plants grow huge, so space them at least 2 feet apart. Leaves are prickly, so use gloves when handling the plants. For fresh flowers, harvest when at least three-fourths of the flowers in the head are open. Vase life is six to twelve days, but the foliage will decline before the flowers. For drying, harvest just before the tiny florets open, but after the heads have turned a lavender-blue. Hang them upside down to dry.

EMILIA JAVANICA (ee-MIL-ee-ah), Tasselflower

Annual 12–24 inches

Emilia is a little-used cut flower because the individual red or orange blossoms are small, less than a half-inch in diameter. They make a bright addition to a bouquet, though, and they're easily grown. Start the seed indoors and plant out after danger of frost. Harvest when several flowers on the stem are half-open.

ERYNGIUM (air-IN-jee-um), Sea Holly

Perennial, Zones 4–7 24–36 inches

E. planum has steel-blue globular flowers that are surrounded by spiky bracts. A biennial species, *E. giganteum,* has smaller flowers but wider, silvery bracts that look great in a landscape planting. Both species can be used for cutting and drying. Wait until the flower heads have turned blue before cutting. Storing them in a 40°F (4°C) cooler will intensify the color. To dry, hang or stand them upright in a dark, dry place.

EUPHORBIA MARGINATA (you-FOR-bee-ah), Snow-on-the-Mountain

Annual 36 inches

This euphorbia has thick, succulent leaves like the other spurges, but it is tall and upright. It is used for its variegated foliage. It should be direct-seeded after danger of frost. Harvest when the upper leaves are almost pure white and larger leaves beneath are lined in white. Like all euphorbias, it can cause allergic skin reactions because of its milky sap. To stop the sap from bleeding, plunge the cut stems into hot water for a few minutes. Vase life is about one week.

EUSTOMA GRANDIFLORUM (you-STOH-ma, YOU-stoh-mah), Lisianthus

Annual ❧ 24–36 inches

One of the most elegant, valuable, and—unfortunately—difficult cut flowers is lisianthus. When well grown, it produces sprays of 2-inch flowers that look like roses. Lisianthus is available in pinks, white, yellow, purple, and bicolors, both singles and doubles. The cultivars most widely grown commercially are 'Heidi' and 'Flamenco', with single flowers, and 'Echo', with double flowers.

The trick to growing lisianthus well is to ensure that it never becomes rootbound. Once the roots begin to curl around the bottom of the pot, it's too late—the plant will never reach its potential height in the field. Lisianthus is extremely slow-growing at first, and is easy to overwater for the three months or so that it will sit in the greenhouse. Unless you can pay constant attention to your seedlings, you're better off buying plugs from a reputable dealer and planting them out in the field immediately to prevent them getting rootbound. The plants require excellent drainage in the field.

Lisianthus produces many buds at the top of its thin stem, so the plants tend to be heavy-headed and need to be grown on support netting. They should be planted about 6 inches apart. If you pinch the terminal bud, you will get a spray of flowers all blooming at the same time. If you let the terminal bud go, wait until it is in full bloom and the secondary buds are fully colored before you pick it. Vase life in preservative is up to two weeks, as buds continue to open indoors.

GEUM QUELLYON (JEE-um)

Perennial, Zones 5–8 ❧ 24 inches

A small but bright addition to bouquets, geum produces 1-inch blooms in bright yellow or red. It thrives in cool, moist climates. Plant 12 inches apart. Harvest when the flower is just beginning to open.

GLADIOLUS (glad-ee-OH-lus)

Perennial, Zones 8–10 ❧ 36 inches

Glads are widely grown as a cut flower both in the United States and abroad. In this country, Michigan and Florida are the main production areas, and when the crops come in there, the price of glads drops to 25 cents per stem or less.

Despite their saturation in the floral trade, glads can be a good crop for local growers selling at farmers' markets. Because of their size, they command up to $1 per stem from the consumer.

Gladiolus corms are priced according to size, with #1s being largest and most expensive. Most commercial growers plant #2 or #3 corms. Plant them after the last frost, spacing as closely as 2 inches apart, 4 to 5 inches deep. Planting an assortment of cultivars will spread the bloom time over a longer period. Al-

Eustoma
grandiflorum
Lisianthus

though glads can be overwintered in Zones 8 through 10, the corms must be dug up after frost everywhere else. Or you can just let them get killed by the cold; with the corms costing just a few cents each, it may be cheaper to buy new ones every year than to dig the old ones.

Glads should be harvested when half the flowers are open, if you're selling at a farmers' market. If selling to florists, harvest when one or two flowers are open. Glads exhibit what is known as negative geotropism, which means they turn away from gravity. Laid flat on their sides, the tips will bend upward, giving the stems a nasty 90-degree bend. Allowed to lean in a bucket, the tips will curve upward in a more appealing arc. If you want ramrod-straight glads, you must keep them straight up at all times.

If your water is fluoridated, fill your buckets and let them sit at room temperature for several hours before putting glads into them. Even low concentrations of fluoride can cause tip burn and leaf burn in glads. Glads need extra sugar in the water to get buds to open. They should not be put in a cooler until nearly all flowers are open.

GODETIA (go-DEE-shee-uh), Satinflower

Hardy Annual ❧ 18–30 inches

A flower best grown in cool, wet climates, godetia has satiny petals in intense colors. It has become widely available to florists in recent years, thanks to abundant West Coast production. It does not like temperatures over 75° (24°C), which limits its potential for most of the country. Godetia can be grown as a single stem with close spacing, or as a spray when planted 2 feet apart. Harvest when the first flower on the stem is fully open. Vase life can be up to two weeks, as new flowers continue to open.

GOMPHRENA (gom-FREE-nah), Globe-Amaranth

Annual ❧ 24 inches

The clover-like blossoms of gomphrena are not very glamorous as a cut flower, but they are so prolific and reliable that they are widely grown anyway. There are several species, comprising several different colors. *G. globosa* is the mixture of pink, white, and purple, plus the aptly named 'Lavender Lady' and a new soft pink-and-white called 'Bicolor Rose'. *G. haageana* is orange and less rounded than *G. globosa*. There is also a bright red cultivar called 'Strawberry fields'.

Gomphrena is easily grown from seed started in the greenhouse. It should be transplanted to the field after all danger of frost, and given at least 9 inches of spacing, as the plants branch low to the ground and can become tangled in one another if grown too close together.

Gomphrena produces a few flowers in early summer, but really starts blooming in midsummer. Harvest when most of the flowers on the stem have good

177

color. They can be harvested as single stems, about 15 inches long, or entire branches can be cut near the ground. They can be used as filler in fresh bouquets, and will last one week. To air-dry, strip the foliage and hang them upside down.

GYPSOPHILA (jip-SOFF-il-ah), Baby's Breath

Annual and Perennial, Zones 3–7 ⚬ *24–48 inches*

The annual species of baby's breath, *G. elegans*, has half-inch blossoms in a range of colors. It should be direct-seeded in spring, and thinned to about 10 inches, with successive plantings made every week until midsummer.

The perennial species, *G. paniculata*, has smaller flowers in white or pink, and the sprays create an excellent, airy filler. Give the plants 2 feet of space in each direction to prevent tangling of the highly branched stems. Harvest when two-thirds of the flowers are open, but before the older flowers begin to turn brown. For drying, harvest when most flowers are open, then stand them upright in buckets with just an inch of water. As the water evaporates and is taken up by the stem, the flowers will dry slowly. For a softer look, preserve with glycerine (see chapter 5).

HELIANTHUS ANNUUS (hee-lee-AN-thus), Sunflower

Annual ⚬ *24–120 inches*

At least thirty cultivars of sunflowers are available to growers, from the 2-foot-tall 'Teddy Bear' to the 10-foot 'Russian Giant'. The best sunflowers for cutting are the pollenless cultivars, which at this writing include 'Sunbright', 'Moonbright', 'Sunbeam', 'Sunrich Orange', and 'Sunrich Lemon'. Because sunflowers are one of the hottest items in the flower world, you can expect to see more pollenless introductions in the future (see chapter 1).

Direct-seed or transplant small plants 9 to 12 inches apart after danger of frost. Harvest when petals are just beginning to unfurl and put in preservative to finish opening, or wait until they are fully open and put in water. Flowers last seven to ten days, although the foliage declines more quickly.

For drying, the best cultivar is 'Sunbright'. It should be harvested when half-open and hung upside down to air-dry. The petals will curl up around the disc.

HELICHRYSUM BRACTEATUM (heli-KRI-sum), Strawflower

Hardy Annual ⚬ *36–48 inches*

I was about 10 years old the first time I saw a strawflower, and I remember how amazed I was that a living plant could produce something so stiff and static. Over the years, my appreciation for strawflowers has deepened. They are essential for the dried-flower grower, and they make a great cut flower if harvested at just the right time. Alas, I find them difficult to grow well because of the disease aster yellows, and I have eliminated them from my commercial planting. But I still sneak a few plants in at the end of a row most years, hoping they might surprise me.

Strawflowers can be direct-seeded after danger of frost, or set out as small plants 10 to 12 inches apart. Some cultivars can grow to over 4 feet tall, and they are not particularly good-looking plants, so don't put them in a prominent place. 'Monstrosum' produces bigger flowers on shorter plants and is a good choice for most purposes. You will find several color selections, including pearly pastels and brights.

For fresh use, cut the flowers when they are almost, but not quite, fully open. If you let them fully open, the centers turn brown. But when cut partially open, the flowers will finish opening in water, and you will have a bright yellow center surrounded by the cheerful strawlike petals.

For drying, harvest when the outer petals start to open; they will continue opening as they dry. You can hang them by the stems, but the heads will prove top-heavy when they're dry, so you might as well wire them while they're fresh. Just push a florist wire into the back of the flower and stand it upright in a can. The flower will tighten onto the wire as it dries. If you know you'll be using just the blossom, you can simply pinch off the flowers and dry them in a basket, with plenty of air circulation to prevent mold.

HESPERIS MATRONALIS (HES-per-is), Sweet Rocket

Biennial, Zones 3–8 ∿ 36 inches

Hesperis is one of the first flowers to bloom in my garden in early spring. Although it is technically a biennial, the plants reseed themselves readily, and so will appear in approximately the same place every year. The purple, white, and mauve flowers are fragrant and similar in appearance to phlox. They are easily started from seed.

HEUCHERA (HEW-kerr-ah), Coral-Bells

Perennial, Zones 3–8 ∿ 18–24 inches

There's no denying that a spray of coral-bells looks fetching in a spring bouquet. But they are such tiny flowers that most commercial growers don't bother with them. They like cool, protected, partially shady spaces. They should be planted 12 inches apart, as they will spread in hospitable places. Harvest when most of the flowers on the stem are open.

HOSTA (HOS-tah), Plantain Lily

Perennial, Zones 3–8 ∿ 18–48 inches

The hostas are a useful and diverse group of plants, ranging from tiny mounds for edging a garden to huge plants used as an understory in woodland settings. They do well in deep shade to part sun, and some can even handle full sun. Both foliage and flowers are used in arrangements. Harvest the leaves when they are fresh and unmarred by insects, and cut the flowers when the first three or four flowers on the stem are fully open.

IRIS (EYE-ris)

Perennial, Zones 3–8 ∾ 12–36 inches

The genus *Iris* is one of the largest groups of garden plants, and several species are popular as cut flowers. Iris are divided into two categories: those grown from bulbs and those grown from rhizomes.

The most commonly grown bulbous types are the Dutch iris. They are shorter than most other iris species, and are beardless. They usually produce only two flowers per stem, in colors that include white, yellow, blue, and bronze. Plant them in the fall, 3 to 6 inches apart, as they produce some foliage before winter sets in. Late frosts are a threat to the emerging flowers in spring. They should be harvested in the "pencil stage," that is, when a pencil of color is visible but before the flower opens.

Among the rhizomatous iris grown for cutting are the Siberian and spuria iris. Siberian iris bloom early, along with the tall bearded types, on stems up to 4 feet tall. Spuria iris come into bloom just as the Siberians are ending, with a large number of flowers on long stems. The rhizomatous iris need to be planted in early fall, so they have enough time to get established before the freeze-and-thaw cycle of early winter. They also can be planted in early spring before growth begins.

Bearded iris, sometimes mistakenly called German iris, are wonderful, fragrant flowers with several blooms that open in succession in the vase. However, they don't sell well because most people don't want to have to pinch off the wet flowers that have died. The dark purple ones, in particular, can drip an inky fluid as they die.

KNIPHOFIA (nye-FOE-fee-uh), Red-Hot Poker

Perennial, Zones 5–9 ∾ 36 inches

These rocket-shaped spikes of tubular flowers in bright yellows and oranges are sometimes still sold under their former botanical name *Tritoma*. Most cultivars bloom in late summer. I have one unidentified variety given to me by a friend that blooms in early summer, along with the larkspur.

These unusual flowers are a matter of taste. Some people really like them, while others find them bizarre. They may be more useful if you use them in bouquets than if you attempt to sell them outright to florists or wholesalers. Start with plants and space them 18 inches apart, as they multiply rapidly. Cut when the inflorescence is fully colored but before the bottom tier of flowers deteriorates. Plunge the hollow stems into water quickly. Vase life is seven to ten days.

LATHYRUS (LATH-ir-us), Sweet Pea

Annual ❧ *Climbs to 10 feet*

Recently a watercolor artist told me that she had been thinking about a vase of sweet peas she had seen on my dining room table six months earlier. The image of those flowers kept coming back to her, she said. Sweet peas, with their glowing colors and heady fragrance, make an impression on people. The world would be a better place if we all had sweet peas on the breakfast table. Unfortunately, they're a tough crop to grow in the hotter regions of the country; they prefer cool, moist climates. You will find them blooming riotously in July in New England or Northern California, but in most places they are an early summer crop.

Prepare the planting beds in the fall, making sure you have good drainage— sweet peas will not tolerate wet feet. Install a strong trellis, 8 to 10 feet tall, depending on how long your cool season lasts. Before planting, the seeds should be soaked in warm water for twenty-four hours. If you live in the North or in coastal California, you can plant the seeds directly into the field at the same time you plant garden peas. In hotter climates, start sweet-pea seeds indoors in 4-inch peat pots six weeks before pea-planting time. Start them at 68°F (20°C), but lower the temperature to 50°F (10°C) when the plants are a few inches tall. Two weeks before planting out, put them in a cold frame, but be sure it doesn't go below 32°F (0°C). Then plant them along the trellis, about 4 to 6 inches apart.

Harvest sweet peas when one flower is fully open and one is starting to open. Each flower will last only a few days, but other buds will open on the stem, providing a vase life of six to ten days.

LAVANDULA (lav-AN-djew-lah), Lavender

Perennial, Zones 5–9 ❧ *18–36 inches*

Lavender is widely grown for drying, and it makes a good fresh flower as well. There are several species with different colors and scents, but not all are hardy to Zone 5, so check hardiness when selecting plants. Lavenders need well-drained soil and plenty of sun. They have a vase life of eight to ten days fresh, or can be hung upside down to dry.

LAVATERA TRIMESTRIS (la-va-TEER-uh)

Annual ❧ *24–36 inches*

The shimmery, mallow-shaped flowers of lavatera are a great cut flower for cool climates. Elsewhere, they're chancy: some years, you'll get tall, full plants, and other years they'll be stunted and crispy. But they're worth the effort, in my opinion.

'Silver Cup' is a rose-pink; 'Mont Blanc' is a pearly white. Plant seeds directly outdoors in early spring and thin to 2 feet apart, because the plants grow like rounded shrubs. Harvest when the flowers are just beginning to open. Vase life is about one week.

LEPIDIUM (le-PID-ee-um), Peppergrass

Annual ∿ 24 inches

Lepidium is a genus of plants that are generally known as mustards. They are considered spring weeds by most farmers, but there are several cultivars grown for drying that are much taller and more dramatic than the natives. Lepidium is grown for the hundreds of tiny seedpods on each stem, which dry well and lend an airy look to dried floral designs. Flowers should be picked when the terminal bloom is nearly complete and the pods are immature.

LIATRIS SPICATA (lye-A-triss), Blazing-Star, Gayfeather

Perennial, Zones 3–9 ∿ 18–48 inches

Liatris is a native of the North American prairies, but it is the Dutch who produce it in huge quantities for the floral trade. The spiky purple or white flowers don't command a good price; they are easy to grow, however, so raising them is a judgement call for small commercial growers.

Plant corms 2 to 4 inches apart and 2 to 3 inches below the surface of the soil. Harvest when half the flowers on the stem are open, and they will last seven to twelve days in the vase. For drying, pick when three-fourths of the flowers are open, and hang them upside down.

LILIUM (LIL-ee-um), Lilies

Perennial, Zones 3–8 ∿ 24–72 inches

There are many kinds of lilies, but those most commonly available to florists are the Asiatics and Orientals. Most of them are grown in greenhouses under carefully controlled conditions, producing long stems with many flowers on each. They usually are not commercially grown in the field, but it can be done.

With hundreds of cultivars to choose from, you should look for stem length, color, and time of bloom. Remember that you have to leave a third of the plant intact if you expect it to come back next year, so choose cultivars that will have adequate stems even with those harvesting constraints. Color selection is a matter of marketing: if you do weddings, grow pastels; if you do mixed bouquets, brights might be better. Aim for a long period of harvest by choosing cultivars that will bloom in succession.

Lilies absolutely require well-drained soil. Buy 10- to 12-centimeter bulbs; plant Asiatics six to seven bulbs per square foot, and Orientals four to five per square foot. Plant in spring as soon as the soil can be worked. Erect support netting over lilies if your climate is windy in summer.

Keep the plants well watered, even after the flowers have been harvested. The number of flowers per stem will decrease the second year, but the plants can be divided for greater yield.

Lilies can be cut when the first flower on the stem is fully colored, but not yet open. Vase life is five to nine days. When cutting lilies after they open, be careful of the pollen, which leaves a stain that is hard to remove. Some florists cut out the anthers, particularly when lilies are going to be carried or worn. If you do get lily pollen on your clothes or other fabrics, don't touch it with your hands or put water on it, which will set the stain. Instead, brush it gently with a tissue and place the fabric in direct sunlight for a few hours. The stain will disappear.

LIMONIUM SINUATUM (lim-OH-nee-um), Statice

Annual ∼ *18–24 inches*

Statice both fresh and dried is a standard in the floral industry. It is easily grown in most climates. There are dozens of cultivars and color mixes, from brights to pastels. Although they go by various names, the differences are slight.

Start the seed indoors and plant out after danger of frost. Many growers plant their statice on black plastic or black paper because the ground-hugging rosettes make weeding difficult.

The colorful parts of the flower are the sepals; the petals are the white parts within. Harvest when the white petals are visible. Vase life is two weeks.

Most commercial dried statice is glycerinized and stem-dyed (see chapter 5). However, statice also is easily air-dried by hanging it upside down in small bunches.

Limonium suworowii is another annual statice species, commonly known as Russian statice or pink pokers. Unlike *L. sinuatum*, it requires cool weather in order to flower well. It can be started inside and planted out after danger of frost. The wavy, pink spikes are lovely fresh, and they can be hung upside down to dry. The dried spikes, however, are likely to rehydrate and droop if they are not supported by other materials in the arrangement.

In addition, there are several perennial statice that are all good either fresh or dried as airy filler material. One of the newest is *L. sinensis* 'Lace Veil', which produces long sprays of tiny flowers with yellow petals and white calyxes. One of the most widely grown commercially is *L. perezii*, or seafoam statice, which has violet-lavender florets; caspia, a hybrid, is another in this group with bluish-white plumes. An essential for dried-flower work is *Statice tatarica*, known as German statice, which bears stiff, triangular sprays of tiny white flowers. Keep in mind that many of the perennial statice species are so commercially available that crafters may find it more cost-effective to buy these varieties than to grow them.

LOBELIA (loh-BEE-lee-ah)

Perennial, Zones 3–8 ❧ *24–48 inches*

Lobelia is a base-branching plant that produces long spikes of star-shaped flowers in shades of red, purple, and pink. Several species and hybrids are available to the cut-flower grower; the best known is the native cardinal flower, *Lobelia cardinalis.* Most recently, growers have been excited about the 'Compliment' series and the 'Fan' series, which have taller, fuller stems than the native species.

Start the seeds indoors or buy plants and space 12 inches apart. Harvest when the first few flowers on the spike have opened; the others will continue to open in the vase.

LUNARIA ANNUA (loon-AIR-ee-ah), Honesty

Biennial ❧ *24–36 inches*

Lunaria is grown for its shimmering, translucent seedpods that look like silver dollars when the pods are fully developed and the papery covering is removed. They also can be used fresh, with the purple pod unstripped. If you direct-seed, you'll get flowers and pods the second year; you also can purchase one-year-old plants that will produce that season.

LUPINUS (loo-PIE-nus), Lupine

Perennial, Zones 4–8 ❧ *36–60 inches*

Lupines have spikes of pealike flowers in beautiful pastels and bicolors. They like a cool, moist climate. If you have trouble with the unopened buds shriveling, try putting them in cold water after cutting and spraying them with a mist of cold water. Some gardeners go to great lengths to increase the vase life of this sometimes difficult flower: They prick the stem with a pin just below the flower, then turn it upside down and fill the hollow stem with water, and plug it with a piece of cotton or Oasis floral foam. That's not feasible on a commercial scale, but home gardeners can do it.

LYSIMACHIA CLETHROIDES (lie-sim-AK-ee-ah), Gooseneck Loosestrife

Perennial, Zones 3–8 ❧ *36 inches*

Spikes of white flowers are produced on 3-foot stems. The plants spread like wildfire, so give them at least a foot of space when planting. Support netting is necessary to keep them from tumbling over. Harvest when a third of the flowers are open. Vase life in plain water is only five days, but can last up to twelve days with preservative.

MALVA SYLVESTRIS (MAL-vah), Cheeses, High Mallow

Annual ∿ 36 inches

Malva sylvestris 'Zebrina' is a small hollyhock with purple-striped flowers. It has sturdy stems and a good vase life. Although it is not grown commercially, I have had good luck selling this flower to florists and using it in bouquets. Start with plants, spaced 12 inches apart. Each stem produces hundreds of buds that open over a long period of time. The flowers will start opening low on the stem, and the top will still be all foliage. Wait until the buds on the top are open before harvesting. Cut the stem long, leaving two or three nodes at the base of the plant, and the plant will send up a new flush of tall stems that are even more useful because they aren't as thick as the central stem.

MATTHIOLA INCANA (ma-THY-oh-lah), Stock

Annual ∿ 18–30 inches

Stock is a beautiful, fragrant flower and very much in demand with florists. However, it needs either mild winters or cool summers, and is grown in the field commercially only on the West Coast, in Arizona, and in Florida. In those places, it can be direct-seeded in the field, but many of the plants—sometimes as many as half—will not have the double flowers that are considered desirable. Instead, flowers will be small and single, and not especially attractive. If you start your own seed in the greenhouse, though, you can often select the plants that are doubles: in general, the singles are gray-green and less vigorous as seedlings than the doubles. Seedlings need to be exposed to temperatures of 50 to 55°F (10° to 13° C) for ten weeks before planting out; they will flower best if temperatures never exceed 60°F (16°C). Stock should be planted 6 to 10 inches apart. Harvest when half the flowers on the stem are open and place immediately in water.

MOLUCCELLA LAEVIS (moll-yew-SELL-ah), Bells-of-Ireland

Annual ∿ 36 inches

These bright green columns of bells are increasingly popular in the floral trade. Their color is fresh and combines beautifully with the hot colors of summer flowers. Green-and-white arrangements also benefit from bells-of-Ireland, because what other green flower is so tall and straight?

Seeds should be started in the greenhouse in cool climates, or direct-seeded after the soil has warmed in warmer climates. (I always direct-seed mine here in Kansas.)

Flowers should be harvested for fresh use when the bells are fully open. Removing the leaves will increase vase life, but this is a lot of work for a commercial grower. Perhaps you can just inform your customers that it's a good idea to pluck them.

For dried flowers, harvest when the bells are firm to the touch and hang them to dry. They will retain their green color for a while. Or let them dry on the plant, in which case they will bleach to the color of parchment. Moluccella also preserves beautifully in glycerine. Let the stems stand in glycerine solution, with or without a green dye, for three or four days; then hang them upside down to dry.

MONARDA DIDYMA (moe-NAR-da), Bee Balm, Bergamot

Perennial, Zones 4–9 ꙮ 24–48 inches

The flowers of monarda remind me of fireworks, with tubular petals bursting out from the center. Their fragrance is sharp and clean. There are a number of colors, including red, pink, white, blue, and purple. The newest cultivar to be touted by the seed companies as a great cut flower is 'Lambada', which produces whorls of lavender flowers in tiers up the stem. I haven't grown it, but have seen it in other growers' gardens and found it much more refined than it appeared in photos, so I'll be growing it in the future.

Start with plants and give them 18 inches of space, as monarda—being a member of the mint family—likes to spread. It also needs good air circulation to prevent powdery mildew. Cut when the petals are just beginning to open.

NARCISSUS (nar-SIS-us), Daffodil

Perennial, Zones 3–9 ꙮ 18–24 inches

Daffodils are a large group of plants divided into eleven classes. Those grown commercially for cutting are described as trumpet or large-cup daffodils. Bulbs are planted in the fall about 6 inches deep and 6 inches apart.

Many commercial growers pull the flowers, bulbs and all, to get a longer stem. Small growers might prefer to leave the bulbs in the ground to perennialize. Harvest when flowers are in the "gooseneck stage"; that is, hanging at a 90-degree angle from the stem—showing color, but not yet open. Daffodils secrete a sap that can harm other flowers, so put them in water by themselves for at least twelve hours, then rinse the stems before mixing them with other flowers.

NIGELLA (nye-JELL-ah), Love-in-a-Mist

Annual ꙮ 14–18 inches

Nigella damascena is a favorite of dried-flower growers because of its puffy, purple-striped seedpods. It can be used as a fresh flower, too, if tall stems are not required. The delicate flowers, in glowing shades of blue, pink, and white, seem to hover on the lacy foliage. They should be direct-seeded as soon as the soil can be worked in spring, with several succession plantings made to extend the harvest. Cut when the flowers are just beginning to open, or wait until the pods form and cut them for drying. In addition to *N. damascena*, there is *N. orientalis*, which has unusual, pointed seedpods. Hang to dry.

PAEONIA (pee-OH-nee-ah), Peony

Perennial, Zones 3–8 ~ *24–48 inches*

The genus *Paeonia* is huge with thirty-three species and about eight hundred cultivars. The most popular species for cutting is *P. lactiflora*, or Chinese peony. Within the species, peonies are divided by their form—singles, Japanese, semidoubles, and doubles (or "bombs")—and by their time of bloom—early, midseason, or late. Peonies need a certain amount of cold before they will flower, with the earliest bloomers needing fewer hours of cold than the late-blooming types. In Zones 4 through 6, just about all kinds of peonies will do well. Farther north, the hardiest late-bloomers are preferable; farther south, the early bloomers will perform better. Although the chilling requirements vary with the cultivar, you can probably grow peonies if you get six weeks of 40°F (4°C) nights.

Within those major divisions of bloom season and form, there are many named cultivars. I visited a peony-breeding farm on Memorial Day—peak peony season—and wandered among the dozens of cultivars in bloom. There were many differences in color and form but, to be honest, the variations within those categories were imperceptible: One white bomb looked pretty much like another. That's why it's so important to talk with other people in your area who grow peonies before deciding which cultivars to purchase. See page 99 for the peonies with the best vase life; then check with city gardeners, botanical gardens, garden-center horticulturists, and other peony growers about whether those preferred cultivars will perform well in your area.

Peonies should be planted in fall, and roots with at least three eyes will establish best and give you blooms by the third year. Peonies need good drainage and full sun to bloom well. Space them 4 feet apart. In the North, place the roots so the eyes are 2 inches below the soil surface; in the South, the eyes should be only 1 inch below the surface.

For information on harvesting and storing peonies, see page 96. They also are easy to air-dry by hanging them upside down in a warm, dark place.

PAPAVER (pah-PAY-vur), Poppy

Annual and Perennial, Zones 2–7 ~ *12–48 inches*

Papaver is a large genus, but most of the species within it are similar in overall appearance, with waving stems topped by big buds that burst open to reveal crinkly, broad petals. They are not a commercial cut flower because the vase life is so short, usually three days at most. However, home gardeners can rush poppies right from the garden into the house, sear the cut stems with a flame or by plunging into boiling water, and enjoy their luminous colors for a few days.

Paeonia, Peony

The pods can be dried for fall arrangements. *P. somniferum,* the opium poppy, is illegal in the United States, although it may still be found in seed catalogs (see chapter 5).

PENSTEMON (PEN-stem-awn), Beardtongue

Perennial, Zones 4–9 ∿ 24–48 inches

Several species of *Penstemon* are useful, though not commonly grown, as cut flowers. One that bears exploring in your locale is *P. digitalis,* a prairie native that has white to light rose, tubular flowers on red stems. The cultivar 'Husker Red' has red foliage and a vase life of seven to ten days. *P. barbatus* hybrids also produce long stems good for cutting. Start with plants and space them 12 inches apart.

PEROVSKIA (pe-ROF-skee-ah), Russian Sage

Perennial, Zones 3–9 ∿ 36–48 inches

The flowers are a lovely shade of pale lavender, and the foliage is a lacy silver-green. Unfortunately, the plant has a strong smell that some people just can't stand; I'd categorize it as being similar to marigold foliage. A florist once told me he thought it smelled like the cat's litter box. So plant it at your own risk. Perovskia is a big plant and should be given at least 18 inches of space. The flowers bloom for a long season, and can be cut at just about any point in their development.

PHLOX (FLOX)

Annual and Perennial, Zones 3–8 ∿ 20–48 inches

Phlox drummondii is an annual that loves cool weather. The clusters of small flowers have a sweet fragrance. At most, this plant will reach 20 inches, so it's most useful in bouquets and for selling to local florists, who don't demand 3-foot stems. It can be either direct-seeded or started indoors from seed.

Summer phlox *(P. paniculata)* is a big, bold flower that is loved by florists. The big heads are composed of many small flowers, many with pink or red centers, so that the flower takes on a different appearance depending on whether you are viewing it from a distance or inspecting it up close. Phlox's big problem is with powdery mildew; fortunately, many of the newer varieties are resistant. At the moment, the most popular "new" phlox with commercial growers is the pure white 'David', which has large heads and is quite mildew-resistant. But a new series of cultivars with the same characteristics is expected on the market shortly.

Start with plants and space them 24 inches apart to insure good air circulation as a preventive measure against powdery mildew. First-year plants may flower, but their stems will be short. In subsequent years, the plants will expand somewhat and grow much taller, up to 4 feet. Harvest when half the flowers on the inflorescence are open. Vase life is five to seven days.

PHYSOSTEGIA VIRGINIANA (fy-soh-STEE-jee-ah), Obedient Plant

Perennial, Zones 3–9 ∾ *36–48 inches*

Physostegia has spikes of small, tubular flowers in white, purple, or rose. The stiff stems make it useful for arranging, and it has another characteristic that florists love: The flowers will stay where they are pushed, hence its common name.

Start with plants and space them 12 to 24 inches apart, as physostegia spreads rapidly. Divide and replant after three years. Harvest when just a few flowers at the base of the spike are open, and plunge them immediately into floral preservative. Vase life is more than a week. In fall, the seedpods of uncut flowers will turn a beautiful red and may be even more desirable to florists than the flowers.

PLATYCODON GRANDIFLORUM (plat-ee-KOH-don), Balloonflower

Perennial, Zones 3–8 ∾ *24–36 inches*

I know some people who really like platycodon as a cut flower, but I'm not one of them. It seems to me that the bloom is pretty sparse, because only one flower on the stem opens at a time. If you cut when the first flower is open, you have a lot of tight buds on the stem. If you wait, you have the browned petals of the first few that opened. Nevertheless, I've included it because the way the buds swell into little balloons as they color up, then burst into star-shaped flowers is intriguing. The blue is a nice color. Flowers last about a week in the vase.

POLIANTHES TUBEROSA (pol-ee-AN-theez), Tuberose

Perennial, Zones 7–10 ∾ *24–48 inches*

Tuberoses are lovely flowers, with many white flowers on thick stems. Their fragrance is sweet and strong; some people find even one flower inside the house to be overwhelming, but others love the fragrance. These flowers are among the few that can be smelled from a distance, so they are popular with farmers'-market sellers as a way to catch the customer's attention. They are grown from tender tubers that must be lifted in the fall north of Zone 7, stored in a dry place at 40–50°F (4–10°C), and replanted in spring after danger of frost. Plant 9 to 12 inches apart for large tubers; smaller tubers can be planted closely to propagate them. The clumps of tubers can be as big as 8 inches across before they need to be divided.

Tuberose flowers late in summer, and its straplike foliage doesn't shade the ground, so weeds are a constant problem for the organic grower. Tuberoses do command a good price, however, so the labor cost to weed them all summer long may be recouped.

Harvest when two or three flowers have opened, or wait till half the flowers have opened, as long as the bottom flowers haven't yet started to die. Buds will continue to open in the vase for up to two weeks.

RUDBECKIA (rood-BECK-ee-ah), Black-Eyed Susan

Annual and Perennial, Zones 3–9 ⌒ 24–30 inches

The perennial rudbeckia most often grown for cutting is *R. fulgida* 'Goldsturm', which produces 3- to 4-inch flowers over a long period in summer. The annual most popular for cutting is *R. hirta* 'Indian Summer', with blooms up to 8 inches across. I prefer the softer look of the annual to the stiff look of the perennial. sorists really like these flowers—they resemble sunflowers closely enough to be used with them or in place of them, and their vase life is astonishing. I've had 'Indian Summer' rudbeckia last ten days in a pitcher in the kitchen, and they actually look more exuberant every day.

I find that rudbeckia attracts a lot of pests that want to munch those bright yellow petals. So I cut blooms before the petals are fully open, and leave them at room temperature in a bucket of preservative. They open within a day or two.

SALVIA (SAL-vee-ah)

Annual and Perennial ⌒ 24–48 inches

There are dozens of *Salvia* species, from the short, red bedding plant, *S. splendens,* to the towering spires of blue perennials. The problem with many salvias, particularly the perennials, is that they tend to drop their petals. Some are great flowers for cutting and drying, though. The following species are the ones that are most widely grown.

Salvia horminum, an annual also known as tri-color sage, is a candelabra-shaped plant with 18-inch stems of brightly colored bracts in pink, purple, and white. They are a bit difficult to use in arrangements because their stems are weak, but they make great bouquet filler. And they retain their color well when air-dried. 'Pink Sundae' and 'Oxford Blue' are widely available varieties.

Another annual species, *S. farinacea,* has spikes of blue to violet flowers. The color deepens in cool weather. Both foliage and flowers have a nice fruity fragrance. 'Blue Bedder' and 'Victoria' are about the same color, but 'Blue Bedder' is taller. There is also a white selection and a blue-and-white one, called 'Strata'. All make good dried flowers. Many growers report that 'Blue Bedder' is perennial, but the flowers don't form as nicely the second year, so it's advisable to plant a fresh crop each spring.

S. coccinea 'Coral Nymph' is an annual with delicate coral-pink flowers. The plants grow about 2 feet tall. I saw them planted in front of *S. farinacea* 'Victoria', and it was a lovely combination.

S. leucantha, known as Mexican bush sage or velvet sage, has fuzzy lavender sepals and white petals. It is a tender perennial that can be grown as an annual; however, it flowers only under short-daylength conditions, so in the North it may get hit by an early frost before it blooms. I've grown it successfully here in Kansas, where our first frost usually comes around Halloween. The plants are huge and should be spaced 2 to 3 feet apart.

SCABIOSA (skab-ee-OH-sah), Pincushion flower

Annual and Perennial, Zones 3–8 ∿ 12–30 inches

Both annual and perennial scabiosas are excellent and highly desirable cut flowers. The 1-inch mounded blooms look like little pincushions and the stems are long and wiry. The annual scabiosa, *S. atropurpurea,* comes in a mix of many colors, ranging from the predominant blue, white, pink, and lavender to the occasional maroon and coral. Start the seed in the greenhouse or purchase plugs. Space the plants 9 inches apart, and erect support netting over them before the flower stems start to shoot up. They absolutely need support, but the netting makes harvest difficult. I plant mine just two rows to a bed so that every plant can be reached from the side. Then I cut the stems with one hand and, using the other hand, pull them down through the netting and out. (If you try to pull them up through the netting, the many side shoots will get caught. Be gentle pulling them through—the flowers will pop right off if you pull them against the netting.) They can be cut when the flowers are half-open to fully open.

The perennial scabiosa, *S. caucasica,* also produces good cut flowers in cool climates. Flowers are bigger than those of the annual species and most varieties are blue. Stems grow to only about 20 inches, so support isn't necessary.

SEDUM SPECTABILE (SEE-dum), Stonecrop

Perennial, Zones 3–9 ∿ 24 inches

Although there are many types of succulent sedums, the one most commonly grown for flowers is 'Autumn Joy'. The flat clusters of tiny flowers are pink in the bud, deepening to peach, then rust, then brown in winter. Start with plants, which are easily divided. Space them about 15 inches apart, and they will soon fill in. Sedum can be used fresh or dried. To dry, harvest when the flowers are open, strip off the leaves, and hang the stems in small bundles. The fleshy stem takes a long time to dry.

SOLIDAGO (soh-li-DAY-goh), Goldenrod

Perennial, Zones 4–10 ∿ 36–72 inches

Goldenrods are wildflowers throughout much of the United States, but there are several cultivars with a more refined look for the cutting garden. Some florists really like goldenrod, but, for others, it's a hard sell because of its reputation for causing hay fever. In fact, this plant doesn't cause hay fever any more than other pollen-producing flowers, but it's gotten mixed up in people's minds with ragweed (*Ambrosia* spp.), which blooms at about the same time of year. *Solidago* may become more acceptable as people are made aware of the confusion. Start with plants and space them 18 inches apart to provide good air circulation, as goldenrod is susceptible to powdery mildew and rust. Harvest when half the flowers on the inflorescence are open. Vase life is about a week.

TAGETES ERECTA (tay-GEE-teez), Marigold

Annual ∾ 36 inches

The only marigolds grown for cutting are the African types, particularly 'Gold Coin' or 'Jubilee' mix. The fully double flowers measure up to 5 inches across, in shades of yellow, gold, and orange. They are a good fall crop because these golden colors are most popular then. The African types do, however, have the strongly scented foliage typical of marigolds. You can always strip it off if it offends you or your customers.

THALICTRUM (thah-LICK-trum), Meadow Rue

Perennial, Zones 4–7 ∾ 36–72 inches

Long sprays of fluffy flowers make meadow rue a good filler. Colors run from white to purple, with pastel shades in between. The plant is poisonous, so be careful where you grow it. Start the seed indoors or purchase plugs. Space plants 18 inches apart and use support netting to keep the flowers from getting tangled. Meadow rue likes moist soil and partial shade. Harvest when almost all the flowers are open.

TRACHYMENE COERULEA (tray-ki-MEE-nee), Blue Laceflower

Annual ∾ 24 inches

These blue, umbrella-shaped blooms measuring 3 inches across were formerly known as *Didiscus.* They can be grown well only in cool climates. Start seed in the greenhouse in peat pots, as the roots should not be disturbed when transplanting. Harvest when half the flowers in the umbel are open.

TROLLIUS (TROH-lee-us), Globeflower

Perennial, Zones 3–8 ∾ 24–36 inches

The ball-shaped, golden flowers like cool, wet weather and will produce well in a boggy spot. Trollius also is one of the few cut flowers that will grow in shade. Start with plants and space them 12 inches apart. Cut when the flowers are starting to open.

TULIPA (TOO-lip-ah), Tulip

Perennial, Zones 3–7 ∽ *18–30 inches*

Tulips should be planted in fall. The types used for cutting include Darwin, Triumph, Rembrandt, and peony-flowered. Plant bulbs 6 inches deep and spaced 6 inches apart. Many commercial growers pull the bulbs to increase the stem length and storage life of the flowers. However, small growers may want to leave the bulbs in the ground because some tulips will perennialize. Harvest when the flowers are colored but not opened. Tulips will continue to grow after they've been picked, and will last more than a week in the vase.

VERBENA BONARIENSIS (ver-BEE-nah), Vervain

Perennial, Zones 7–10 ∽ *36–48 inches*

This is an odd plant with long, square stems topped by clusters of tiny, bright purple flowers. It blooms the first year from seed, so it can be grown as an annual north of Zone 7. Space the plants 12 to 18 inches apart to keep the many branches from getting tangled. Cut when the inflorescence is bright with flowers, and place immediately in floral preservative. Some of the flowers will shatter, but new ones will open quickly.

VERONICA LONGIFOLIA (ver-RON-ik-ah), Speedwell

Perennial, Zones 4–8 ∽ *24–36 inches*

Veronica produces pointed spikes of blue, pink, or white flowers. Seed is easily started in the greenhouse, or you can buy plugs. Plant them 12 inches apart. If planted in spring, it will bloom in fall, but the bloom time in subsequent years will be spring or early summer. Cut when about half the tiny flowers on the inflorescence are open, and put them in preservative. Flowers are ethylene-sensitive, so keep them away from fruits and vegetables, cigarette smoke, and gas fumes.

ZANTEDESCHIA (zan-te-DES-kee-ah), Calla Lily

Perennial, Zones 7–10 ∽ *24–48 inches*

Calla lilies come in white, yellow, orange, peach, pink, and rose. They are grown from rhizomes that must be lifted in the fall north of Zone 7, cleaned, and left to cure in a warm place with good air circulation. When the roots have shriveled, they can be packed in dry peat moss and stored over the winter in a place where temperatures will not go below 40°F (4°C).

Plant the rhizomes 4 to 8 inches apart, depending on their size. They require well-drained soil. They will flower about ten to twelve weeks after planting. Harvest when the flowers are open and fully colored; they will last two weeks or more in the vase.

ZINNIA ELEGANS (ZIN-ee-ah)

Annual ⌇ *24–36 inches*

One of the workhorses of the flower garden, zinnias show up on the Top Ten lists of flower growers all over the country. They particularly like hot, dry weather, so they are a natural for the Midwest and Southwest; but they also can be grown in the cool, wet climates of the Northeast, Southeast, Northwest, and coastal California.

Zinnias are available in many cultivars that encompass all sorts of sizes and shapes, from big dahlia-flowered ones, to little button-shaped ones, to raggedy cactus-flowered types. Nearly every color except blue is represented, too.

In the dahlia-flowered types, the top choice among flower growers these days is a cultivar called 'Giant Dahlia Blue Point'. I have grown it beside other cultivars such as 'State Fair' and have found it superior in many ways. It blooms earlier, on taller stems; blooms longer without getting powdery mildew; and has uniform flowers and the clearest colors. If you can't find it for some reason, 'State Fair' is a close second choice.

Another good choice for cutting is the new cultivar 'Oklahoma'. It is a smaller zinnia, similar to 'Ruffles', but on stems much longer than most small zinnias. It is available in five colors and a mix. 'Oklahoma' was dedicated by the breeder, Benary Seed Company, in late 1996, and became available from retail seed companies in 1997.

Zinnias can be direct-seeded; I use an Earthway push seeder, which makes planting even easier. Once the seeds are in the ground, stand back. You don't have to do a thing until it's time to cut them. They don't really need to be thinned, because you can just cut long stems on the early bloomers, in effect thinning as you cut. Plant every two weeks until midsummer to ensure high-quality flowers until your first frost.

Harvest zinnias when the flowers are fully opened, and put them in floral preservative. They don't like to be put in a cold cooler; rather, keep the cooler above 45°F (7°C), or even let the flowers rest in an air-conditioned room. They will last five to seven days in the vase.

Recommended Cut Flowers

Zinnia elegans,
Zinnia

Sources and Resources

The following information is organized by the chapter to which it most closely relates. However, many of these references cover more than one aspect of flower farming, so feel free to browse.

CHAPTER 1

Seed Companies

Seed companies are your first resource for getting acquainted with the many cut-flower cultivars available. In the alphabetical list that follows, companies that publish a color catalog of flowers are marked with an asterisk (*). Commercial seed companies that sell seed in bulk rather than packets are marked with a plus (+).

Abundant Life Seed Foundation
P.O. Box 772, Port Townsend, WA
98368; 360-385-5660, Fax 360-385-7455

Bountiful Gardens
18001 Shafer Ranch Rd., Willits, CA 95490
707-459-6410

*W. Atlee Burpee
300 Park Ave., Warminster, PA 18991-0002
800-888-1447, Fax 800-487-5530

D. V. Burrell
P.O. Box 150, Rocky Ford, CO 81067
719-254-3318, Fax 719-254-3319

The Cook's Garden
P.O. Box 535, Londonderry, VT 05148
802-824-3400, Fax 802-824-3027

Fedco Seeds
P.O. Box 520, Waterville, ME 04903
207-873-7333, Fax 207-426-9005

Garden City Seeds
778 Hwy. 93 N., Hamilton, MT 59840
406-961-4837, Fax 406-961-4877

+Germania Seed Company
5952 N. Milwaukee Ave., Chicago, IL 60646-5424
773-631-6631, Fax 773-631-4449

*+Fred C. Gloeckner & Co., Inc.
600 Mamaroneck Ave., Harrison, NY 10528-1631
800-345-3787

*+G. S. Grimes Seeds
201 W. Main St., Smethport, PA 16749
800-241-SEED, Fax 814-887-2150

*Harris Seeds
P.O. Box 22960, Rochester, NY 14692-2960
716-442-9386, Fax 800-544-7938

*Horticultural Products and Services
P.O. Box 10, Graniteville, SC 29829
800-322-7288

*Johnny's Selected Seeds
Foss Hill Rd., Albion, ME 04910-9731
207-437-4395, Fax 800-437-4290

*Mellinger's
2310 W. South Range Rd., North Lima, OH 44452
800-321-7444, Fax 330-549-3716

+Modena Seed Company
5727 Mission St., P.O. Box 12007
San Francisco, CA 94112
415-585-2324, Fax 415-585-6820

Nichols Garden Nursery
1190 N. Pacific Hwy., Albany, OR 97321
541-928-9280, Fax 541-967-8406

+Norman Seed Company
3303 Harbor Blvd., Suite B12
Costa Mesa, CA 92626
714-498-3537, Fax 714-498-5969

*Park Seed
Cokesbury Rd., Greenwood, SC 29647
Wholesale Division 800-845-3366,
Fax 800-209-0360

Prairie Oak Seeds
P.O. Box 382, Maryville, MO 64468-0382

Redwood City Seeds Company
P.O. Box 361, Redwood City, CA 94064
415-325-7333

*Seeds of Change
P.O. Box 15700, Santa Fe, NM 87506-5700
888-762-7333, Fax 888-329-4762

*Seymour's Selected Seeds
 P.O. Box 1346, Sussex, VA 23884
Shepherd's Garden Seeds
 30 Irene St., Torrington, CT 06790-6658
 860-482-3638
*R. H. Shumway Seedsmen
 P.O. Box 1, Graniteville, SC 29829
 803-663-9771, Fax 803-663-9772
Southern Exposure Seed Exchange
 P.O. Box 170, Earlysville, VA 22936
 804-973-4703, Fax 804-973 8717
*Stokes Seeds, Inc.
 Box 548, Buffalo, NY 14240
 716-695-6980, Fax 716-695-9649
Territorial Seed Company
 P.O. Box 157, Cottage Grove, OR 97424
 541-942-9547, Fax 541-942-9881
*Thompson & Morgan
 P.O. Box 1308, Jackson, NJ 08527-0308
 800-274-7333
*Otis S. Twilley Seed Company
 P.O. Box 65, Trevose, PA 19053
 800-622-7333, Fax 215-245-1949
Westcan Horticultural Ltd.
 Bay 5, 6112 30th St. S.E., Calgary, Alberta,
  Canada T2C 2A6
 403-279-5168, Fax 403-236-0854

CHAPTER 2

Organic Growing Reference Books

Because *The Flower Farmer* covers the broad subjects of both growing and marketing flowers, I have been forced to limit the amount of information included about general organic growing practices such as composting and soil fertility. However, I strongly urge inexperienced organic growers to read the references that have guided me in my growth as a market gardener.

The most important book for market growers is *The New Organic Grower: A Master's Manual of Tools and Techniques for the Home and Market Gardener* by Eliot Coleman, published in 1995 by Chelsea Green Publishing Company. You can order it from your local bookstore or call the publisher directly at 800-639-4099.

You can also order *Backyard Composting: Your Complete Guide to Recycling Yard Clippings* (published by Harmonious Technologies, 1992) from Chelsea Green at the number above.

Another excellent guide to biointensive growing is *How to Grow More Vegetables* by John Jeavons (Ten Speed Press, 1995). You can get it through local book-

stores or order it for $19.95 postpaid from Ecology Action, 5798 Ridgewood Rd., Willits, CA 95490; 707-459-0150, Fax 707-459-5409.

A more detailed treatment of organic soil fertility is available in *Fertile Soil: A Grower's Guide to Organic and Inorganic Fertilizers* by Robert Parnes, published in 1990 by agAccess, P.O. Box 2008, Davis, CA 95617; 916-756-7177, Fax 916-756-7188.

For large-scale composting, see *The On-Farm Composting Handbook,* available from Northeast Regional Agricultural Engineering Service, 152 Riley-Robb Hall, Cooperative Extension, Ithaca, NY 14853.

Cover-Crop Seeds

Many of the plants grown as cover crops for fertility in organic systems are the same as the row crops grown by farmers in your area. Consequently, those cover crops can probably be purchased cheaply at your local farmers' coop. When you talk to your Cooperative Extension agent about which cover crops to grow, be sure to ask about local suppliers.

There are also several mail-order companies that supply cover-crop seeds. Here are a few:

Harmony Farm Supply
 3244 Hwy. 116, Sebastopol, CA 95472
 707-823-9125, Fax 707-823-1734
Peaceful Valley Farm Supply
 P.O. Box 2209, Grass Valley, CA 95945
 916-272-4769
Snow Pond Farm Supply
 RR 2, Box 1009, Belgrade, ME 04917
 800-768-9998

CHAPTER 3

Plant and Bulb Suppliers

There are hundreds of nurseries that sell plants and bulbs useful to the cut-flower grower. If you are looking for specific types of plants, such as peonies or chrysanthemums, consult *Andersen Horticultural Library's Source List of Plants and Seeds,* available at most libraries or from the Andersen Horticultural Library, Minnesota Landscape Arboretum, 3675 Arboretum Dr., Box 39, Chanhassen, MN 55317-0039. This excellent reference book lists, by variety, every seed and plant company that sells it.

The following list includes companies that sell a wide selection of cut-flower varieties. The types of plant material each sells is noted in italics at the end of the listing. Plug suppliers sell both annual and perennial flowers grown in small cells, ready to be planted into larger containers in the greenhouse or directly into the field. Perennial suppliers sell bareroot plants or container-grown plants, usually in larger sizes than plugs. Companies that sell bulbs and rhizomes are also included. Again, wholesale companies are marked with a plus (+).

+Ball Seed Company
  622 Town Rd., West Chicago, IL 60185
  800-TRY-BALL, Fax 630-231-3871
  Plugs, perennials, bulbs
+Bluebird Nursery, Inc.
  P.O. Box 460, 519 Bryan St., Clarkson, NE 68629
  800-356-9164, Fax 402-892-3738
  Container-grown perennials
+Bradbury Farm
  19738 W. Bradbury Rd., Turlock, CA 95380
  209-668-7584, Fax 209-668-7928
  Plugs
Daffodil Mart
  7463 Heath Trail, Gloucester, VA 23061
  800-ALL-BULB, Fax 800-420-2852
  Bulbs
+DeVroomen Bulb Co., Inc.
  P.O. Box 189, 14867 W. Russell Rd., Russell, IL 60075
  847-395-9911, Fax 847-395-9920
  Bulbs
Fedco
  P.O. Box 520, Waterville, ME 04903
  207-873-7333, Fax 207-426-9005
  Shrubs and bareroot perennials
+Germania Seed Company
  5952 N. Milwaukee Ave., Chicago, IL 60646-5424
  773-631-6631, Fax 773-631-4449
  Plugs, plants, seeds
+G. S. Grimes Seeds
  201 W. Main St., Smethport, PA 16749
  800-241-SEED, Fax 814-887-2150
  Plugs, plants, bulbs
+Gro 'n Sell
  307 Lower State Rd., Chalfont, PA 18914
  215-822-1276, Fax 215-997-1770
  Plugs
+Headstart Nursery
  4860 Monterey Rd., Gilroy, CA 95020
  408-842-3030
  Plugs
+Here & Now Gardens
  P.O. Box 6, Gales Creek, OR 97117
  503-357-5774, Fax 503-357-3858
  Perennial divisions

High Country Garden
  2909 Rufina St., Santa Fe, NM 87505-2929
  800-925-9387
  Plants
Mountain Valley Growers
  38325 Pepperweed Rd., Squaw Valley, CA 93675
  209-338-2775, Fax 209-338-0075
  Herb and flower plants
Patchwork Gardens
  2999 U.S. 35 S.E., Washington Court House, OH 43160
  614-335-0018, Fax 614-335-5338
  Plugs
+Vandenberg Bulb Company
  1 Black Meadow Rd., P.O. Box 532, Chester, NY 10918-0532
  800-221-6017, Fax 914-469-2015
  Bulbs
+Walters Gardens, Inc.
  P.O. Box 137, Zeeland, MI 49464
  800-421-0333, Fax 800-752-1879.
  Plants
Wayside Gardens
  1 Garden Lane, Hodges, SC 29695-0001
  800-845-1124, Fax 800-457-9712
  Plants
White Flower Farm
  P.O. Box 50, Litchfield, CT 06759-0050
  800-503-9624
  Plants

Seed-Starting Suppliers

Seed-starting supplies such as flats, cell packs, pots, and so forth, can be purchased from local garden centers if you're just buying a few. If you need larger quantities, ask your local garden center about purchasing a case from them, and if that's not possible, ask for the name of the nearest distributor. You can also buy supplies from mail-order suppliers, such as the following companies:

G & M Agricultural Supply
  5301 N. 82nd St., Scottsdale, AZ 85250
  602-947-0096
Gardener's Supply
  128 Intervale Rd., Burlington, VT 05401
  800-863-1700, Fax 800-551-6712
Harmony Farm Supply
  3244 Hwy. 116, Sebastopol, CA 95472
  707-823-9125, Fax 707-823-1734
A. M. Leonard, Inc.
  P.O. Box 816, Piqua, OH 45356
  800-543-8955, Fax 800-433-0633

Peaceful Valley Farm Supply
P.O. Box 2209, Grass Valley, CA 95945
916-272-4769
Snow Pond Farm Supply
RR 2, Box 1009, Belgrade, ME 04917
800-768-9998

Greenhouse Information and Equipment

Greenhouse structures and supplies are available from many companies, and it pays to compare price lists before buying. Because freight can be a big part of the cost of a new structure, you should look first at the companies nearest you. The list below includes many of the largest greenhouse manufacturers; for other manufacturers, read the advertisements and buyer's guides in the greenhouse magazines listed below.

Magazines:

Greenhouse Business, McCormick Communications Group
P.O. Box 698, Park Ridge, IL 60068
847-823-5650, Fax 847-696-3445

Greenhouse Grower, Meister Publications
37733 Euclid Ave., Willoughby, OH 44094-5992;
216-942-2000

Greenhouse Management and Production, Branch-Smith Publishing
P.O. Box 1868, Fort Worth, TX 76101
800-434-6776

Grower Talks, Ball Publishing
335 N. River St., Batavia, IL 60510
708-208-9080

Manufacturers:

Atlas Greenhouse Systems, Inc.
P.O. Box 558, Alapaha, GA 31622
800-346-9902, Fax 912-532-4600

Charley's Greenhouse Supply
1569 Memorial Hwy., Mt. Vernon, WA 98273
360-428-2626

Crop King, Inc.
5050 Greenwich Rd., Seville, OH 44273
330-769-2002, Fax 330-769-2616

Ex-Cel Greenhouses
P.O. Box 3095, Greenwood, SC 29648
800-234-3301

E. C. Geiger, Inc.
Rt. 63, 189 Main St., Box 285, Harleysville, PA 19438-0332
800-443-4437, Fax 800-432-9434

Gardener's Supply
128 Intervale Rd., Burlington, VT 05401
800-688-5510
Janco Greenhouses
9390 Davis Ave., Laurel, MD 20723
800-323-6933, Fax 301-497-9751
Ludy Greenhouses
Box 141, New Madison, OH 45346
513-996-1921, Fax 513-996-8031
Stuppy Greenhouse Mfg.
P.O. Box 12456, North Kansas City, MO 64116
800-877-5025, Fax 800-423-1512
United Greenhouse Systems
708 Washington St., Edgerton, WI 53534
800-433-6834, Fax 608-884-6137

CHAPTER 4

Specialty Tool and Equipment Suppliers

The tools and supplies you need for small-scale, intensive flower production can be purchased from mail-order suppliers. The companies listed in the preceding section about greenhouse supplies also carry supplies for field growing, and I recommend you send for their catalogs if you haven't done so already. Many seed companies also carry supplies. The list below includes specialty suppliers and the numbers of manufacturers to call to find out your nearest distributor.

Chapin Watermatics, Inc.
740 Water St., Watertown, NY 13601
315-782-1170, Fax 315-782-1490
Irrigation supplies
DeWitt Company
800-888-9669
Weed barrier fabrics, shadecloth. Call for names of local suppliers
Dripworks
380 Maple St., Willits, CA 95490
800-522-3747, Fax 717-459-6323
Irrigation and pond and tank liners
Ferrari Tractor
P.O. Box 1045, Gridley, CA 95948
916-846-6401, Fax 916-846-0390
European and specialized small-scale farm equipment
Gardener's Supply
128 Intervale Rd., Burlington, VT 05401
800-863-1700
Organic fertilizers and pest controls, row covers, tools, and more. Specialty catalog of irrigation supplies with free design service

Gardens Alive

5100 Schenley Pl., Lawrenceburg, IN 47025

812-537-8650, Fax 812-537-5108

Organic soil amendments and pest controls

Langenbach Fine Tool Company

P.O. Box 1420, Lawndale, CA 90260-6320

800-362-1991, Fax 800-362-4490

High-quality hand tools

A. M. Leonard, Inc.

P.O. Box 816, Piqua, OH 45356

800-543-8955, Fax 513-773-9993

Tools and supplies for nurseries, landscapers, foresters, arborists

Market Farm Implement

RD 2, Box 206, Friedens, PA 15541

814-443-1931

New and used farm machinery

Mechanical Transplanter Company

1150 South Central Ave., Holland, MI 49423

800-757-5268, Fax 616-396-3619

Implements and farm supplies

Millcreek Manufacturing

2617 Stumptown Rd., Bird-in-Hand, PA 17505

800-311-1323

Farm equipment

North Country Organics

RR 1, Box 2232, Bradford, VT 05033

802-222-4277, Fax 802-222-9661

Fertilizers and soil amendments

Seasons Irrigation Supply

P.O. Box 2158, Valley Center, CA 92082

800-396-0100, Fax 800-396-0122

Irrigation equipment

Tenax Corporation

4800 E. Monument St., Baltimore, MD 21205

800-356-8495, Fax 410-522-7015

Makers of support netting, bird netting, and plastic trellis

Valley Oak Tool Company

448 W. 2nd Ave., Chico, CA 95926

916-342-6188

Wheel hoes

Pest Controls

In my efforts to experiment with organic pest controls, I have relied heavily on information from the Bio-Integral Resource Center (BIRC), an organization that seeks to identify alternatives to chemical pest controls. BIRC publishes two monthly newsletters: *The IPM Practitioner,* with scientific yet comprehensible information for farmers, and *Common Sense Pest Control,* with information geared to the layperson. *The IPM Practitioner* includes an annual directory of least-toxic pest controls for every pest you are likely to encounter, with addresses for dozens of companies that supply beneficial insects and other biological controls. BIRC founders William Olkowski, Sheila Daar, and Helga Olkowski are the authors of *Common Sense Pest Control* (Taunton Press, 1991), a valuable reference work packed with ideas for fighting pests in the garden and in the home without using chemicals. Contact BIRC at P.O. Box 7414, Berkeley, CA 94707; 510-524-2567, Fax 510-524-1758.

For help in identifying pests, I rely on three books:

Pests of the Garden and Small Farm: A Grower's Guide to Using Less Pesticide by Mary Louise Flint (University of California Publication 3332, 1990). For ordering information, call 415-642-2431.

Rodale's Pest and Disease Problem Solver by Linda Gilkeson, Pam Peirce, and Miranda Smith (Rodale Press, 1996).

Rodale's Color Handbook of Garden Insects by Anna Carr (Rodale Press, 1979).

Organic pest controls are available from some of the farm supply companies listed under chapter 3, and from many seed companies.

CHAPTER 5

Drying and Preservation Supplies

Glycerine can be purchased in very small quantities at drug stores, if you just want to experiment. Larger quantities of glycerine and stem dyes can be ordered from:

Robert Koch Industries, Inc.

4770 Harback Rd., Bennett, CO 80102-8834

303-644-3763, Fax 303-644-3045

Westcan Horticultural Ltd.

Bay 5, 6112 - 30 St. S.E., Calgary, Alberta T2C 2A6, Canada

403-279-5168, Fax 403-236-0854

Silica gel crystals are available at large craft shops. One mail-order source is Prairie Oak Seeds, P.O. Box 382, Maryville, MO 64468.

To learn more about freeze-drying, either starting your own business or finding suppliers of freeze-dried materials, contact the International Freeze-Dry Floral Association, c/o Jacquelyn Leaman, Leaman's Green Applebarn, 7475 N. River Rd., Freeland, MI 48623; 517-695-2465, Fax 517-695-4560.

CHAPTER 6

Woody Ornamental Information and Nurseries

The woody ornamentals are a huge category of plants, certainly deserving of their own book with an emphasis on cutting for the floral trade. Unfortunately, no such book exists at this writing. The best reference on woodies as landscape plants is a voluminous book that you should be able to get on interlibrary loan or at a college library: *The Manual of Woody Landscape Plants* by Michael Dirr, published by Stipes Publishing Company, Champaign, IL.

To purchase shrubs, you have several options, depending on the size of your garden. For the hobby gardener, local and mail-order nurseries will have most of the plants you're looking for. If you know what cultivar you're seeking, you can find out which nurseries supply it in *The Andersen Horticultural Library's Source List of Plants and Seeds*, available at most libraries or from the Andersen Horticultural Library, Minnesota Landscape Arboretum, 3675 Arboretum Dr., Box 39, Chanhassen, MN 55317-0039. Another source for locating specific plants is *Gardening by Mail* by Barbara J. Barton (Houghton Mifflin, 1994).

The commercial grower also can purchase one or two specimens, then take cuttings—provided they are not cultivars protected by plant patents. If you want more plants quickly, you can purchase container-grown stock from nurseries in your region. Find out where the local garden center buys its plants. Or you can buy "liners"—that is, rooted cuttings—and grow them in a seedbed until they are about 18 inches tall. A good source of information about nurseries that sell liners is the classified advertising section of *American Nurseryman* magazine, 77 W. Washington, Suite 2100, Chicago, IL 60602; 800-621-5727.

CHAPTERS 7 AND 8

Floral Preservative Manufacturers

These suppliers will also test water for growers.

Floralife Inc.
120 Tower Dr., Burr Ridge, IL 60521
800-323-3689
Gard Environmental Group
250 Williams Rd., Carpentersville, IL 60110
800-433-4273
Pokon & Chrysal USA
3063 NW 107th Ave., Miami, FL 33172
800-247-9725
Robert Koch Industries
4770 Harback Rd., Bennett, CO 80102
303-644-3763

Smithers Oasis
919 Marvin Ave., P.O. Box 118, Kent, OH 44240
330-673-5831

Floral Design Supplies and Information

The floral supplies mentioned in these chapters, including arranging supplies and floral preservatives, are available at most wholesale floral-supply houses. To be able to shop at one of these wholesalers, you probably need a tax number or whatever form your state uses to show that you're a reseller. If you are located far from a wholesaler, one mail-order source of floral supplies is Floral Supply Syndicate, 3800 Via Pescador, Camarillo, CA 93012.

Other suppliers include:

A-Roo Company
963 Schriewer Rd., Seguin, TX 78155
800-446-2766
Floral packaging, including sleeves and bags
Action Bag Company
1422 Stone Hollow, Kingwood, TX 77339
800-824-2247, Fax 800-400-4451
Polybags, cotton drawstring bags, ziplock, tissue paper, cellophane wrap, shipping supplies
Dorothy Biddle Service
HC 1 Box 900, Greeley, PA 18425-9799
717-226-3239, Fax 717-226-0349
Flower arranging supplies are sold in quantities and packages most useful to small retailers, but some items are useful to the home or small commercial grower

Books on flower arranging:

Many beautiful books are available on flower arranging, and a trip to the public library should provide enough material to get you started. One of my favorite books for both technical instruction and design ideas is *The Complete Flower Arranger* by Pamela Westland (Smith Mark Publishers, 1992). Two mail-order sources of books on all facets of horticulture, including floral design, are:

American Nurseryman Horticultural Books
77 W. Washington St., Suite 2100, Chicago, IL 60602
800-621-5727
Timber Press
9999 S.W. Wilshire, Suite 124, Portland, OR 97225
503-227-2878

Magazines for the floral industry:

The following publications provide ideas for floral designers, and are helpful for the grower who wants to become familiar with the businesses likely to buy his or her flowers. Call and ask for a sample copy.

Floral & Nursery Times
P.O. Box 8470, Northfield, IL 60093
708-441-0300

Flowers &
12233 West Olympic Blvd., Suite 118,
Los Angeles, CA 90064
310-442-3090

Florist & Grower
1296 Hamilton St., Springfield, OR 97477
503-746-6615

Florist Magazine
29200 Northwestern Highway, Southfield, MI
48037
810-355-6291

Florists' Review
3641 S.W. Plass, Topeka, KS 66611
913-266-0888

Flower News
120 S. Riverside Plaza, Suite 464, Chicago, IL
60606
312-258-8500

Super Floral
10901 W. 84th Terr., Lenexa, KS 66214
800-255-5113

CHAPTERS 9 AND 10

Trade Information and Marketing Supplies

Information:

Growing for Market is a monthly newsletter for small-scale growers of produce and flowers. It contains a monthly column written by experienced cut-flower farmers. In summer, it includes flower prices on the wholesale market. Every issue contains a profile of a successful grower as well as feature articles about various aspects of market gardening, news briefs, and advertising from appropriate suppliers. Information is practical and geared to the small organic farmer. Write or call GFM, P.O. Box 3747, Lawrence, KS 66046; 800-307-8949.

The Association of Specialty Cut Flower Growers is an international organization of commercial flower farmers, ranging in scale from less than an acre to hundreds of acres. ASCFG publishes a bimonthly newsletter and holds an annual conference with educational sessions, a trade show, and opportunities for networking with fellow growers. Proceedings of past conferences are available, and they are packed with useful information. An annual directory lists members according to what they grow, so that potential customers can make contact. Membership is pricey—$125 a year at this writing—but the cost is worthwhile for the serious commercial grower. For more information, contact ASCFG, MPO Box 268, Oberlin, OH 44074-0268; 216-774-2887, Fax 216-774-2435.

Wholesale-flower price information is available from several U.S. cities, but the USDA has been cutting back recently on its price reporting services, so you should check to see what is currently available. Contact Market News Service, Room 2503, South Building, P.O. Box 96456, Washington, DC 20090.

California growers have done a superb job of commercializing flowers that were once considered "garden flowers." Many of the flowers now becoming common in upscale floral shops are supplied by California growers. Many of the flowers you see in home magazines were supplied by the California Cut Flower Commission. The commission publishes a Buyer's Guide that contains color photographs of the flowers produced by its members. Write the California Cut Flower Commission, 2339 Gold Meadow Way, Suite 101, Gold River, CA 95670.

Florists' Review is a monthly magazine covering the floral industry. It contains industry news, business advice, and expertly photographed designs that showcase the latest trends in flowers. It's an excellent resource for any grower, no matter where you're marketing, and it's indispensable if you sell to florists. Write or call *Florists' Review*, 3641 S.W. Plass, Topeka, KS 66611-2588; 913-266-0888, Fax 913-266-0333.

Marketing supplies:

Bannerscapes
P.O. Box 21924, Santa Barbara, CA 93121
800-832-7707, Fax 805-684-9708
Banners, flags

Growers Discount Labels
800-693-1572 *Product labels*

Made In The Shade
P.O. Box 231, Cool, CA 95618
800-742-3328
Canopies for farmers' markets

A. Steele
Rt. 1, Box 190, Stockholm, WI 54769
800-693-3353
Market canopies, scales and cash registers

Wheeler Arts
66 Lake Park, Champaign, IL 61821
217-359-6816, Fax 217-359-8716
Computer art for horticultural businesses

Index

Index

Index

206

Index

Chelsea Green Publishing Company

The sustainable world is one in which all human activities are designed to co-exist and cooperate with natural processes rather than dominate nature. Resources are recognized as finite. Consumption and production are carefully and consciously balanced so that all of the planet's species can thrive in perpetuity.

Chelsea Green specializes in providing the information people need to create and prosper in such a world.

Sustainable Living has many facets. Chelsea Green's celebration of the sustainable arts has led us to publish trend-setting books about organic gardening, solar electricity and renewable energy, innovative building techniques, regenerative forestry, local and bioregional democracy, and whole foods. The company's published works, while intensely practical, are also entertaining and inspirational, demonstrating that an ecological approach to life is consistent with producing beautiful, eloquent, and useful books, videos, and audio tapes.

For more information about Chelsea Green, or to request a free catalog, call (800) 639–4099, or write to us at P.O. Box 428, White River Junction, VT 05001.

Chelsea Green titles include:

The Man Who Planted Trees	Jean Giono
Beyond the Limits	Donella Meadows, Dennis Meadows, and Jørgen Randers
Loving and Leaving the Good Life	Helen Nearing
The New Organic Grower	Eliot Coleman
Solar Gardening	Leandre Poisson and Gretchen Vogel Poisson
Four-Season Harvest	Eliot Coleman
The Contrary Farmer	Gene Logsdon
Forest Gardening	Robert Hart
Who Owns the Sun?	Daniel Berman and John O'Connor
The Independent Home	Michael Potts
The Straw Bale House	Athena Swentzell Steen, Bill Steen, and David Bainbridge
The Rammed Earth House	David Easton
Independent Builder	Sam Clark
The Passive Solar House	James Kachadorian
Whole Foods Companion	Dianne Onstad
A Patch of Eden	H. Patricia Hynes